SPECTACULAR PERFORMANCES

Manchester University Press

SPECTACULAR PERFORMANCES

Essays on theatre, imagery, books and selves in early modern England

STEPHEN ORGEL

Manchester University Press
Manchester and New York

*distributed in the United States exclusively
by Palgrave Macmillan*

Published by Manchester University Press
Oxford Road, Manchester M13 9NR, UK
and Room 400, 175 Fifth Avenue, New York, NY 10010, USA
www.manchesteruniversitypress.co.uk

Distributed in the United States exclusively by
Palgrave Macmillan, 175 Fifth Avenue, New York,
NY 10010, USA

Distributed in Canada exclusively by
UBC Press, University of British Columbia, 2029 West Mall,
Vancouver, BC, Canada V6T 1Z2

British Library Cataloguing-in-Publication Data
A catalogue record for this book is available from the British Library

Library of Congress Cataloging-in-Publication Data applied for

ISBN   978 0 7190 8168 2 hardback

First published 2011

Typeset
by Carnegie Book Production, Lancaster
Printed and bound by
CPI Group (UK) Ltd, Croydon, CR0 4YY

For
Michael Wyatt
and
Giorgio Alberti

Contents

Illustrations

Note: all illustrations not otherwise credited are in private collections.

Previously published essays

Previously published essays have appeared as follows:

"Jonson and the Amazons," in *Soliciting Interpretation*, ed. Elizabeth D. Harvey and Katharine Eisaman Maus (University of Chicago Press, 1990)

"*Othello* and the end of comedy," *Shakespeare Survey 56: Shakespeare and Comedy*, ed. Peter Holland (Cambridge University Press, 2003)

"*King Lear* and the art of forgetting," under the title "Shakespeare and the art of forgetting," in *Memory and Invention: Medieval and Renaissance Literature, Art and Music*, ed. Anna Maria Busse Berger and Massimiliano Rossi (Leo S. Olschki, 2009)

"The case for Comus," *Representations*, no. 81 (Winter 2003)

"Textual icons," in *The Renaissance Computer*, ed. Neil Rhodes and Jonathan Sawday (Routledge, 2000)

"Not his picture but his book," in a much truncated version, Commentary, *Times Literary Supplement* (London), no. 5238 (August 22, 2003)

"Plagiarism revisited," under the title "Plagiarism and original sin," in *Plagiarism in Early Modern England*, ed. Paulina Kewes (Palgrave Macmillan, 2003)

"Ganymede Agonistes," in a shorter version, *GLQ: A Journal of Lesbian and Gay Studies*, vol. 10, no. 3 (2004)

Introduction

This is a volume of essays on performance construed in the largest sense, as theatre and pageantry, as the deployment of a personal style, as imagery of various kinds, and even as books, which in the early modern era often include strongly performative elements. Most of the essays are recent, and five are unpublished. They fall logically into four groups: on personal style and the construction of the self, on drama, on books, and on the visual arts.

Personal style is performative in the simple sense that it is expressive and in the more complex sense that it thereby implies that there is something *to* express. The essays in my first section, on style, begin with the construction of the sovereign. "I am Richard II" is a discussion of courtly imagery, and of the ways in which the English monarchy imagined itself through the visual arts and through the culture of royal entries, masques and triumphal arches. It begins with a reconsideration of Elizabeth's famous characterization of herself as her tragic ancestor, and then focuses on several striking examples of courtly display in which something went wrong – the actors subverted the text, the monarch refused to play his assigned role, the audience rebelled. "Seeing through costume" takes a broad view of the question of performance through disguise. Disguises in Elizabethan drama are nearly always presumed to be impenetrable, effectively concealing the self, whereas costume is designed to adorn the self, to make the self more strikingly recognizable. Both concepts are essential elements of theater, though costume, as a defining feature of almost any social role, is also essential to the functioning of every human culture. The permanence and impenetrability of the self beneath the costume, and therefore the essential superficiality of the costume, however, has not always been taken for granted. The essay considers the changing effects of disguise and costume both on concepts of the self and on assumptions about the kind of reality represented by theater. "Jonson and the Amazons" focuses on the growing influence of women on literature and drama in the English Renaissance, and is a chapter in the complex history of patronage, the strategic performance of poets for their most immediate audiences.

As a practice that makes performance visible as such, theater is characterized by an ongoing reflection on the very norms that make dramatic performance legible and indeed possible. The book's second section, on those shifting norms, includes essays on *King Lear, Othello, Hamlet* and *Comus*. "*Othello* and the end of comedy" starts from the familiar observation that *Othello* is a tragedy that has the structure of a comedy and, indeed, opens where traditional comedies end, with the secret lovers publicly united in a happy marriage. One of Shakespeare's two or three most perennially popular plays, it became the norm of tragedy in the later seventeenth century, but at the end of the century it was savagely and wittily attacked by Thomas Rymer, who denounced the play as irrational and pernicious, a dangerous norm. Rymer's critique appears to us an exercise in lunacy, but it is not entirely misguided and gives a clue to the sources of the play's unique intensity and to the peculiar power it has always exercised over audiences. In "*King Lear* and the art of forgetting" I propose that forgetting, or the suppression or subversion of memory, is an essential creative principle. I have in mind both really big creative acts like forgetting that the Lear story has a happy ending, and really small but even more baffling creative acts such as in *As You Like It* introducing a character named Jaques and forgetting that there is already a character named Jaques in the play. There are many more such examples in Shakespeare, and they have yet to receive their critical due. Indeed, the process of constructing the Shakespeare we want has for the most part been itself a process of forgetting about such moments and, generally, this side of Shakespeare's creative process. But forgetting is key to the act of creation and even in certain respects the essence of drama itself. "The case for Comus" offers a radically unorthodox reading of Milton's *Maske*, focusing on both the nominal villain and the place of women in the society for which the work was composed. Most discussions of Milton's early masque focus on its political or religious implications, and its status as a precursor to Milton's ethical and revolutionary thinking in his prose pamphlets and major poems. I am concerned here, on the contrary, with its implications specifically as a family affair; it is this that seems to me most significantly Miltonic. "Completing *Hamlet*" is basically a *jeu d'esprit*, a tribute to two of my favorite incarnations of Shakespeare's most inexhaustible play.

Although books have often been seen primarily as repositories of meaning, they also behave as complex performances, whether through the shifting relations among the parts that make up a book's whole or in the relation of book to reader and reader to book. The first essay on books is "Open secrets" and concerns magic in early modern England. Sixteenth-century English household books include a good deal of magic in their recommendations for staying healthy and keeping the house safe and clean. It is customary to argue that this was not "really" thought of as magic in the period, that magic was something much more serious and professional, such as alchemy; but a reading of two of the most popular handbooks, Thomas Lupton's *Thousand Notable Things* (1577, and innumerable subsequent editions) and the English version of Girolamo Ruscelli's *Segreti d'Alessio, Secrets of Alexis* (1562, and innumerable subsequent editions) explicitly belie this claim. The volumes give a fascinating perspective on an everyday world explicitly said to be full of magic – what Lupton and Ruscelli say they are purveying is "natural magic," which is useful for everything from curing toothaches to undoing the effects of witchcraft. The idea that magic was both natural and a part of everyday life allows us to reassess the fantasy worlds of *Doctor Faustus*, *A Midsummer Night's Dream* and *The Tempest*, as well as Jonson's satire on the popular faith in magic in *The Alchemist*. "Textual icons" is concerned with the practice of early modern book illustration. We tend to consider pictures in books peripheral, decorative, an adjunct to the text. But, in the history of printing, the illustrated book is as old as the book itself. Woodblock books, such as the *Biblia Pauperum*, employed pictures to epitomize, recall and even control the interpretation of the scriptural histories. The image as epitome of the text becomes increasingly significant as the book develops. But also, with the development of the caption, the image becomes free-standing, no longer dependent for its interpretation on the narrative or discursive movement of the text. Moreover, pictures have a tendency to migrate from text to text, illustrating or epitomizing widely divergent books – it is the text in these cases that is ephemeral, the pictures that are stable and continuous. "Not his picture but his book" examines the development of the concept of the author-portrait in early modern England, of ways of imagining and constructing authorship, looking beyond the familiar examples of Sidney, Shakespeare, Jonson and Donne. The idea of the author is considered from another aspect in "Plagiarism revisited," which returns to an early essay of mine on the subject, and discusses the history of attitudes toward plagiarism, and its relation to concepts of literary creativity.

Images are never more performative in and for a culture than when they offer a view onto the differences through which culture is made. My first essay on the visual arts, "Devils incarnate," takes its title from Roger Ascham's famous dictum that Italians are wicked but the Italianate Englishman is the devil incarnate. I consider a group of English Renaissance artists and connoisseurs with a particularly intense relationship to Italian culture, including Inigo Jones, Ben Jonson, and the first notable British collectors of Italian painting, the Earl and Countess of Arundel, Henry Prince of Wales and King Charles I. And "Ganymede Agonistes" offers a reading of the history of interpretations of the Ganymede myth in the Renaissance through both literary and iconographic evidence, arguing that the story's homosexual component played a much larger role, and was much more often and openly acknowledged, than modern literary and art historians have been willing to allow.

I conclude with acknowledgments to several indispensable friends. There is not an essay in this collection that has not benefitted from the wisdom and generosity of my most constant reader Bradin Cormack. I owe scarcely less to both the care and the learned and vigilant attention of Michael Wyatt. My friend and research assistant Ryan Zurowski negotiated the minefields of pictures and permissions with ingenuity, patience and unfailing good humor, with the assistance at a particular emergent occasion of my old and valued friend Clark Hulse. I am infinitely grateful to Peter Davidson and Jane Stevenson for endless hospitality and conversation about a number of these essays, all in the splendid comfort of Burnside House in the far north of Scotland, and most of all for recommending me to my exemplary editor Matthew Frost, who won me away from all other publishers with the siren song "You can have as many illustrations as you want."

Finally, a word about Anne Hollander's exquisite costume sketch, which she has kindly permitted me to reproduce on the cover. In 1969 the the poet John Hollander, my oldest friend, wrote an Elizabethan masque for the New York Pro Musica entitled *An Entertainment for Elizabeth*, and dedicated it to me. Anne Hollander, art historian and designer, then his wife, did the costumes for the work, which were based on Elizabethan and Jacobean models. In the performance, a dancer impersonating Queen Elizabeth was on stage, in a dress based on her gown in the Ditchley portrait. She was entertained by Terpsichore, the goddess of dance, with embodiments of the seven Motions: Up, Down, Back, Forth, Right, Left and Around. Eventually Elizabeth joined in the dance. The work was beautiful and the production was a notable success; the group toured widely with it, and it remained in the repertoire for several seasons. The drawing reproduced here is an early sketch of the costume for Up, revealed as the Sun, a spectacular performance in itself.

Part I

The construction of the self

1

I am Richard II

My title alludes to William Lambarde's well-known account of his interview with Queen Elizabeth in August, 1601, seven months after the Essex rebellion and Essex's execution for treason. Lambarde was the royal archivist, and had brought Elizabeth a summary of the historical documents stored in the Tower of London. She paused at the reign of Richard II, and when Lambarde asked why, she replied, memorably, "I am Richard II, know ye not that?" Lambarde acknowledged that he understood this to be an allusion to the actions of the late earl of Essex, who had commissioned Shakespeare's company to revive the old tragedy of *Richard II* on the eve of the rebellion. Lambarde responded, "Such a wicked imagination was determined and attempted by a most unkind gentleman, the most adorned creature that ever your majesty made." This was obviously the right response, and Elizabeth continued, "He that will forget God will also forget his benefactors; this tragedy was played forty times in open streets and houses." In fact, that season Shakespeare's tragedy was played only that once: as the actor Augustine Phillips later explained to the authorities, the play was "so old and so long out of use that they should have small or no company at it" (that is, it would have attracted no audience), but Essex's men had subsidised the performance to the tune of forty shillings – 480 groundling tickets, or 240 seats in the gallery – and so the company "at their request were content to play it." Clearly Elizabeth saw the implications of that single performance extending well beyond the confines of the Globe and a particular afternoon. "Forty times in open streets and houses": her fantasy made the whole of London a huge civic theater in which she was continually mimed and deposed.

Most accounts of the interview with Lambarde end there. But Lambarde's memorandum continues, and it is the next bit I wish to focus on. "Returning to Richard II," Lambarde says, "she demanded 'Whether I had seen any true picture, or lively representation of his countenance and person?'" "None," Lambarde replied, "but such as be in common hands." The queen said she had a portrait of Richard. "The Lord Lumley, a lover of antiquities, discovered it fastened on the backside of a door of a base[ment] room; which he presented unto me, praying, with my good leave, that I might put it in order with the ancestors and successors; I will command Thomas Kneavet, Keeper of my House and Gallery at Westminster, to show it unto thee." [1]

Figure 1.1 is the painting, now in Westminster Abbey. It is the earliest known painted portrait of an English monarch, and is ascribed to André Beauneveu, a Valenciennes painter resident at the English court in the late fourteenth century. The portrait, therefore, could have been done from life – it was, at any rate, done while the king was still living. It shows him in full formal regalia, holding the orb and scepter. His age is difficult to guess. He has no facial hair, and it has the look of a coronation portrait. Richard ascended the throne at the age of ten, but the image is so stylized that, though he is clearly in coronation robes, it could represent him at any point in his twenty-year reign. The lack of facial hair is not unusual for royal portraits of the period – figures 1.2 and 1.3 are Richard III and Henry V, both depicted clean-shaven, as is, at the end of the century, Henry VII in Torrigiano's superb bust (figure 1.4). All these monarchs are unambiguously mature. Figure 1.5 is a miniature of the young Henry VIII, aged twenty-two, in 1513. It is he who subsequently changes the facial convention, in emulation of the monarch he most envied: according to a Venetian envoy in 1519, "hearing that King Francis wore a beard, he allowed his to grow." [2] Nevertheless, the earliest miniature of the king painted by Lucas Hornebolte in 1525, when Henry was thirty-four (figure 1.6), still shows him as clean shaven. In another Hornebolte miniature painted only a few months later (figure 1.7), however, he is bearded and, to the modern eye at least, much improved. The pattern is definitively established by Holbein in the 1530s (figure 1.8) and since most of the portraits from this period are done in the context of marriage negotiations, they emphasize his virility and patriarchal ambitions, with the beard as an obviously relevant accessory. Figure 1.9 dates from the year of his brief and disastrous marriage to Anne of Cleves – the beard in this case must have been especially disillusioning, for both of them.

Let us return now to Elizabeth's portrait of Richard II. All the other representations of the king done during his lifetime, such as that in the Wilton diptych (figure 1.10), are similarly beardless – he is twenty-three years old here. The later portrait in figure 1.11, however, probably sixteenth century, and obviously based on the Westminster painting, has facial hair added – modestly in this case, nothing assertively masculine in the Henry VIII style, but enough to establish that the king is not a child. On his tomb effigy in figure 1.12 he is elegantly bearded – the facial hair that, until Henry VIII, was inappropriate to portraits of the living dignified him in death.

1.1 Attributed to
André Beauneveu,
Richard II in
coronation robes,
late fifteenth century.
Westminster Abbey.

1.2 Anonymous, Richard III.

1.3 Anonymous, Henry V.

1.4 Pietro Torrigiano, Henry VII, portrait bust from a death mask, 1509.

1.5 Anonymous, Henry VIII at the age of twenty-two, 1513.

1.6 Lucas Hornebolte, Henry VIII at the age of thirty-four, 1525.

1.7 Lucas Hornebolte, Henry VIII growing a beard, 1525

1.8 Hans Holbein the younger, Henry VIII aged forty-nine, 1537.

1.9 After Holbein, Henry VIII c. 1540.

1.10 Anonymous, Richard II presented to the Virgin and Child (the "Wilton diptych"), detail, c. 1395–99.

Elizabeth, coming to the throne with a compromised claim, certainly had as her greatest asset her protestantism; but she also brought to the succession her youth and her gender, which probably generated the assumption among her powerful supporters that, unlike her half-sister Mary, she would be both fecund and manageable. This was of course an illusion, and she thoroughly redefined the monarchy, largely through her extraordinary personal style. An essential element of that style was aesthetic and sartorial, beginning with her coronation portrait in figure 1.13. The original is lost; this is a copy from the beginning of the seventeenth century. In comparison with the individualized and assertive Holbein and Hornebolte portraits of her father, or the

1.11 Anonymous, Richard II, posthumous sixteenth-century portrait.

1.12 Richard II's tomb effigy. Westminster Abbey.

1.13 Anonymous, Elizabeth I in coronation robes. Copy c. 1600 of a lost original.

domesticated portraits of her sister by Antonio Mor, the painting is strikingly iconic. It employs a pictorial formula used occasionally on royal documents, but it is most strikingly similar to the Westminster portrait of Richard II. Roy Strong says that the medieval conventions of the representation of royalty were being revived here,[3] which is doubtless true; but in fact the only comparable earlier English royal portrait is the portrait of Richard; there *are* no other medieval English coronation portraits. The model that was being revived was that of the portrait of Richard II. Since the painting must always have been in the royal collection, was it in fact available to the painter in 1559, and did it disappear into the basement only after it had served its exemplary function? Perhaps Elizabeth had even seen it at the time of her accession; and in that case, it was not discovered by Lord Lumley, but rediscovered, and restored to its place in her lineage.

"I am Richard II" indeed. The two paintings document the creation of a carefully crafted ideology. Elizabeth's coronation portrait returns to the model of the last English monarch with an unquestioned claim to the throne – it goes back beyond her parents' dubious marriage and her own bastardization, beyond her grandfather Henry VII's seizure of the throne by conquest, beyond the disputed claims of York and Lancaster and the Wars of the Roses, beyond Henry IV's usurpation and deposition of the last unquestionably legitimate English king, whose model she adopts despite the fact that he was not her ancestor. The painting, in short, iconographically abolishes a century and a half of both English history and royal iconography, and returns us to the last moment when the legitimacy of the monarchy was not a problem. Indeed, Elizabeth's claim was always more exemplary than genealogical. Half a century later, ironically, in the context of the Essex rebellion, the image had become relevant again, in the worst way.

The story of Elizabeth's self-fashioning has been well covered, particularly by Janet Arnold in her study of the royal wardrobe, by Roy Strong on the portraits, and more generally by Susan Frye in her excellent book *Elizabeth I*, tellingly subtitled *The Competition for Representation*.[4] Competing versions of the queen were visible throughout the reign. The iconic, unapproachable, doll-like figure of the coronation portrait existed simultaneously with the endlessly desireable heiress in figure 1.14, the most eminently marriageable woman in Europe, demure and virtuous, but also wonderfully accomplished, as in figure 1.15, more and more splendidly dressed and displaying astonishing jewelry, an indication of how rich a prize she would constitute for any husband – the accoutrements, indeed, increasingly pre-empted the woman, as in the painting in figure 1.16 at Hardwick Hall, attributed to Nicholas Hilliard and dated 1592. Her virtues are summed up in the well-known reworking of the Judgment of Paris in figure 1.17, where she combines the virtues of Venus, Minerva and Juno, everything one could want in an aristocratic wife; but in which the golden apple of love, no longer in the gift of some irresponsible shepherd prince, has become the orb of state and is firmly in her grasp.

But of course the power inherent in the promise of marriage was dependent on her never exercising it – her strategy was the opposite of her half-sister's, who thought that marriage to the most powerful man in Europe was the key to controlling the course of her own realm. It was a strategy that, once determined upon, left her no other options. Elizabeth elected to leave all her options perpetually open – she raised flirtation to an instrument of policy. It was an instrument that was effective as long as she remained marriageable but unmarried. Figure 1.18 shows the last time she represented herself as a marriageable woman, the magnificent frontispiece to Saxton's *Atlas*, the

1.14 William Scrots, Elizabeth I as princess, c. 1546–47.

1.15 Nicholas Hilliard, Elizabeth I playing the lute.

1.16 Attributed to Nicholas Hilliard, Elizabeth I, 1592.

1.17 Hans Eworth, Elizabeth and three goddesses, 1569. The painting, despite its monogram HE, had been attributed by Roy Strong to Joris Hoefnagel, but is now accepted by the Royal Collection, which owns it, as the work of Eworth.

first comprehensive survey of England and Wales and the first national atlas undertaken anywhere, published in 1579, in the midst of her two-year flirtation with the Duc d'Alençon. She takes possession of her realm as patron of geography. As A. B. Hind has shown, she was actively involved in the design of this portrait, a humanized and sexualized refiguration of the formula of the coronation painting.[5] The imagery surrounding her places the masters of geography and astronomy at her service; but most striking of all are the implications of the impresa at the center of the frieze, figure 1.19.

I have written in detail about this in my essay "Gendering the Crown"[6] Above the queen, in an oval at the center of the frieze, is a group of three figures. A naked woman bearing an olive branch and an armed woman bearing a sword embrace; behind the armed woman, a putto holds a set of scales. This represents the loving union of Justice and Peace, as predicted by Psalm 85, "iustitia et pax deosculatae sunt" (there are all sorts of problems with this interpretation, but I

Clemens et Regni moderatrix iusta Britani
Hac forma insigni conspicienda nitet.

An. Dni

Tristia dum gentes circum omnes bella fatigant,
Cæciq́ errores toto grassantur in orbe.
pace beas longa, Vera et pietate Britannos:
Iusticia moderans miti sapienter habenas.
Chara domi, celebrisq́ foris, longævaq́ regnû
Hic teneas, regno tandem fruitura perenni

1579

1.18 *(opposite)* Remigius Hogenberg (?), frontispiece to Christopher Saxton's *Atlas of England and Wales, 1579.*

1.19 Justice and Peace embracing. Detail of Figure 1.18.

have sorted them out and I believe resolved them in "Gendering the Crown," to which I refer readers who want the whole argument). This was an impresa invented for Pope Julius III, widely circulated and often reproduced. Figure 1.20 shows its usual form, on one of the title-pages to another atlas, Georg Braun's magnificent *Civitates Orbis Terrarum* (1572). To appropriate the papal emblem and redefine it for the queen, Peace has been undressed, and the putto bearing Justice's scales has been added. The English version makes the issue of female sexuality insistently manifest. A naked woman accompanied by a putto inescapably suggests Venus and Cupid; and, indeed, one's first impression of the impresa is that it represents the more commonplace coupling of Venus and Mars – in the topos, the armed woman, Pallas or Bellona standing in for Justice, has replaced the god of war. The association of Venus with Elizabeth was surely intentional: Saxton's *Atlas* was published, as I have said, in the midst of the negotiations over the Alençon match, the last time the queen was to represent herself as a marriageable woman. The allusion to Venus, moreover, makes a genealogical claim: Elizabeth is descended from Venus, the mother of Aeneas and the great-grandmother of Brutus, legendary founder of Britain and therefore Elizabeth's ancestor. The goddess of love is the source of the British royal line. The impresa prefixed to this survey of Elizabeth's kingdom insists on the absolute authority of the feminine, embodied in the English queen.

But of course one cannot control the implications of imagery, or close it off to interpretation. The claim of programmatic chastity always had to compete with the assumption of aristocratic promiscuity, especially when the aristocrat was an unmarried woman; and doubtless the introduction of Venus and Cupid

1.20 Georg Braun and Remigius Hogenberg, title page to *Civitates Orbis Terrarum*, 1572, detail of Justice and Peace.

into the royal impresa was a way of both acknowledging the queen's sexuality and at the same time attempting to keep it under control. Nevertheless, scurrilous stories – for example, that she had had a child by Leicester – made the rounds; and that particular one was still circulating in the next century. In the same way, her first chosen image of royal legitimacy, Richard II enthroned, also always carried with it the spectre of his deposition – the farther Elizabeth got from her accession the more dangerous the ancient precedent became. Is it surprising that the portrait was banished to the basement, out of sight?

The dangers of deposition were secondary, however, to the reality of Elizabeth's remaining unmarried and without an heir. At a strange moment near the end of Shakespeare's celebratory history *Henry VIII* an old lady appears before the king, interrupting some business of state. "I guess thy message," he says; "Is the queen delivered?/ Say ay, and of a boy." The old lady, astonishingly, complies: "Ay, ay, my liege, and of a lovely boy." A moment later she amends the message: "'Tis a girl/ Promises boys hereafter" (V.1.163–6). The king is not pleased, and undertips the messenger, who grumpily departs.

The incident has no parallel in the historical sources – it is all Shakespeare – and even among audiences at the Globe in 1613, with a king and a male heir finally in place again, it must have resonated strangely. For Henry's posterity, after all, Elizabeth represented the end of the line; and she certainly did not promise the accession of James I, whom she declined to name as her successor until she was on her deathbed – and it is not clear that she did so even then. Not only was the Scottish king not Henry VIII's descendant, he derived from a branch of the family specifically excluded from the succession by the king's will. Elizabeth's father had done everything he could to preclude the Scottish succession. James's presence on the throne represented the ultimate failure of Henry's dynastic dream. The dramatic moment introduces a strange blip into the play's triumphal rhetoric. The original title under which it was performed at the Globe was *All Is True*. What kind of truth does this incident, indeed, does the whole of the triumphal drama, represent?

In short, who believed in all the age's idealizing iconography? Did Elizabeth herself believe it? Spenser's endless epic encomium *The Faerie Queene* promised to immortalize her royal mythology, but it earned the poet little: not the laureateship, not a place at court, only a modest payment and a ticket back to Ireland. Ben Jonson told William Drummond that "Q. Elizabeth never saw herself after she became old in a true glass; they painted her, and sometimes would vermilion her nose. She had always about Christmas evens set [i.e. loaded] dice that threw sixes or fives, and she knew not they were other, to make her win and esteem herself fortunate."[7] This describes a queen trapped in her image and manipulated by her servants; and even if the stories were untrue, the very fact that they were in circulation argues a skeptical public.

The Puritan barrister John Stubbs's *Gaping Gulf Wherein England is Like to Be Swallowed*, published in 1579 at the height of the Alençon negotiations, heartlessly deconstructed the royal mythology. The pamphlet included nothing that was not a popular commonplace, but it became notorious because of Elizabeth's explosive reaction to it, which was outraged, panicky and vindictive. Stubbs is undeniably rude about Alençon, whom he despises as an adventurer and a Papist, but his attitude toward Elizabeth, while certainly not reverent, is unquestionably loyal and loving. The tone he takes might best be described as fraternal: scolding and impatient, but also affectionate, indulgent, full of care and concern; above all, straightforward and commonsensical – about matters like Elizabeth's advanced age, for example. What, Stubbs asks, in effect, does a young man like that want with an old woman like you? Young men only pursue older women for their money; and so forth. Such arguments are certainly tactless, but scarcely treasonable. The queen, however, was furious, and wanted Stubbs and the publisher charged with seditious libel and hanged. This turned out to be legally impossible – the case proved to be an important test of the limits of sovereignty, and constituted a defeat for the queen – but the perpetrators were imprisoned (ironically, charged under a statute of Mary Tudor's providing penalties for those who libelled her husband Philip II of Spain) and their right hands were cut off by the public executioner, a sentence which, however grisly and symbolically appropriate, cannot have given Elizabeth much satisfaction. Stubbs on the scaffold waved the bloody stump and shouted "God save the queen," still infuriatingly affirming that he had only her interests at heart, that he knew best; and the crowd agreed. He was a popular hero. A reading of the pamphlet reveals no intention of either sedition or libel, but it does tell a good deal about Elizabeth's sense of the crucial importance, both political and personal, of the fictions with which she surrounded herself, the fictions that were to be enshrined in *The Faerie Queene*. Stubbs's model for his relation to the sovereign is not the chivalric court, but the family. Spenser sets his fiction in the distant past to keep it safe, he says, from the envy of present time – that, for Spenser, is the reality. We surely err in taking the queen's version of herself as a working model for the life of the commonwealth.

1.21 Nicholas Hilliard, James I c. 1605.

1.22 James I, *Workes*, 1616, frontispiece.

1.22 James I, *Workes*, 1616, frontispiece.

The accession of the king of Scotland to Elizabeth's throne was greeted with enthusiasm and a certain amount of relief – the issue of what was to happen next had at last been resolved. James made his way to his new kingdom with all deliberate speed, stopping along the way at various great houses to be congratulated and feasted, bestowing honors, and promising much more. He appeared a grateful choice; certainly he was a generous one. There is no formal coronation portrait – he disliked sitting for painters – but the early portraits from his reign avoid the traditional royal iconography of crown, orb and scepter, in favor of the attributes of a rich aristocrat. In the Hilliard miniature in figure 1.21 he wears the Order of St George and a complex jewel in his feathered hat. He might be one of the stylish young men he doted on and was continually ennobling. It was not until late in the reign that he adopted the royal iconography, on the frontispiece to his *Workes* (figure 1.22), published in 1616.

As for his accession to the English crown, the difference between Queen Elizabeth's enthusiastic and carefully crafted response to the pageantry that celebrated the beginning of her reign and James's delayed, reserved and grudging one to his is notorious, and in both cases the response itself was performative, part of a show for the much larger audience of spectators who lined the route. It was also, probably more significantly, a performance for the audience who footed the bill – in the case of civic pageantry, the guilds, city fathers, Inns of Court, foreign merchants, or private magnates, for whom the production was an investment; and the responses of both the chief actor/spectator and the civic audience should be considered in that context, as the return on the investment.

When King James balked at participating in London's pageant celebrating his accession, both the refusal and the response to it were matters of public policy, and the whole project could not simply be abandoned. The entry had originally been planned for July, 1603, to coincide with his coronation. But the plague was raging, and the entry was repeatedly postponed – so long that the seven triumphal arches, which had been erected along the route at great expense, had to be dismantled and stored. James finally consented to submit to what he made clear he considered an ordeal in March, 1604.

What did the City want the king to see and hear; and, more important, what did the City want to display him seeing and hearing? The pageant constitutes an exemplary case for considering the interaction of symbolic fictions and their subjects. To begin with, much of the auditory part was notional, since (as Thomas Dekker reports in his account) many of the speeches could not be heard – acoustics were always a problem at these events; moreover, because of time constraints some were omitted entirely. This means that, for the spectators, there was effectively no elucidation: this was spectacle without meaning. By far the most important element was the arches, created by the architect Stephen Harrison, who published engravings of them that constitute the best record we have of an English royal entry before the Restoration. I shall not here walk through the whole of the entry, but will rather indicate some particular points of tension. Figure 1.23 is the first arch, at Fenchurch, at the east end of the City – the design was Ben Jonson's, realized by Harrison. It is an epitome of London, crowned with a model of the city, and including two little stages for musicians and niches for actors. Initially it was covered with a silk curtain painted with thick clouds. As the king approached, the curtain was drawn. Jonson (who wrote the speeches) explains that the clouds represent the City's "long want of his wished sight," but the king's appearance at last is the sun that has dispersed the mists. Queen Elizabeth might have managed a gracious impromptu reply to the implied criticism of

1.23 Stephen Harrison, the arch at Fenchurch, from *The Arch's of Triumph*, 1604.

1.24 The Genius of the City, and the River Thames, detail of Figure 1.23.

the royal dilatoriness, but the king listened, as he did throughout the day, in silence. The allegorical figures on the arch are Monarchia Britannica with a globe and scepter; Divine Wisdom, with dove and serpent and the motto *Per me reges regnant*, kings reign through me; and Tamesis, the river Thames, the life blood of the city. Genius Urbis (figure 1.24), the Spirit of the City, however, delivers an unexpected sting. He holds a goblet and a bundle of twigs, "to signifie increase and indulgence" (presumably in reverse order); but he is accompanied by two figures representing the City's counsel and its military strength – through these, Jonson says, the City is able "to extinguish the king's enemies and preserve his citizens"; but they also clearly imply the City's power and the dangers of ignoring it.[8]

1.25 Stephen Harrison, the Italian arch, from *The Arch's of Triumph*, 1604.

1.26 Henry VII welcomes his descendant James I, detail of Figure 1.25.

On the next arch (figure 1.25), erected by the Italian merchants in London, Henry VII is invoked in a large central panel (figure 1.26): the first Tudor monarch, seated, receives James I on horseback and passes the royal scepter to him. The motto, *Hic vir hic est*, this is the man, he is here, declares James both the right man and a true counterpart to his ancestor: *this* man is also *this* one. As Elizabeth's iconography had gone back to the last legitimate English monarch, James's goes back to the usurping monarch from whom his own legitimacy derives. James is declared Henry's true heir, and Henry and James are identified as uniters of the realm and bringers of peace.

Near the Royal Exchange the large and prosperous community of Dutch merchants had erected their arch (figure 1.27). It is vastly more elaborate than the Italian arch (it filled the entire width of the street), combining painting, sculpture and living figures. At the top stands Providence; below her is a portrait of King James, and below this, in a central niche, seventeen children in native costume represent the seventeen provinces of the Netherlands. Various paintings on the structure depicted scenes of Dutch industry, clothmaking, fishing and shipping. The arch's complex allegorical scheme was elucidated at length by a boy orator exhorting the king to remember that he is subject to Providence, and recalling Elizabeth's military support for the Protestant cause

1.27 Stephen Harrison, the Dutch arch, from *The Arch's of Triumph*, 1604.

in the Low Countries. This was a message that the pacifist king who believed he ruled by divine right could not have found at all sympathetic.

The king proceeded in sullen silence through three more arches. The final arch (figure 1.28), at Temple Bar, the west end of London, was dedicated to Janus, the god of new beginnings, looking forward and backward. Designed and described by Jonson, it is learnedly classical, and his account of it is heavily annotated with citations from scholarly authorities. This was Jonson's bid for the scholar-king's attention, but the message was very much the City's: Eirene, Peace, has at her side Plutus, a boy carrying "a heap of gold ingots to express riches." Through James's peace and the City's wealth, Mars lies defeated at Eirene's feet. Jonson's speakers, a Roman flamen or priest and the Genius of the city, observe the date of the performance – the Ides of March. The flamen has kindled a fire to celebrate the distinctly inauspicious day (there is of course no allusion to the death of Caesar; but the anniversary would not have gone unnoticed). The Genius, however, stops him: "these dead rites/ Are long since buried, and new power excites/ More high and hearty flames."[9]

New Power – it is precisely that new power that the whole pageant, from one end of the City to the other, both celebrates and exercises: the power of the king, but also power *over* the king. James's reaction to the crowd, as a sign of the city's force, is telling here. The courtier Arthur Wilson recalled the occasion half a century later:

> The King, with the Queen and Prince ... rode from the Tower to Whitehall; the City and Suburbs being one great Pageant, wherein he must give his ears leave to suck in their gilded Oratory, though never so nauseious to the stomach. He was not like his Predecessor, the late Queen of famous memory, that with a wel-pleased affection met her peoples Acclamations ... . He endured this days brunt with patience, being assured he should never have such another.[10]

James hated and feared crowds, and had no talent for manipulating them. His biographer David Harris Willson quotes a visitor to the court who reported that "the King ... would swear with passion, asking his attendants what the people would have. He was told they came of love to see him. 'Then would he cry out in Scottish, "God's wounds! I will pull down my breeches and they shall also see my arse."'"[11]

It is clear why it was important for the City to put on this show, a public declaration on the one hand of allegiance and support, and on the other of the royal dependence on the commercial and financial powers of the kingdom. But when the king resisted, what was in it for the City and the guilds to force him

1.28 Stephen Harrison, the final arch of Janus at Temple Bar, from *The Arch's of Triumph*, 1604.

to give the performance, as he eventually did with such bad grace? Obviously this performance was not for the king's benefit; the king became, unwillingly, an actor in a larger drama presented by the City, the central element of which was precisely the City's ability to produce the king as a participant in the pageantry. The show was ultimately less a celebration than a show of force.

Theater is a two-way affair, action and reaction, and both inventors and audiences have their own purposes. In the case of festival modes the interaction with the various audiences – subject, patrons, onlookers – is far more complex, essential and palpable than it is in the case of books, or even of drama in performance. In interpreting such performances, we are inevitably limited by our evidence, which is invariably a written text, whether a script or a description. As should already be clear, I am especially interested in those cases where something goes wrong, and where the text gives us no help in understanding what happened. I now turn in conclusion to three examples, two from the courtly world of the masque and one from the commercial theater.

Sir John Harington's satiric account of the masque of Solomon and the Queen of Sheba, devised for the entertainment of James and his brother-in-law Christian IV of Denmark on their visit to the Earl of Salisbury at Theobalds in 1606, has become a touchstone for the indecorum of the Jacobean court; and since the text of the masque does not survive, Harington's letter has in effect become the masque. Indeed, there is no other reference to the performance, though the visit is quite well documented. It is entirely possible that the whole event was an invention of Harington's, a satiric epitome of the new court's excesses.[12] Fantasy masques, however, are no less enlightening than real ones if it is cultural assumptions we are concerned with, and in any case Harington had certainly participated in enough masques for his fiction to be enlightening. I am quoting rather more of the account here than usual, since I want to focus on some things that are generally overlooked:

> after dinner the representation of Solomon his temple and the coming of the Queen of Sheba was made, or (as I may better say) was meant to have been made, before their majesties, by device of the Earl of Salisbury and others [note that credit for the 'device' belongs to the patrons, not the poet and architect]. But, alas! … The lady who did play the queen's part did carry most precious gifts to both their majesties; but forgetting the steps arising to the canopy, overset her casket into his Danish majesty's lap, and fell at his feet, though I rather think it was in his face. Much was the hurry and confusion. Cloths and napkins were at hand, to make all clean. His majesty then got up, and would dance with the Queen of

Sheba; but he fell down and humbled himself before her, and was carried to an inner chamber and laid on a bed of state; which was not a little defiled with the presents of the queen which had been bestowed on his garments, such as wine, cream, jelly, beverage, cakes, spices, and other good matters.

The account continues to tell how most of the speakers bungled their parts through incompetence or drunkenness. King James, moreover – this is worth stressing – was decidedly uncooperative:

Victory, in bright armor … presented a rich sword to the king, who did not accept it, but put it by with his hand; and …did endeavor to make suit to the king … but after much lamentable utterance, she was led away like a silly captive and laid to sleep in the outer steps of the anti-chamber.

Harington concludes that "I never did see such lack of good order, discretion and sobriety as I have now done."[13]

This is all that survives of a masque embodying King James's most deeply felt persona, the Solomonic monarch, and the only masque recorded from his reign on a biblical subject. Even in Harington's mind, James could not have been ignorant of the text. Why did the king refuse the sword of Victory? He must have known it was to be presented. Was he simply so offended by the indecorum that he withdrew from the game? Or was there a deeper meaning that Harington either missed or unwittingly revealed, the pacifist king refusing the martial image – if the masque did take place, was this even perhaps part of the show? What spectators see often differs significantly from what inventors intend.

Here is an example in which the audience refused to play its part. Ben Jonson's masque *Love Restored* was performed on Twelfth Night 1612, in the presence of the king and Prince Henry. The masquers were ten lords, "the spirits of Court, and flower of men" led by Cupid, and when they went to take out the ladies to dance the revels, John Chamberlain reports, "beginning with the ladies of Essex and Cranbourne, they were refused, which set an example to the rest, so that the lords were fain to dance alone and make court to one another."[14]

The only way we know about what must have been a real fiasco is from Chamberlain's letter. Jonson's published text is understandably silent about it. Gossip here is of the essence. At this remove, it is very difficult to know what the problem was. The Countess of Essex (who was not yet the notorious divorcée) and Viscountess Cranborne were sisters, Frances and Catherine

Howard, stars of James's court, daughters of the Earl of Suffolk, a powerful and very influential peer. Suffolk apparently was embarrassed by their behavior, but since the rest of the ladies followed their lead, the problem they perceived cannot have been theirs alone. Martin Butler suggests, plausibly, that the lords, most of whom were Scots, were seen by the Howard ladies as upstarts and insufficiently aristocratic, and, if this is correct, the incident gives us a good insight into the limits of protocol and the extent of courtly privilege and independence at such events – Frances Howard was in the process of divorcing her husband to marry one of James's Scots favorites, Robert Carr, created Earl of Somerset in the following year, and she may have been especially touchy about the number of rapidly enobled Scots at court. But this cannot be the whole story. What happens when the audience refuses to play its part? The work was jointly sponsored by the king and Prince Henry, and the Scottish masquers were members of their households, favorites and protégés; so the ladies were offending not merely the upstart lords, but their royal patrons as well. One can imagine circumstances in which such behavior would have been considered deeply disruptive, even perhaps treasonable – like Cordelia's behavior at the opening of *King Lear* – but if we understand Chamberlain correctly (the letter is not entirely legible) all the apologies were directed at the mortified parent, Suffolk; Chamberlain says nothing about the reaction of the king and prince. In short, the implications of this affair seem more private than public. And yet, the whole point of the masque – any masque – was precisely that public assertion of aristocratic solidarity: everybody joins in the game celebrating the glories of the crown and court. But even the gossips seem to be silent about what happens when they don't. Is this because nothing happens, or is the lacuna simply in our evidence – or in what we must, perforce, treat as evidence?

When King James came to the English throne he placed the theatrical companies under royal patronage because he loved theater and believed in its efficacy as an attribute of royal authority; and no doubt when the actors, poets, designers and musicians provided court masques celebrating his wisdom and glory, the investment looked like a good one. But, in fact, in the period the alliance between court and theater worked both ways, and theater, even the theater of the court masque, is too anarchic to be confined by patronage. Often enough the protection of the crown was interpreted by the participants to be protection *from* the crown. Take, as a final example, the strange case of the Children of the Revels producing plays at the Blackfriars satirizing the king, his favorites and his new Scottish knights. One particularly offensive production, which I have discussed in my essay "The Spectacles of State," depicted James himself, according to the French ambassador, "ivre pour le moins une fois le jour" – drunk at least once a day.[15] This play so enraged the king that he swore he would never have the company play before him again and would make them "beg their bread."[16] In fact, the players were back at court within the year: the incident reveals how little we really understand what must have been a very complicated and ambivalent relationship.

Why did the company produce such plays to begin with? They pitted what were apparently the prejudices of the Blackfriars audience against the wishes and authority of their own patron: how was this in their interest? Why did they not anticipate the king's displeasure, or, if they did, why were they willing to risk it – what was in it for them? Where was the censor: why did the Lord Chamberlain allow such a production? And surely most baffling of all, why did the king cool down? Consider a few dates: the play depicting the king drunk was produced in March, 1608. The boys next played at court on January 1 and 4, 1609, the Christmas season of the same year. But their *last previous* appearance at court had been in the season of 1604/5: they were not a company that regularly played before the king. The invitation to perform at New Year's 1609 was therefore extraordinary, a mark of special favor. The troupe's insolence had greatly advanced their standing.

What are we to make of all this? James was used to being attacked and insulted to his face by ministers preaching in his chapel, but surely neither he nor the players could have believed that theatrical companies were like preachers, and served a higher law. Ben Jonson, characteristically, regretted the fact. He told William Drummond that "he hath a mind to be a churchman, and so he might have favor to make one sermon to the King, he careth not what thereafter should befall him, for he would not flatter though he saw Death."[17] Like the Children of the Revels Jonson dreamt of attacking with impunity; and the target of the satire in both cases was not the playhouse audience but the king. In overlooking the players' offense in 1608, James was at the very least acknowledging his own complicity in the fictions of the revels. Queen Elizabeth's players were less fractious and had always been flattering – George Peele in *The Arraignment of Paris* once again gave her the golden apple intended for Venus, Ben Jonson appropriated her wisdom to adjudicate the conclusion of *Every Man Out of His Humour*, *Cynthia's Revels* was a celebration of her court – but she knew well enough that the relationship between the theater and the crown was always a complex mixture of intimacy and danger, and she knew her own place in it. "We princes," she told the Lords and Commons in 1586, "are set on stages" – she was not the audience; she was the spectacle. "This tragedy was played forty times in open streets and houses." "I am Richard II."

Notes

1 Both Lambarde's memorandum and Phillips's testimony are cited in Peter Ure's Arden II *Richard II* (London, 1956), pp. lvii–lix.

2 *Calendar of State Papers Venetian 1509–19*, p. 559.

3 Roy Strong, *Gloriana: The Portraits of Queen Elizabeth I* (London, 1987), p. 20.

4 Janet Arnold, *The Queen's Wardrobe Unlock'd* (Leeds, 1988); Strong, *Gloriana*; Susan Frye, *Elizabeth I: The Competition for Representation* (New York, 1993).

5 A. B. Hind, *Engraving in England in the Sixteenth and Seventeenth Centuries* (Cambridge, 1952), 1.73.

6 Stephen Orgel, "Gendering the Crown," in *The Authentic Shakespeare, and Other Problems of the Early Modern Stage* (New York, 2002), pp. 107–28.

7 Conversations with Drummond, in Ian Donaldson, ed., *Ben Jonson* (Oxford, 1985), p. 602.

8 Ben Jonson, *Part of the Kings entertainment, in passing to his Coronation*, in C. H. Herford, and P. Simpson, *Ben Jonson*, volume VII (Oxford, 1941), pp. 85–6.

9 Herford and Simpson, *Ben Jonson* VII, p. 102.

10 Arthur Wilson, *The History of Great Britain, Being the Life and Reign of King Iames the First* (1653), pp. 12–13.

11 David Harris Willson, *King James VI and I* (Oxford, 1967), p. 165.

12 The case has tentatively but persuasively been made by Martin Butler, *The Stuart Court Masque and Political Culture* (Cambridge, 2008), pp. 125–7.

13 John Nichols, *Progresses ... of King James the First* (1828), 2.72–3.

14 *Letters of John Chamberlain*, ed. Norman E. McClure, 2 vols (Philadelphia, PA, 1939), 1:328. There is an excellent discussion of the incident in Butler, *The Stuart Court Masque and Political Culture*, pp. 205–7.

15 The essay is in *The Authentic Shakespeare*, pp. 71–88. I summarize a section of the argument here.

16 E. K. Chambers, *The Elizabethan Stage*, 4 vols (Oxford, 1923), 4:500.

17 Conversations with Drummond, in Donaldson, *Ben Jonson*, p. 602.

2

Seeing through costume

Disguise is by definition superficial, the misrepresentation of one's appearance, though etymologically it imagines something much more radical, a "dis-appearance," which can imply anything from a mere move out of sight to the total annihilation of the person whose appearance is undone. It also assumes that there is always an essence beneath the appearance, something being concealed, misrepresented or denied. Corollary to this is that the essence is different from the disguise, and that what is concealed is what is real – this is not quite as axiomatic as it appears: consider such a construction, from *Henry v*, as "Then should the warlike Harry like himself/ Assume the port of Mars…", where the self is entirely congruent with the persona. Clearly, however, being like oneself is different from being oneself – the self is a role one plays. The congruence is, in any case, acknowledged to be all but impossible, requiring a "muse of fire." When the change of appearance includes a fictional or theatrical element and is not intended to render the person unrecognizable – intended not to conceal the real but to adorn it, even to make the person more strikingly recognizable – we call the disguise a costume, a relatively new term, existing in English only since the mid-eighteenth century, deriving from French and Italian words for "custom," and involving notions of the fashionable. This too assumes that though the externals may change, there is a self within that does not. Disguise is the essence of theater, and thereby of drama in performance, and it is enabled by, though not subsumed in, costume – what we are meant to see beneath the costumes on stage is the characters, not the actors. But costume, as a defining feature of almost any social role, is also essential to the functioning of every human culture.

I begin, however, with a few examples to remind us that the permanence and impenetrability of the self beneath the costume, and therefore the essential superficiality of the costume, has not always been taken for granted. The history of anti-theatricalism from Plato onward assumes that actors are indeed changed by their costumes; and Renaissance polemicists in England were especially exercised by the transvestism of the Elizabethan stage, arguing from both platonic and patristic examples that the wearing of female garments necessarily resulted in an effeminization of the actor's masculine self, and from that to the corruption of the audience. The self, in such arguments, is the most fragile of entities, acutely permeable by externals. In the context of Shakespeare's England, this claim was eccentric, even pathologically so, a defining feature of a lunatic fringe, and the urban mercantile audience to whom it was directed was largely unpersuaded, since it also constituted the principal audience for the popular theater of the age. But its assumptions nevertheless resonated in significant ways throughout the culture. Indeed, they have continued to do so: Robert Merrill, a leading baritone at the Metropolitan Opera for thirty years, was an orthodox Jew, and when he sang in *Don Carlo* or *La forza del destino* he always refused to wear a cross, lest this attribute of the role somehow penetrate and violate his inner self. The stage property, for this performer, had a dangerous interiority; which argues a striking belief in the power of the Christian symbol coming from an orthodox Jew. In contrast, for Caruso, singing Eléazar in *La juive*, the Jewish ritual garments were an essential element of the role, and he made much of them. Was Caruso's self less fragile than Merrill's, or did he simply take the role less seriously – or was Merrill, like Shakespeare's imagined Henry v, always playing himself?

As these examples suggest, it is not always clear what distinguishes the external from the internal. In the case of a light-skinned black who passes as white, for example, what is the relation between the skin color and the true self? The disguise, if there is one, is entirely internal – the person has undergone no visible change, but presents himself, or thinks of herself, in a new way. New ways of self-presentation are the very essence of fashion, which constantly reinvents itself, often blatantly, commanding attention through attempts to shock. What exactly is shocking in unconventional hair styles, revealing clothing, tattoos, body piercings? What fears are parents expressing in their alarm at the unexpected ways their children present themselves? The fear must be that the rebelliousness is not merely external; that the costume does express an inner reality, that our children are no longer versions of ourselves; but somewhere in the course of that reasoning must also be a conviction that the costume is the problem, that without the external transformation the inner rebellion would cease to exist, as Hamlet's mother urges him to cast his nighted color off, as if that would restore him to sociability. Culturally, the change, in fact, tends to work in the opposite direction: the transformations of fashion quickly cease to be shocking and become simply stylish – since the late twentieth century, when black has been fashionable, most of the court in productions of *Hamlet* has been costumed like Hamlet, and even the parents of my students now occasionally sport tattoos and nose studs.

How deep can disguise go? What is the effect of costume on the self? Here is an instance in which the effect is as esssential as it can be in a narrative – in which, that is, the effect is linguistic and, specifically, grammatical. Barnabe Riche, in his *Farewell to the Military Profession*,[1] tells the story of Apolonius and Silla. Silla and Silvio are twins, children of the Duke of Cyprus. Silvio is off at the wars; Silla falls in love with Apolonius, the duke of Constantinople, who is visiting at her father's court. When Apolonius departs, Silla determines to follow him, and persuades a faithful servant to accompany her on a ship about to sail for Constantinople. She disguises herself "in very simple attire," but the captain, struck by her exceptional beauty, proposes either to make love to her or, if she refuses, to rape her. Silla contemplates suicide, but a violent storm arises, the ship is wrecked, and Silla, clinging to a chest full of the captain's clothes, is washed ashore. Realizing the dangers faced by a young woman traveling alone, she disguises herself this time as a young man, wearing the sea-captain's clothes. She takes the name of her twin brother, Silvio, makes her way to Constantinople, seeks out the Duke Apolonius, and enters his service.

As most readers will be aware, this is the plot of *Twelfth Night*, though it is, for all its conventional romance elements, a far more rational version of the story than Shakespeare's. This heroine has already known and fallen in love with the duke who was to become Orsino, and she has a cogent reason for her cross-dressing, to avoid a repetition of the fate she has so narrowly escaped – Shakespeare cleans up the story, and in so doing removes the motive for the disguise.

Rational or not, however, the disguise turns out to be far more problematic for Silla than for Viola. After some months, when we are well into the plot, Silvio appears in Constantinople: he has been traveling the Mediterranean searching for his sister. Julina, Shakespeare's Olivia, encounters him, and naturally thinks he is his twin. She takes him home and entertains him; she is delighted with him – for once he is not undertaking to woo her on his master's behalf, and, indeed, Apolonius's name is not mentioned at all. And Silvio, overcoming his astonishment at the attention he is getting from a total stranger, is enchanted with her beauty and charm. One thing leads to another, and they spend the night together. The next morning, Silvio leaves, to continue his search for Silla. Two months later Julina realizes that she is pregnant.

She confronts Apolonius, demanding justice: his servant has taken advantage of her. Silla is summoned, and denies everything; but it is clear to Apolonius that Julina is telling the truth, and he insists that his servant now marry Julina.

Silla refuses, offering no reason for the refusal, and Apolonius imprisons "him." Julina visits the prisoner, berating and pleading; her oaths and absolute conviction are so persuasive that Silla herself "was like to beleeve that it had bin true in very deede; but remembryng his owne impediment, thought it impossible that he should committe such an acte" – notice both that Silla's disguise here is grammatical (the narration continues to refer to her with a masculine pronoun) and that she herself has to stop to remind herself that she is not what she appears – and even in doing so, contemplating the one thing that guarantees her innocence, she remains male, "remembryng his owne impediment." Even the eventual, ultimate revelation to Julina, Silla's confession of the genital truth about herself, does not undo the disguise: "And here with all loosing his garmentes doune to his stomacke, and shewed Julina his breastes and pretie teates ... saiyng: ... See, I am a woman ..." Silla only finally becomes grammatically female when Apolonius, "amased to hear this strange discourse of Silvio, came unto him, ... perceived indeede that it was Silla ..., and embracing her" – at last a feminine pronoun – orders a definitively feminine wardrobe for her and proposes marriage.[2] The true nature of the character here, even syntactically, is determined by the name and the provision of an appropriate costume.

In *Twelfth Night*, Viola and Sebastian are indistinguishable merely because they are identically dressed, and Viola is never in any doubt about the gender of the self beneath the costume. Nevertheless, the costume is still of the essence: at the very end of the play, when all the revelations have been made, Orsino still declares that the concluding marriage cannot take place until Viola's original clothes have been recovered; these have been hidden by the sea captain, who, in a plot twist introduced out of nowhere at the last minute, has been arrested on some unknown charge of Malvolio's, and will not reveal the whereabouts of the clothes until he is released, which only Malvolio can effect – and Malvolio has stormed out of the play, declaring that he will "be revenged on the whole lot of you." It is not, moreover, merely female garb that is required for this happy ending; it must be the original costume in which we first saw Viola – no one suggests that she borrow a dress from Olivia, or buy a wedding gown. The costume, the play insists, is Viola, and therefore it must be the right costume.

Disguises in Shakespeare are almost always absolute – with a small number of exceptions, nobody ever sees through a disguise (the exceptions are Falstaff in drag in *The Merry Wives of Windsor*, Tamora's impersonation of the allegorical figure of Revenge in *Titus Andronicus*, Tybalt recognizing Romeo behind his mask at the Capulets' ball, and, the most significant one, the Muscovite masquerade in *Love's Labour's Lost*, which the ladies penetrate with ease, though their own disguises are impenetrable to the men – Shakespeare's testimony, perhaps, to the superior perspicacity of French women). But for the most part, in Shakespeare's drama, people are as they present themselves. We treat this as a theatrical trope, a point where we are simply required to suspend our disbelief – my students often ask me whether Orlando in his scenes with the disguised Rosalind in *As You Like It* really thinks he is talking to a boy. My reply, that on Shakespeare's stage he really was talking to a boy, only reveals to them how unimaginable the conditions of the Elizabethan stage are, and how far Shakespeare is from being credible. But there are some striking cases in the world outside the theater that suggest that the device has more to do with cultural assumptions than with theatrical convention. I have discussed two of these in my book *Impersonations*,[3] and I return to one of them now for a closer look.

The cases concern Lady Arbella Stuart and Elizabeth Southwell. Both these aristocratic women escaped the bondage of patriarchy and arranged their own marriages through successful transvestite disguises – disguises as impenetrable, and impenetrable in the same way, as those of Rosalind, Jessica, Portia, Viola, Imogen. I am focusing here on Arbella Stuart, whose case has ramifications that I did not discuss in *Impersonations*.

Arbella Stuart was the granddaughter of the famous and formidable Bess of Hardwick, Countess of Shrewsbury, so loyal a supporter of Queen Elizabeth that for twenty years she and her husband were entrusted with the custody of Mary Queen of Scots. In 1574, however, Bess married her daughter, in haste and in secrecy, to the Scottish queen's brother-in-law, the young Charles Stuart, Duke of Lennox, brother of Mary's murdered husband the Earl of Darnley and therefore uncle to James VI of Scotland, who even at this period was being spoken of as the presumptive successor to the English throne. Lennox himself had the same claim to the English throne as his brother Darnley had had, through their grandmother Frances Brandon, Duchess of Suffolk, the niece of Henry VIII – it was chiefly this claim that had recommended the disastrous Darnley as a husband for Mary, who had always had her eye on the throne of England. Any marriage with Lennox, therefore, affected the line of succession to the English throne, and could not be performed without the crown's permission. Nevertheless the match was solemnized at Hardwick Hall in Derbyshire, Bess's estate – a long, hard ride from London; it took several weeks for the news to reach the capital. Elizabeth was enraged, and imprisoned the bridegroom's mother, but her trust in the Shrewsburys was such that, beyond a stern rebuke, they suffered no consequences. The young couple were left alone, and the marriage was allowed to survive.

Lennox died after only two years, and the sole child of that marriage was the Lady Arbella Stuart, who was therefore a first cousin to King James and a distant cousin to Queen Elizabeth. Much of her life was taken up with attempts to find a suitable husband, one who would be acceptable to the English crown. Needless to say no such person could be produced: neither Elizabeth nor James had any interest in increasing the pool of candidates for their throne.

So Arbella finally took matters into her own hands. In 1610, at the age of 35, she secretly married William Seymour, a grandson of the Earl of Hertford with a distant claim to the throne – in 1603 she had proposed marriage to his brother Edward, a boy of 16 whom she had never seen, but she had received only a curt and frightened dismissal from his father. This time no parental permission was solicited, but the match was still illegal, requiring the king's permission, and when it became known, Seymour was imprisoned in the Tower and Arbella placed under house arrest, initially at Lambeth. When it was found that this made it too easy for her to communicate with her husband, she was ordered to be sent to Durham. As the journey began, she took ill, and the party stopped at Barnet, in north London, for some weeks. As the move once again seemed imminent, Arbella took action. She persuaded one of her attendants that she was stealing out to pay a final visit to Seymour, and would return before morning. She disguised herself as a man, with trousers and boots, a doublet and a black cloak. She wore a man's wig that partially concealed her features, and a black hat, and she carried a rapier. In this disguise she fled, successfully deceiving an innkeeper and an ostler as to her sex, and headed for the coast for a rendezvous with Seymour, where they intended to take a boat to freedom in France.

Seymour escaped the Tower through an equally ingenious disguise plot. Seymour's barber, who regularly attended on him, appeared at the Tower thoroughly disguised, and asked for himself (that is, asked for Seymour's barber), saying that he was with Seymour. He was admitted, together they disguised Seymour in the barber's usual clothes, and both then went out together. The guards asked no questions, since the disguised barber was the man who had just gone in; nor did they say anything to the man they took to be the barber, because he was accustomed to go in and out almost daily.[4]

For Arbella this comedy did not have a happy ending: the couple missed their rendezvous, and though both took ships separately for Calais, Arbella's was pursued; she was arrested at sea, and spent the rest of her life – only five years – imprisoned in the Tower. Seymour, however, disembarked safely in France and lived abroad until Arbella's death. He then returned to England, and within the year married the daughter of the Earl of Essex.

The disguises of Shakespearean drama look less conventional if we consider them with these cases in mind. It is scarcely hyperbole to say that disguise offered Arbella Stuart the only hope of an escape from the intolerable situation her paternity had placed her in – Imogen's case in *Cymbeline* is hardly more melodramatic. And both Seymour's and Arbella's disguises were genuinely impenetrable, quite as impenetrable as any in Shakespeare. Arbella had a long, hard ride from Barnet to the coast, during which she and her servant stopped at an inn and changed horses – the ostler later reported only that the young man seemed unwell, and had difficulty with the horse (Arbella would have been accustomed to riding side-saddle), but he had no inkling that there was a woman beneath the clothing and hair. And though both Seymour and his barber were well known to the guards of the Tower, it was nevertheless perfectly possible to disguise Seymour as his barber and his barber as somebody unknown, both impenetrably. These cases are a good index to how much the sense of who one was in the period depended precisely on externals, on costume, wigs, facial hair, attributes such as jewelry and accessories – on everything that constituted the representation of a social role. But, beyond this, there must be a presumption in the culture that such superficies represent realities, and are the closest we can come to knowing somebody.

But now let us consider two counter-examples, the first from two centuries later. In the last act of *Le mariage de Figaro*, in which Suzanne and the Countess are disguised as each other, Figaro, at a moment of high drama, suddenly penetrates Suzanne's disguise. In Beaumarchais, it is Suzanne who accidently lets her identity slip out; but in Da Ponte's libretto for Mozart, Figaro recognizes his wife's voice – "io conobbi la voce che adoro" ("I knew the voice that I adore"). The two women have been imitating each other, but there are limits to mimesis.

The limits, however, to both mimesis and recognition, are only those of Enlightenment aesthetics: consider a Renaissance analogue. *Don Quixote* is full of people in disguise, and the eventual revelation of the truth beneath the disguise constitutes one of the main narrative principles of the work. The revelation, however, is hardly ever a matter of the disguise being penetrable, save of course in the case of Don Quixote himself, whose chivalric persona is constantly coming undone – the hero is a credible knight only to himself. Near the end of Part 1, however, in the course of the extended episode of Cardenio, comes the story of Doña Clara and the mule boy. Doña Clara is traveling with her father, a judge; they are staying at an inn with a number of other guests, including Cardenio, Dorothea, Don Quixote and Sancho Panza. Dorothea and Doña Clara are sleeping together, and in the middle of the night Dorothea is awakened by a song. Cardenio enters to tell them that it is a mule boy singing, with the most beautiful voice he has ever heard. Dorothea wakes Clara to hear the mule boy, and Clara immediately identifies the voice as that of Don

Luis, a noble youth who is in love with her – like Figaro, she has no difficulty recognizing the voice that she adores. He has indeed disguised himself as a mule driver, but the disguise is basically irrelevant. Here is the story.

Don Luis lived in a house opposite Clara's, and though her father kept the windows of his house carefully curtained, the youth saw Clara, perhaps at church, and fell in love with her. He never spoke with her, but made her understand by gestures from his window that he wanted to marry her. She loved him too, but she was well aware that his aristocratic family would never agree to such a match for their son, and she never told her father about it. When her father determined on the journey they are now taking, she could not even see Don Luis to wave farewell. But after they had been on the road for two days, she says, "I saw him ... dressed as a mule-lad; and so much like one that if I had not borne his portrait in my heart, I should have found it impossible to recognize him. I knew him; I was amazed; I was delighted ... . I have never spoken a word to him in my life, but ... I love him so much that I cannot live without him."[5]

The disguise, therefore, is impeccable, but she sees through it because of the portrait in her heart – it is that that she recognizes, the projection of her innermost self. And, adoring him as she does, she also immediately identifies his singing, although she has never heard his voice: they have never exchanged a word. This is magically romantic, a testimony to the mystical power of true love.

It all seems much more routine the next morning, however, when Don Luis's father's servants appear at the inn to apprehend him and bring him home. They have found him easily, and have no difficulty penetrating his disguise. They berate him for his socially degrading costume, and at this point even Doña Clara's father recognizes him. In fact, the concept of disguise itself undergoes a significant transformation in the course of this story. Initially it appears as the essence of romance, epitomizing the love that pierces to the heart, the truth of the self that can be known only by the beloved. But as the plot unfolds and the young man's scheme unravels, the disguise appears more and more a mere gesture toward the conventions of romance. It has scarcely concealed the youth at all; everyone who knows him recognizes him, not only Doña Clara. The disguise has at most briefly enabled him to travel without attracting attention. Even the motive for the concealment turns out to have been greatly exaggerated: in the morning, hard pressed to explain himself, the young man finally confesses his love to Doña Clara's father, who, mastering his astonishment, is delighted with so fine a match for his daughter, and the story becomes positively banal as the episode ends with the whole group of travelers discussing ways of persuading the young man's father to approve the marriage. Presumably they will succeed: the romance dissipates with the disguise, and we never hear the end of this story. Without the disguise, the episode is of no further interest.

So disguise here is a metonym for romance, both the romance of love and the romance of storytelling, a metonym for the novel itself. It seems axiomatic that the point of any disguise plot is the penetration of the disguise, the revelation that constitutes the plot's resolution; but in this case the revelation simply aborts the story. In the same way, when the old gentleman from La Mancha with the uncertain surname, Quexada or Quesada, stops impersonating the chivalric knight Don Quixote, which is the only identity he has for us, the immense novel is finally over.

One can imagine a romance in which the plot does not ultimately undo itself in this way; where disguise becomes the reality, the true expression of the self – where the impersonation becomes the person. This actually happens in Beaumont and Fletcher's play *Philaster* (1609), in which the embattled heroine Euphrasia, disguised as the page Bellario, decides to remain permanently in drag and serve her lord and lady as an epicene youth, equally attractive to men and women. There are gestures toward this sort of essentialization of costume in Shakespeare. In *As You Like It*, when Rosalind disguises herself as the youth Ganymede to accompany Celia in their flight into the forest of Arden, it is for the same practical reasons offered by Barnabe Rich's Silla: women on the road are always in danger, and the presence of a man – any kind of man, even a prepubescent youth – is a sufficient deterrent to predators. The disguise subsequently becomes a cover for her meetings with Orlando; but why is the cover necessary? It would appear, indeed, to be self-defeating: by the middle of the play, when Orlando is tacking love-poems to Rosalind on every tree, Rosalind is perfectly well aware of his feelings for her. She even acknowledges the pointlessness of continuing her disguise: "Alas the day, what shall I do with my doublet and hose?" (III.2.214–15). Why not at this point reveal herself, and consummate the love? But the play is scarcely half over; for another two acts, always as Ganymede, she puts Orlando through a series of tests and catechisms, good for comedy but only serving to delay the ultimate erotic satisfaction. Disguise here, as in the episode of Doña Clara from *Don Quixote*, is the essence of romance, and when the disguise is discarded the romance has ended – in this case in marriage, though if we think about what happens after marriage in Shakespeare, for example in *Othello* and *Romeo and Juliet*, it is not clear that abandoning the disguise necessarily constitutes a happy ending.

In *Twelfth Night* Viola is initially quite explicit about the relevance of her disguise to her inner state. It will be, she says, "the form of my intent"

(I.2.55). By the middle of the play she has changed her mind, calling disguise "a wickedness/ In which the pregnant enemy [Satan] does much" (II.3.27–8): she is now trapped in a costume that misrepresents the form of her intent, that makes it impossible for her to express her feelings. But she too maintains the disguise long after its utility in the plot has been exhausted. In the middle of Act III, when Antonio intervenes in her duel with Sir Andrew and calls her Sebastian, it is clear to her that her brother is alive and in Illyria – she concludes the scene with the recognition "That I, dear brother, now be ta'en for you" (III.4.361). The resolution, the unmasking, could occur at any point after this; but she retains her disguise for another two acts, even in the final confrontation with her twin, putting him through a pointless exercise comparing details about their parentage. The eventual unmasking, moreover, does nothing to change the terms on which the play has operated throughout: appearances remain of the essence. Olivia has fallen in love with the cross-dressed Viola, and when Sebastian appears, identically costumed, she instantly, effortlessly, transfers her feelings to him – the twins are, for Olivia, interchangeable. But if falling in love with a cross-dressed woman is the same as falling in love with a man, what is a man except the costume?

There are very few plays that are willing to acknowledge that gender is in fact more than the costume – that that part of the self that is defined by gender is ultimately and absolutely real and knowable. Viola, challenged by Sir Andrew, laments that "a little thing would make me tell them how much I lack of a man" (III.4.282–3), invoking in that lack a very old anatomical fantasy that women are men with something missing (the fantasy is as old as Galen, but it is still present in Freud). The play alludes to this assumption elsewhere, in its puns on "cut" and "cunt." This is obviously a male fantasy, not a female one, though in this case Viola's failure of nerve is not merely a function of the missing genital organs: in the duel, Sir Andrew turns out to be no more of a man than Viola. In a much more substantial example, John Fletcher's strange play *The Honest Man's Fortune* (1613), a very attractive young man named Veramour is propositioned by an elderly lecher. To repel his attentions Veramour claims he is really a woman, and proceeds to dress accordingly. This stratagem is only marginally successful, since the lecher is equally attracted to women, and as the play nears its climax a good deal of discussion takes place over the difficulties of distinguishing attractive boys from women. The argument is short-circuited when one of the participants tartly observes that a hand thrust into the subject's underpants would easily settle the matter – a piece of common sense that would demolish a good many disguise plots.

Even in the real world, however, common sense is not always the bottom line, and the boundaries of mimesis are far more extensive than they are in the theater. The witnesses who were deceived by Arbella Stuart saw nothing more intimate than her hair and her clothing, but they also detected nothing in her manner to suggest that any surprises might lie hidden beneath the clothing: gender here was a matter of behavior and costume. There are a number of famous cases of people who successfully lived cross-gendered for years, for example the Chevalier d'Eon as a woman, and the jazz pianist Billy Tipton as a man. Tipton's sex was discovered only after his death, by the medical examiner; his wife and children (the children were adopted) had been entirely unaware of it. This means, obviously, that the marriage was without the usual sorts of intimacy, but his wife explained that this suited both of them, and the marriage was long and happy. This all sounds quite inconceivable, but Diane Middlebrook's superb biography of Tipton renders the story both credible and touchingly human.[6] Initially Tipton passed as a man because in the 1930s for a woman to perform in jazz clubs as anything but a vocalist was simply impossible – the elderly band members from her early years, whom Middlebrook tracked down and interviewed, said they of course knew she was a woman; her cross-dressing was what made the band viable. Gradually the impersonation became the person. Tipton's wife, a stripper, said she was initially attracted to him precisely because he was unlike the other men she had known, gentle and affectionate, and not eager for sex – an unusual kind of man, in her experience, but not an inconceivable one, and since she had been badly mistreated by sexually aggressive men in the past, she was grateful for his manner and found him easy to fall in love with. He explained his physical aloofness by saying he had been seriously injured in an accident, and was obliged to wear heavy elastic bandages around his chest all the time; obviously they never saw each other naked. Out of this fiction Tipton constructed an entirely satisfactory life with a wife, and later with children, for whom the fiction was fact.

It would be incorrect here to say that all Tipton's family knew of him was his costume. The costume represented an inner truth. That truth was constructed, certainly, but all our selves are surely constructed. The Billy Tipton story is no more incredible than the innumerable stories of people with aristocratic pretensions who turn out to have come from humble origins – the facts of gender seem to us much more basic and undeniable than the facts of social class, but surely this is an illusion. Billy Tipton's or Arbella Stuart's sexual anatomy would have been the ultimate reality only for the purposes of one particular type of sexual intercourse; for all other forms of social interaction, most of what constitutes life, gender is not a matter of anatomy but of self-presentation. There is, moreover, some degree of deception in every form of self-presentation – appearing naked is rarely an option in human society, and decisions about what to wear are decisions about the power of costume to make us look better than we look to ourselves, better than we know we are. "All the world's a stage" indeed, as Shakespeare's Jaques says, "And all the men and women merely players," though one could pause at length over that "merely," as if the theatricality of everyday life were simple or superficial, rather than essential. On Jaques's stage, the actors are everything: his theater has players but no playwright.

Over the centuries, the stage has gone to great lengths to insist on its coincidence with reality, initially through illusionistic scenery, and, from the eighteenth century, increasingly, through the invocation of history, specifically realized in historically informed costumes. In fact, it is probably not overstating the case to say that whatever historical relevance theater has claimed has been expressed through costume. The move into history, however, was neither direct nor consistent. The famous Peacham drawing for *Titus Andronicus* (figure 2.1) gestures toward ancient Rome in the costume of Titus, in the center; but queen Tamora's costume is quite generalized, vaguely medieval, certainly neither Roman nor Elizabethan. Her sons and Aaron the Moor, on the right, are in outfits that combine Elizabethan and Roman elements, and the guards on the left are Elizabethan soldiers. The costumes here identify the characters according to their roles and their relation to each other, not to their place in a historical era – there is no attempt here to make the stage a mirror of the Roman world. Within two decades of this drawing, however, Inigo Jones was consulting the best available authorities on ancient Roman dress for his

.1 Henry Peacham, drawing based on *Titus Andronicus*, c. 1614.

2.2 Inigo Jones, a Roman priest, costume design for Aurelian Townshend's *Albion's Triumph*, 1631; with Jones's source in Onofrio Panvinio, *De Ludis circensibus*, Venice, 1600.

costumes for masques at the court of Charles I (figure 2.2). If the king was to be idealized as a classical hero, the classical context had to be authentic.

On the dramatic stage, however, for the next two centuries, costume was either contemporary, or retained the syncretic character of the Peacham sketch. In figure 2.3, the frontispiece to *Henry VIII* in the first illustrated Shakespeare, Nicholas Rowe's edition of 1709, Henry wears an early sixteenth-century costume based on the famous Holbein portrait, but his courtiers wear eighteenth-century formal dress, with frock coats and wigs. The first attempt at a systematic change of the sort Inigo Jones had introduced into the masque did not come until 1731, when Aaron Hill's *The Generous Traitor, or Aethelwold*, set in Anglo-Saxon times, was staged in Old English costume – this was the author's idea, not the producer's. A *Macbeth* in historical Scottish costume was performed in Edinburgh in 1753, but the first Shakespearean production in historic dress came to the London stage only in 1773, in Charles Macklin's *Macbeth* (figure 2.4), in which Macklin, for his first entrance, wore a plaid scarf, tartan stockings and a knee-length tunic (the tartans were anachronistic for eleventh-century Scotland, but less so than a kilt would have been). This was not a success, partly because Macklin was too closely

SHYLOCK turnd *MACBETH*.

M: MACKLIN,
In the Character of MACBETH.
Act II.? Scene 3.?

2.3 Title page to *Henry VIII* from Nicholas Rowe's *Works of Shakespear*, 1709.

2.4 Charles Macklin as a Scottish Macbeth, 1773. The print is entitled "Shylock Turned Macbeth."

2.5 Macklin's Act II costume in *Macbeth*.

2.6 Mary Ann Yates's Lady Macbeth, c. 1760, the model for Macklin's Lady Macbeth, Mrs Hartley.

2.7 Francesco Zuccarelli, *Macbeth meeting the witches*, c. 1760.

identified with his famous Shylock – the caricature reproduced here is entitled "Shylock Turn'd Macbeth" – but even more because the costuming was totally inconsistent: by the middle of Act II Macbeth was wearing eighteenth-century breeches (figure 2.5), and his Lady Macbeth, Mrs Hartley, refused to wear Scottish garments at all, and was modishly dressed in a hoop skirt, in the fashion of Mrs Yates's Lady Macbeth a decade earlier, depicted in figure 2.6. Visual artists of the period imagined up-to-date Scottish Macbeths. Figure 2.7 is Francesco Zuccarelli's *Macbeth meeting the witches*, painted in London in the 1760s – this is the first Italian illustration of Shakespeare. Zuccarelli was famous for his landscapes in the tradition of Claude Lorrain, with, as here, a little Salvatore Rosa as well. These usually included mythological subjects, but, in a striking innovation, the mythology here is Shakespeare. But what a Shakespeare! The Scots tartans are striped, rather than checked, and Zuccarelli had clearly never seen kilts, which should just cover the knee and would not be blowing in the wind; and the witches are graceful country girls, not at all

"So withered and so wild in their attire/ That look not like the inhabitants o' th' earth...": this is Shakespeare imaginatively adapted to the requirements of romantic landscape painting. But Zuccarelli's Shakespeare is also adapted to contemporary politics: the blue caps of Macbeth and his troops were the uniform worn by the Jacobite rebels at the battle of Culloden in 1746, when the Jacobite forces were decisively defeated. The costumes give a clear sense of what side Macbeth is on: the wrong side.

By the end of the eighteenth century the vogue for historic costume in drama was well under way. John Philip Kemble played Hamlet in Elizabethan dress in 1783 (figure 2.8), and Talma, in Paris, wore a sixteenth-century German academic gown (figure 2.9). This was in Jean-François Ducis's adaptation of the play, in which authenticity was otherwise not an issue: an urn containing old Hamlet's ashes figures significantly in the action, although cremation in the Middle Ages and Renaissance was reserved for heretics. This *Hamlet*, in any case, had little enough to do with Shakespeare: Hamlet has

2.8 John Philip Kemble's Elizabethan *Hamlet*, 1783.

2.9 François-Joseph Talma in Ducis's French adaptation of *Hamlet*.

been king from the outset, having succeeded his father on his death; Ducis's ghost reveals that the queen, not Claudius, was his murderer; and at the end both Ophelia, who is Claudius's daughter, not Polonius's, and Hamlet remain alive.

The movement toward history was codified by James Robinson Planché's archeologically correct designs for Charles Kemble's *King John* in 1824. The playbill for this production declared that the play will be presented "with an attention to costume never before equalled on the English stage. Every character will appear in the precise habit of the period, the whole of the dresses and decorations being executed from indisputable authorities" – the authorities cited are not textual but material, visual, documentary: tomb effigies, royal seals, manuscript illuminations, all the fruits of Planché's research into costume history. Figure 2.10 shows a group of tomb effigies of medieval British royalty from Planché's *History of British Costume*, which went through many editions and became a standard reference work. These were the models Planché provided for Shakespeare. King John's effigy is on the far right; figure 2.11 shows the king's costume in the 1824 production, based on it. Two decades later, in 1842, the costumes were used again in Macready's production of the same play. This was not parsimony; Macready's productions were quite elaborate. The costumes remained unchanged because

2.10 J. R. Planché, tomb effigies from the reign of King John, from his *History of British Costume*, 1834.

King John 1st dress.   *Elinor, Widow of Henry 2nd.*

2.11 Planché's costume designs for King John and Queen Elinor, from *Costume of Shakespeare's Historical Tragedy of King John*, 1824.

they stamped both productions as authentic. This is what Planché did to theater, and it gives a striking sense of what the attractions of theater were now conceived to be.

Planché's work was a manifesto, backed by a genuine historical impulse and informed by an impressive body of scholarship. He also published "correct" costume designs for *Hamlet*, *Othello*, *As You Like It* and several other plays, for which he selected appropriate, if arbitrary, historical eras. The effect of this sort of historicizing is, of course, to place the plays at a considerable distance from us – theater becomes a mirror of the past, showing us how life was lived in historical eras. In Shakespeare's own theater – though, as we have seen, plays with classical settings had gestures toward the period – for the most part plays were costumed in Elizabethan dress; the Italy of *Romeo and Juliet* was a version of England. There were practical reasons for doing this, but it also meant that the plays were not distanced from the audience, in the way modern Shakespeare is when we do it in any sort of period costume, which is what, thanks to Planché, tends to seem natural to us.

Of course, even when we do the plays in period costume, there remains a problem about the period. The thrilling, visually stunning Franco Zeffirelli films of *Romeo and Juliet* and *The Taming of the Shrew* are set in fifteenth-century Verona and Padua, with historically accurate costumes and sets. Zeffirelli's décor really does work beautifully; but as a version of Shakespeare there is nothing authentic about it: Shakespeare's Romeo and Juliet wore the same clothing their audiences wore; their tragedy did not take place in the distant past, and the society of Verona was a recognizable version of the society of London. If we try to be authentic, however, and emulate Shakespeare by dressing our productions in Elizabethan costumes, in the style of the original *Romeo and Juliet* depicted in the film *Shakespeare in Love*, we simply make the play into another period piece – it is still ancient history, although now the history is Shakespeare's rather than that of the characters. Both sorts of historically correct costuming give a good sense of what the limits of authenticity are for us.

Zeffirelli employed an extremely knowledgeable costume historian for his *Romeo and Juliet*. Watch the ballroom scene – many of the costumes derive quite directly from Perugino paintings. The women's headgear was especially striking, because the designer was willing to use authentic styles that risked looking faintly ridiculous to modern audiences (figure 2.12). For *The Taming of the Shrew* Zeffirelli moved about half a century later in time, and went for sumptuousness in addition to authenticity, but there was lots of period detail – for example a courtesan who flirts with one of the newly arrived suitors is shown wearing chopines, fashionable high-soled shoes (figure 2.13). They look preposterous to us (and they constitute a visual joke in the film), but they are included precisely because they are authentic 1540 footwear of the Veneto – like Planché's effigies, they give the film the stamp of authenticity. The women's costumes were especially elaborate, but Elizabeth Taylor's were less authentic than everyone else's, because she insisted on having her own designer provide her clothes. Her dresses tended to be much less voluminous than everyone else's, making her appear more slender, and thus, to modern eyes, more attractive than the other women in the film (figure 2.14).

Shakespeare in Love did a beautiful re-creation of Elizabethan costumes. The climax of the film involves the first performance of *Romeo and Juliet*. This was, correctly, played in contemporary costume; that is, what went on onstage looked just like what went on offstage (figure 2.15). But the film's devotion to authenticity went only so far. Ben Affleck played the actor Edward Alleyn (figure 2.16), who took the role of a very impressive Mercutio, and Joseph Fiennes played Shakespeare playing Romeo (which is probably incorrect, since the original Romeo seems to have been one of the two actors who produced

2.12 Women's hairstyles in Franco Zeffirelli's *Romeo and Juliet*.

2.13 A courtesan's chopine in Franco Zeffirelli's *The Taming of the Shrew*.

2.14 Katherina (Elizabeth Taylor) with the other Veronese wives in Franco Zeffirelli's *The Taming of the Shrew*.

the somewhat garbled text that was published in the first quarto[7]). The costumes in Mercutio's death scene are perfectly correct (figure 2.17), but the hair is late twentieth-century short, Affleck's a sexy brush cut, and Fiennes's fashionably windblown. Elizabethan men wore their hair long, sometimes down to their shoulders. But the film says as clearly as possible that these are not Elizabethans, they are movie stars, and they have to look glamorous.

2.15 The opening scene of *Romeo and Juliet*, from *Shakespeare in Love.*

2.16 Ben Affleck as Edward Alleyn playing Mercutio, from *Shakespeare in Love.*

2.17 Mercutio's death, from *Shakespeare in Love.*

2.18 Nicholas Hilliard, Sir Walter Ralegh.

2.19 Artist unknown, Henry Wriothesley, Earl of
Southampton, c. 1600.

Figures 2.18 and 2.19 show two very sexy Elizabethan men for comparison:
Sir Walter Ralegh and the Earl of Southampton, Shakespeare's patron. The
more hair, the sexier.

Shakespeare plays are most often performed nowadays in something
approximating modern dress, as a way of restoring that Elizabethan sense of
immediacy, as in the very successful film of *Richard III* with Ian McKellen.
This has become quite routine, though for audiences who do not see much
Shakespeare and who know the plays, if at all, only from reading them, the
modern costumes are a distraction because the language remains archaic –
part of what makes Shakespeare a classic is that he is so firmly in the past.
There are good reasons for using modern settings and costumes – the relations
between the social classes, for example, become much more easily understood
if the dress codes are modern rather than Elizabethan – but there is really
no way around the discrepancy between the language and the setting, and

little way of mitigating it. It is simply something the director has to hope the audience will get used to, and it seems worth taking the risk in order to avoid the sense that the play is safely canonical, merely a classic; in order to restore some of the drama's original energies. From the twentieth century onward, updated Shakespeare has often been highly charged politically – the incendiary productions of *Coriolanus* in Paris in 1934 and of *Macbeth* in East Berlin in 1982 had an authenticity that went beyond décor. In its own time Elizabethan theater was always relevant to current issues, and was assumed to be intended as such, and the costumes themselves on Shakespeare's stage had a kind of authority that was not without its element of danger. I conclude with a passage from my book *Impersonations*.

When Prospero tempts Stefano and Trinculo to their destruction with a closet full of "glistering apparel" he invokes a central cultural topos. Caliban declares the garments to be "trash"; but they are trash only because the conspirators have not yet succeeded, and are not yet entitled to wear them. Robes of office, aristocratic finery, confirm and legitimate authority, they do not confer it. There is obviously, however, a widespread conviction in the culture that they do. Caliban may well be revealing here just how much of an outsider he is – the costumes, after all, belong to Prospero. Prospero himself invests his cape with the enabling power of his magic: "Lie there, my art." Analogously, the wardrobe of Henslowe's company included "a robe for to go invisible," asserting in a culturally specific manner how powerfully garments determined the way one was to be seen, and not seen. These fictions, moreover, reflected an economic reality: the theater company had its largest investment, its major property, in its costumes; and the costumes were for the most part the real cast-off clothes of real aristocrats. As the legitimating emblems of authority, these garments possessed a kind of social reality within the culture that the actors, and indeed much of their audience, could never hope to have. The actors and characters were fictions, but the costumes were the real thing.

Notes

1 Barnabe Riche, *Riche, his Farewell to the Militarie Profession* (London, 1581).
2 Geoffrey Bullough, *Narrative and Dramatic Sources of Shakespeare* (London, 1958), 2.361–2.
3 Stephen Orgel, *Impersonations: The Performance of Gender in Shakespeare's England* (Cambridge, 1996).

4 Sarah Gristwood, *Arbella* (London, 2003), pp. 302–3.
5 Miguel de Cervantes, *Don Quixote*, trans. J. M. Cohen (Harmondsworth, 1990), pp. 389–90.
6 Diane Middlebrook, *Suits Me: The Double Life of Billy Tipton* (Boston, 1998).
7 See Stanley Wells and Gary Taylor, *William Shakespeare: A Textual Companion* (Oxford, 1987), p. 288.

3

Jonson and the Amazons

When James I succeeded as king of England, he came to a throne that had been occupied for more than half a century by women. Both Henry VIII's daughters were legally illegitimate, and their claims to the crown were ambiguous at best; Elizabeth's was especially shaky, since Henry had argued at her mother's trial for adultery and incest that she was not even his daughter. She was queen because she was included in the line of succession established in her father's will, which overrode the earlier illegitimation, though it did not revoke it; but she made good her right to the throne through a combination of policy and extraordinary personal style.

An important component of that style was the chivalric mythology with which she surrounded herself. This had been introduced into the political life of the realm by her grandfather Henry VII, who used Burgundian models of knightly heroism to legitimate the de facto rule by conquest confirmed at Bosworth field. Henry VIII had extended the trope into lavish displays of Arthurian fantasy, asserting through spectacle a parity with Francis I and Charles V that he could not assert with arms. Elizabeth gradually redefined the family mythology, eventually placing herself at the center of a drama in which the essence of knighthood was not the performance of heroic deeds in battle but service to a lady. Chivalry became, in her hands, a myth that disarmed her heroes as it idealized her, and the language of heroism became the language of submissive love. This was not only a way of exerting her control over a large number of active and ambitious men who depended on the crown for employment; it was also a useful element of foreign policy. She supported privateers, not armies. The Armada victory was her major military triumph, and she made the most of it. But she was resolved to keep England out of the European power struggles, and the great cause that fired the enthusiasm of the most idealistic of her submissive subjects, a Protestant league and the freeing of the Netherlands from Spanish domination, she wanted no part of. Despite the general unpopularity of her position, her success for most of her long reign was notable, though it was eclipsed during her last years by the uncertainty of the succession, an issue that she carefully left unresolved until almost the moment of her death. The popular adulation accorded to Sir Philip Sidney for the most meager of military careers, the exaggerated hopes invested in the disastrous Earl of Essex, are indices to how badly the realm yearned for glory as Elizabeth's rule drew to an end.[1]

Despite her presentation of herself as a Petrarchan heroine and the sovereign lady to a band of adoring knights, official representations of her dealt warily with her womanhood. In portraits she appears in the increasingly elaborate gowns that she loved, but the pose and the facial expression tend always to be stylized, cool, impersonal. She herself was distrustful of representations, and attempted to restrict their production; the face in her portraits, indeed, was invariably based on one of a small number of patterns supplied by her authority. Very few paintings of her addressed the realities of her situation as a woman. The most striking of these is the Sieve Portrait, probably painted around 1580 by Cornelius Kettel, and now in Siena (figure 3.1). She holds a sieve, the attribute of Roman vestal virgins, and stands before a column bearing inset scenes from the story of Dido and Aeneas. The allusions have a complex relevance: Elizabeth traced her descent from Aeneas, grandfather of Brutus, the legendary founder of Britain; and Dido has a double and contradictory history, as the chaste founder of Carthage who committed suicide rather than give up her chastity to an importuning suitor, and as the betrayed and abandoned mistress of the Trojan hero. The allusion to the latter story invokes both her royal ancestry and the dangers that threaten her peace and the realm's; the sieve assures us that she is an incarnation of the chaste Dido, not the fallen one.[2] When the monarch was a woman, such reassurance was constantly necessary.

But the language of love was a crucial part of her power. Lord Thomas Howard in 1611 analyzed for Sir John Harington the difference in style between the old queen and her successor: "Your Queen did talk of her subjects love and good affections, and in good truth she aimed well; our King talketh of his subjects fear and subjection, and herein I think he doth well too, as long as it holdeth good."[3] The new king's ideology was as disarming as the queen's had been, and more overtly so. James I was a pacifist; his motto, *Beati pacifici*, blessed are the peacemakers, appears inscribed over his head in the frontispiece to his works, published in 1616. The king's determination to keep his new realm clear of the European wars was as central an element in his foreign policy as it had been in his predecessor's. It was an eminently sensible part of the royal program; but to a nation longing for glory after the decline of Elizabeth's last years, it was again disappointing and unpopular. Eulogists

3.1 Cornelius Kettel, Queen Elizabeth I (the "Sieve Portrait"), c. 1580.

could praise James's wisdom and learning, but the imagery of triumph was not easily applied to this autocratic, withdrawn and uncharismatic monarch. Within a few years after the king's accession, Elizabeth was being recalled with a fervent nostalgia. Sir John Harington in 1606 had already anticipated Lord Thomas Howard, summing up what had passed from the royal style: "We all did love hir, for she said she loved us."[4]

To pursue the ideology of chivalry from Elizabeth's reign into James's is to confront a political dialectic that is almost occult in its complexity. It is also to confront a family drama: by the age of fourteen, James's elder son, Prince Henry, was already emerging as the focus of a militant Protestant opposition. Ben Jonson and Inigo Jones, poet and architect of the spectacles of the Jacobean state, were called on by both sides; here, as so often, we can see the conflicts of the Jacobean politics expressed in the symbolic fables of royal theater.

The first explicitly heroic masque created for the Jacobean monarchy was Jonson's and Jones's *Masque of Queens*, performed at Whitehall in 1609. It celebrated, however, not King James but his queen, by whom it had been commissioned, and included a troupe of Amazonian heroines as supporting roles for her ladies (figure 3.2). It was an unlikely part for Queen Anne, who studiously avoided politics and was unsympathetic to her son's ambitions – she was, indeed, a convert to Catholicism.[5] Nevertheless, through her patronage, Jonson here reconceived in heroic terms the forms he had made peculiarly his own. In his earlier court masques Jonson had placed his performers in arcane symbolic fables, where they danced out philosophical arguments, recreated classical rituals or participated in the creation of cosmic emblems. In 1609, for the first time, Jonson's ideal vision was expressed through a set of martial roles. The Jacobean court became the culmination and embodiment of two thousand years of militant female virtue. In this world of ancient examples, only Queen Anne, the living heroine, played a version of herself, Bel-Anna, Queen of the Ocean. If the epithet was intended to recall the triumphant Elizabeth of the Armada victory, it was the only allusion Jonson allowed himself to the dangerously successful model of the previous reign.

Jonson opens his masque on "a spectacle of strangeness," an ugly hell and a coven of witches, the opposites, he says, to fame and glory. This was his first fully realized antimasque, and he credits its inclusion to the queen, who,

> best knowing that a principal part of life in these spectacles lay in their variety, commanded me to think on some dance or show that might precede hers and have the place of a foil or false masque.[6]

3.2 Inigo Jones, costume design for the Countess of Bedford as Penthesileia, queen of the Amazons, in Jonson's *Masque of Queens*, 1609.

But if it was the queen's idea to have an antimasque, the startling subject of the antimasque must have been determined by the king's interests. The royal treatise on witchcraft, *Daemonologie*, first published in Edinburgh in 1597, had been reissued in two separate London editions in 1603 upon James's accession to the English throne. It was a subject that was of passionate interest to him, and his expertise on the matter formed an important part of his scholarly and judicial credentials.

Jonson presents his own scholarly credentials in a set of elaborate marginalia composed at the request of Prince Henry – the masque in its final form appears as very much a family affair. Sources both classical and modern are adduced for the smallest details of the witches' performance, and the exhaustive citation of authorities naturally includes a reference to the king's book. This was doubtless intended as a compliment, but it displays a subtle antagonism as well. *Daemonologie* deals with general theological and philosophical issues rather than with specific cases or historical precedents; it is, granting its premises, a capable, economical and intelligent discussion. Jonson invokes the royal expertise, however, on a specific point: to justify opening the performance with a dance, he contends on the king's authority that witches commonly begin their meetings in this way.[7] In fact, the matter is not touched on in *Daemonologie*; Jonson's real source appears to be, ironically, Reginald Scot's sceptical treatise *The Discoverie of Witches*, a tract James attacks in his own treatise.

But if Jonson thus marginalized the king's scholarship, usurping the royal authority with a rival expertise, the presentation of witches at court was anything but marginal. James was convinced that there had been, from his youth, a systematic and continuous conspiracy against his throne and his life; those responsible were not any of the multitude of political enemies that did in fact fill the early part of his reign, but witches under the direct control of the devil. He made it a point to be present at the interrogation of witches whenever possible, and the confessions invariably extracted from them under torture always confirmed his belief. English readers were offered an account of the conspiracy, and of the king's involvement in its detection, in a pamphlet published in London in 1591 entitled *Newes from Scotland*. One of the women interrogated, Agnis Tompson,[8] revealed that when James went to Denmark in 1589 to bring back his bride, the delays and extraordinary bad weather he experienced were the result of witchcraft; she herself had caused the storms, and had been designated by the devil to kill the king by sorcery. The latter project failed, she said, only because she was unable to persuade any of his loyal servants to provide her with the necessary piece of the king's soiled linen for her spells.

The king reportedly was initially skeptical of this story, and

said they were extreme liars, whereat she answered she would not wish his majesty to suppose her words to be false, but rather believe them, in that she would discover such matter unto him as his majesty should not any way doubt of. And whereupon taking his majesty a little aside, she declared unto him the very words which passed between the king's majesty and his Queen at Uppsala in Norway the first night of their marriage, with their answer to each other; whereat the king's majesty wondered greatly, and swore by the living God that he believed all the devils in hell could not have discovered the same, acknowledging her words to be most true ... .[9]

If we are concerned with *The Masque of Queens* as a family drama, it is significant that the witchcraft in this account is specifically implicated in the king's marriage. It is designed to prevent his return with his bride, and the crucial evidence is a revelation of the secrets of his wedding night. The story, moreover, is authenticated by the king. James's intense interest in witchcraft is clearly related to his general distrust of women, and his compulsive and public attachment to young men.[10] For all the romance of his winter voyage across the North Sea to fetch his bride, he told his privy council that he was marrying simply to produce an heir; and he added that "as to my own nature, God is my witness, I could have abstained longer."[11] The defeat of the sorcery was a triumph not of true love but of the king's exceptional virtue, as Agnis Tompson testified, asserting that "his majesty had never come safely from the sea if his faith had not prevailed above their intentions."[12] But the battle was never to be won: she also reported that the witches "demanded of the devil why he did bear such hatred to the king, who answered, by reason the king is the greatest enemy he hath in the world."[13] Just as the king provides the crucial testimony to the authenticity of witchcraft, so it is the witch who validates the king's religious faith. James's bride, Anne of Denmark, it will be observed, plays no part whatever in this romantic drama.

There are obvious cultural coordinates to these fantasies. James's own career was determined by his relation to two powerful and threatening women. His mother, the libidinous – and, to Protestants, diabolical – Mary, was the source of his power, but it was a power that depended on her absence: he was king of Scotland because she was not queen. She was also his link to the English succession, but she simultaneously represented the greatest danger to his achieving it. The claim she gave him through heredity she had rendered dubious by her sexual behavior: the charge that James was illegitimate, the child of his mother's secretary, David Rizzio, was widespread in the 1580s; James expressed fears that it would weaken his chances at the English throne, and he never felt entirely free of it. He undertook to replace Mary in his family line with the chaste and regal Elizabeth, whom he was regularly addressing by the mid-1580s as "madame and dearest mother."[14] She was a mother who could give him everything he wanted – safety, wealth legitimacy: in short, the English throne – and he courted her tirelessly; but she made no promises, ever, and would not confirm him as her heir until the moment of her death; and it is not clear she did so even then.

Out of these crucial, unreliable, powerful, dangerous, and – most important – absent women James's imagination constructed a world in which women were controlled by being incorporated. Upon his accession in 1603, he declared to Parliament that "I am the husband and the whole island is my lawful wife; I am the head, and it is my body."[15] The imagery derives from St. Paul on marriage, and the two statements are presented as synonymous. Mothers became unnecessary; he himself would be "a loving nourish-father" who would provide his subjects with "their own nourish-milk."[16] Psychologically, such a conception of his relation to the realm had obvious advantages. But as a political solution, James's patriarchy had a fatal weakness: it required Parliament to allow itself to be conceived as the monarch's children, or wife, or the body to his active mind, to be dictated to where it preferred to dictate. Queen Elizabeth's rhetoric with the men on whom her power and her purse depended had been shrewder, and much more effective: it represented them as her lovers. This was, for James, in every way an impossible act to follow. Jonson's witches and queens represented the limits of the Jacobean patriarchy.

The transformation scene

The transition from witches to queens comes, in Jonson's masque, without even a confrontation:

> In the heat of their dance on the sudden was heard a sound of loud music, as if many instruments had made one blast; with which not only the hags themselves, but the hell into which they ran quite altered, scarce suffering the memory of such a thing. But in the place of it appeared a glorious and magnificent building figuring the House of Fame, in the top of which were discovered the twelve masquers sitting upon a throne triumphal erected in form of a pyramid and circled with all store of light. (ll. 334–41)

The new scene, like the hell it replaces, has its sources in poetry, scholarship and a profoundly personal politics. The design of the House of Fame is based, Jonson tells us, on Chaucer's poem, and as a spokesman to moralize the spectacular transformation he introduces a classic figure of heroic virtue, Perseus.

But Perseus as Jonson presents him is not simply heroic virtue, and he does more than elucidate the antithesis of witches and queens. He greatly complicates it as well. He represents, Jonson says, "a brave and masculine

virtue,"[17] and in the very moment of transition he pre-empts the triumph of
the masque's heroines:

> So should, at Fame's loud sound and Virtue's sight,
> All dark and envious witchcraft fly the light.
> I did not borrow Hermes' wings, nor ask
> His crooked sword, nor put on Pluto's casque,
> Nor on my arm advanced wise Pallas' shield
> (By which, my face aversed, in open field
> I slew the Gorgon) for an empty name.
> When Virtue cut off Terror, he gat Fame.
> And if when Fame was gotten Terror died,
> What black *Erinyes* or more hellish pride
> Durst arm these hags now she is grown and great,
> To think they could her glories once defeat:
> I was her parent and I am her strength.
> (ll. 344–56)

King James would have been pleased to find that the claims to heroic
responsibility were also patriarchal claims: the masque at its most classical is
also most Jacobean. So it is again as Masculine Virtue introduces the historic
queens naming them, and celebrating as their chief and epitome Bel-Anna,
who "alone/ Possessed all virtues." But she wisely keeps her eye on the king:

> She this embracing with a virtuous joy,
> Far from self-love, as humbling all her worth
> To him that gave it, hath again brought forth
> Their names to memory; and means this night
> To make them once more visible to light,
> And to that light from whence her truth of spirit
> Confesseth all the luster of her merit:
> To you, most royal and most happy king,
> Of whom Fame's house in every part doth ring
> For every virtue … .
> (ll. 401–10)

So much, in the Jacobean court, was no more than politic. Queen Anne was
a sensible woman, and Jonson was a sensible poet.

But the moment, if we keep the pyramid of triumphant queens with
Bel-Anna as its apex in view, is also a genuinely subversive one, and to

evaluate it necessitates a look at Jonson's sources. Jonson says in a marginal note that the ancient authorities offer three possible figures symbolic of masculine virtue: Hercules, Bellerophon and Perseus. His choice of Perseus, therefore, is in itself significant. He cites as his sources for information about the hero Hesiod and Apollodorus; but his unnamed intermediate sources are the sixteenth-century handbooks he so often consulted, of Cesare Ripa, Natalis Comes and Vincenzo Cartari, and these are, for our purposes, more informative.[18] The rejected models, Hercules and Bellerophon, are the figures of Virtue elucidated in Ripa, who does not mention Perseus.[19] The passages about Perseus from Hesiod and Apollodorus appear only in Comes, in the expanded edition first published in 1581; this presumably was Jonson's primary reference work.[20] But to find his hero in it he would have had to look not under Perseus, who is not listed in the index, but under *Medusa* and *Gorgones* – under feminine evil, not masculine virtue. He would have found Perseus directly only in Cartari, along with the general points about the relation of terror to heroic success.[21]

Something is significant here by its absence: for a Renaissance classicist, the major source for the story of Perseus would have been Ovid, in books 4 and 5 of the *Metamorphoses*. The fact the Jonson does not cite this account is probably the most revealing index to his interests. Ovid concentrates on the rescue of Andromeda, to which the Medusa story is ancillary, and relatively perfunctory. The Perseus Jonson wants is the victor over dangerous and destructive women, the hero who "cut off terror," that death-dealing female head, and made it an emblem of virtue. This is the Perseus of Comes, for whom Medusa is the embodiment of sensual temptation, lust and illicit sexuality; but it is even more the quite different – and in certain ways more classical, and in every way more Jonsonian – Perseus of Cartari. Cartari's account of Perseus and Medusa is so germane to the masque, and so deeply embedded in its conception, that it will repay close attention. Here is a translation of the relevant section:

> Diodorus writes that the gorgons were warlike women in Africa who were overcome by Perseus, who also killed Queen Medusa; this may be historical. But the fables report, as Apollodorus writes, that the gorgons were three sisters, of whom only Medusa was mortal; the other two, Euriale and Sthenno, were immortal. Their heads were surrounded and covered with scaly serpents; they had huge teeth like those of hogs, hands like branches, and wings of gold, with which they flew as they pleased; and they changed into stone whatever they looked at. Perseus, finding them asleep, cut off Medusa's head, took it away and gave it to

Minerva, who had been of great assistance to him, because she furnished him with his shield, as Mercury had provided his sword and the wings for his heels, and Orcus [Pluto] the helmet that made him invisible. ... It is also said (and this is the most common fable) that the gorgons were three very beautiful sisters, called gorgons after the islands where they lived; Medusa was the most beautiful, with hair of gold. But when Neptune fell in love with her, he slept with her in the temple of Minerva, and the goddess, in her outrage, transformed Medusa from someone beautiful and lovely to see to someone terrible and frightening, and changed her golden hair to serpents. She wished whoever looked at her thereafter to be turned to stone; but since the world cannot endure so alien a monster, Perseus killed her, with the assistance I have described, and gave her head to Minerva, who always carried it on her shield or her cuirass. Thus, when Homer has his goddess arm herself for battle against the Trojans, he says she was surrounded with dreadful terror; and, along with the head of Medusa, she brought with her bold courage, confident valor, and a most threatening appearance – all things appropriate to the goddess of war, as is also victory. Therefore Pausanias says that the Athenians placed her on their breastplates with the head of Medusa. ...

These things show the power of knowledge and prudence, which through wonderful works and wise counsels can astonish men and render them like stone with amazement, a power that can obtain whatever it wishes, provided it can suitably expound it: it is language that is expressed by that terrible head.[22]

This account, obviously, can be read many ways. As Cartari understands it, it is not primarily a story about the dangers of lust and illicit sex: Medusa is punished for attracting the attentions of Neptune, but the concluding moralization ignores this in favor of quite other points. It is also not simply, or even primarily, a story about male valor – Perseus is furnished by the war-goddess Pallas with the crucial mirror-shield that enables him to kill Medusa without looking at her, and it is she who wears it on her armor to betoken martial courage and certain victory – hers, not his: the power of Medusa is quintessentially female power.[23] Cartari gives no support to Jonson's claims for the genetic and functional relationship of Perseus and Fame, "I was her parent, and I am her strength"; Perseus's strength, on the contrary, depends on Pallas. In fact, if one were starting from this account of Perseus, the logical figure for Heroic Virtue would be Pallas, the goddess of both war and wisdom. Why then is Pallas not the guide from antimasque to masque for this celebration of heroic queens?

A simple answer might be that Jonson's focus at this point is on the defeat of the witches; he wants a martial hero whose triumph over evil is a triumph over hideous women, and Medusa is an obvious prototype for feminine evil. Still, as we read Cartari's account, even this assumption grows increasingly problematic. The gorgons prefigure the queens as much as they prefigure the witches: they are, in Cartari's historical allegory, martial women. They were, to begin with, beautiful, and the Medusa head becomes the emblem of Pallas because of its association specifically with militant female power, courage and victory. A very different answer is suggested by the final allegorization. Here Medusa is "knowledge and prudence," "wonderful works and wise counsels" – the emblem now of Pallas as wisdom, not as war; and the emblem as well of the poet and advisor to kings: "it is language that is expressed by that terrible head."

None of this, of course, is original with Cartari. Giovanni Pierio Valeriano in his *Hieroglyphica* allegorizes the Medusa head as prudence, and reports that the Athenians took it as their civic emblem because it was the sign of a strong and prudent city.[24] Coluccio Salutati made Medusa embody "artful eloquence," and the allegory ultimately derives, as Nancy Vickers points out, from a privileged classical source. During still another lighthearted male contest of both drinking and oratory, the *Symposium*, a flattering Socrates tells Agathon, the speaker who immediately precedes him, that he was held spellbound by the dazzling display of Agathon's speech. He compares Agathon to the master rhetorician Gorgias, and then permits himself a witty play on words: "I was afraid that when Agathon got near the end he would arm his speech against mine with the Gorgon's head of Gorgias' eloquence, and strike me as dumb as a stone."[25]

Given this context, Jonson's attraction to Perseus looks more and more marginal, his attraction to Medusa more and more central. Perseus is there because he confers – on the poet – the power of women, the power of the gorgon.

If Jonson's preference for Cartari's Perseus over Comes's subverts the queen's interests, it fully supports the king's. We might observe, to begin with, that for James the defeat and decapitation of the primary sensual and beautiful woman in his life was the crucial act of empowerment. But Jonson's mythography also points to an essential aspect of the poet's sense of himself. For Comes, the story is about the defeat of erotic temptation and illicit sexuality, and the finding of true love in the faithful wife Andromeda. This was not a Jonsonian model. "In his youth," he told William Drummond in 1619, he was "given to venery. He thought the use of a maid nothing in comparison to the wantonness of a wife, and would never have another mistress." His own

wife "was a shrew yet honest; five years he had not bedded with her."[26] He
was lavish in adulation of his noble patronesses, but printed a poem in praise
of the Countess of Bedford immediately after an epigram asserting that the
words "woman" and "whore" were synonyms.[27] By 1610 he had at least two
illegitimate children.[28] The play he wrote directly after *The Masque of Queens*
was the openly misogynistic *Epicoene*. Explaining "Why I Write Not of Love,"
it is Cupid, not Venus, that he seeks to bind in his verse;[29] in another poem,
attempting to find a subject, he banishes Venus to "invent new sports" with
the Graces, "thy tribade trine," a lesbian trio (and thereby introduced into the
language this first English adjective for female homosexuality),[30] concluding,

> Nor all the ladies of the Thespian lake
> (Though they were crushed into one form) could make
> A beauty of that merit that should take
> My muse up by commission ... .[31]

His own fantasy of heroic self-sufficiency is fed by a parallel fantasy of the
misanthropic self-sufficiency of beautiful woman.[32]

Heroic virtue

The triumph of heroic virtue is the triumph of Jonson and the word, and *The
Masque of Queens*, whatever else it says and unsays, unconditionally asserts
the power of poetry. The House of Fame realizes a Chaucerian allegory, but
its implications are characteristically Jonsonian (figure 3.3). Architecturally,
the building is an amalgam of classical and English elements: the Roman
arch below supports the gothic trefoil above. Within the trefoil is a turning
machine, bearing the twelve queens on one side and the winged figure of Fame
on the other. The façade, Jonson tells us, is adorned with statues: on the lower
tier are Homer, Virgil and Lucan, on the upper Achilles, Aeneas and Caesar
– the heroes' fame is supported and preserved by the immortal poets; heroism
(says this architectural emblem) depends on the ordering, transforming, and
preserving power of poetry. Jonson's text, however, maintains a discreet
distance from its performance: the witches of the antimasque are "twelve
women in the habit of hags or witches" (ll. 14–15); Perseus is "a person ... in
the furniture of Perseus" (ll. 341–2) – these, like the triumphant queens, are
all impersonations. But his own invention is authenticated, he writes, by "the
all-daring power of poetry."[33]

And where is the king in this Jacobean triumph? Jonson's claims for himself
are royal claims too: poet and king in this text assert the same authority.

3.3 Inigo Jones, the House of Fame in *The Masque of Queens*, 1609.

Outside the fiction, but at the center of the courtly spectacle, sits the monarch, declaring by his presence that in this masque of queens, heroism may be personified in the royal consort, but the highest virtue is that of the Rex Pacificus, scholar and poet. We confront again both Jacobean politics and the family drama; it is the royal pacificism that has compelled the witches' presence and that they deplore:

> I hate to see these fruits of a soft peace,
> And curse the piety gives it such increase;
> (ll. 132–3)

It is not the martial glory of Perseus and the Amazons – and the ambitious and popular Prince Henry – that Fame's trumpet sounds, but the king's peace (l. 410). It was as a scholar that James had himself represented on the tower of

3.4 James I offering his *Works* to the University on the Tower of the Five Orders, Bodleian Library, Oxford.

Oxford's Bodleian Library, to commemorate his gift to the university of the folio of his works, published (like Jonson's own folio) in 1616 (figure 3.4). The masque, for all its spectacle and martial imagery, celebrates the sovereign word.

Chivalric ideology

It is clear that Jonson's fable of heroic queens is less straightforward than it appears, and if we look further beneath its rhetoric it will reveal a good deal about the complexities of Jacobean ideology. On one level, it expresses erotic idealization through martial metaphors – analogous to the sort of praise Othello gives Desdemona when he calls her his fair warrior. There is a perennial male fantasy behind this; its modern counterpart, at its crudest, idealizes women dressed in leather and spike heels. But the queen's masque, I have also been suggesting, embodies a political fantasy too, and is more a mirror of the king's mind than of the queen's. As such, it may be taken as a good example of an absolutist mystification.

Jacobean chivalry is only superficially a revival of the Elizabethan mystique; beneath the surface the two are crucially different. In 1609, the royal ideology is no longer that of courtly love. For all the military chic of Inigo Jones's costumes, there is no suggestion in *The Masque of Queens* that the power of Bel-Anna and her Amazons derives in any way from their erotic attractions. Jonson's reformulation of the chivalric myth is, in its way, far more radically disarming than Elizabeth's had been. Elizabeth's version expressed a truth: much of the queen's power lay in her desirability as a wife, and for a good part of her reign her control over political factions derived significantly from her ability to treat their leaders as her suitors. Chivalry under King James was quite a different matter, for none of the power of the Jacobean monarchy inhered in the queen, and Jonson's chivalric metaphor in effect deprived Anne and her ladies of the only real source of authority they possessed, their status as desirable consorts. Female chivalry, in this new formulation, leaves male power unaffected: unmoved, unthreatened, uncompromised. As such, the mythology was ideally suited to the purposes of the king, by nature withdrawn and secretive, by ideology absolutist and patriarchal, programmatically pacifist, and far more attracted to men than to women.

Prince Henry too was interested in *The Masque of Queens*, but for different reasons. He asked Jonson for an annotated copy of the text, with detailed information about the poet's authorities. *Evidence* concerned this young man; he saw through the courtly compliment of his mother's masque to the historical reality of heroic examples. Jonson presented the prince with a beautiful manuscript in his own hand, anatomizing, in a way that is all but unique in English, the relation of a Renaissance poet to the sources of his invention. Jonson was as deeply concerned as the prince to establish the authority of his poetic fictions.

And when the chivalric ideology was adopted by Prince Henry, its implications were suddenly disturbing and subversive. Two years after *The Masque of Queens*, at New Year's 1611, he commissioned the masque of *Oberon* from Jonson and Inigo Jones. They presented him as a romantic hero, in a costume adapted from imperial Roman armor (figure 3.5). James's heir had serious military ambitions, and the chivalric mode had now to do not with courtly love but with jousts and tilts, and ultimately with training and leading armies. By the age of fourteen, Henry's military interests were being

3.5 Inigo Jones, costume
design for Prince Henry
as Oberon in Jonson's
masque *Oberon*, 1611.

noted throughout the country with excitement and admiration, making him in
effect a powerful rival to the withdrawn and pacifist king. The prince's militant
Protestantism was something that James, like Elizabeth before him, wanted
no part of. The heroic persona that Jonson and Inigo Jones devised for Henry
thus expressed not only ideals but intentions. If Elizabethan chivalry had been
disarming, the chivalry of *Oberon* was a declaration of war, and King James
did his best to counteract it. The prince had wanted his masque to culminate
in barriers, martial games in which he could distinguish himself. But the king
vetoed this proposal, and insisted that *Oberon* conclude instead with the

dances and songs of courtly society. And as in *The Masque of Queens*, Jonson finally served the king: at the crucial moment of revelation, when Oberon at last appears in a chariot drawn by two white bears, a chorus celebrates the prince's heroic ambition,

> Oberon's desire,
> Than which there nothing can be higher,
> Save James to whom it flies:
> But he the wonder is of tongues, of ears, of eyes.
> (ll. 223–6)

The focus of admiration remains the king in the audience. *Oberon* is thus a curiously double-edged work, creating for its ambitious young protagonist an imperial persona, but disarming him at the same time. James and Jonson contrive to transform the heroic assertions of *Oberon* into the subverted claims of *The Masque of Queens*. Henry, denied his triumph on stage, pursued it in the political world, supporting his sister's marriage to the Elector Palatine and proposing to follow her and her husband to Bohemia at the head of a Protestant army. It was only his sudden death in 1612, probably of typhoid fever, that ensured that the heroic persona of his masque would never be translated into reality. Queen Anne asserted till her dying day that her son had been poisoned.

Notes

1 For a fuller discussion, see my "The Spectacles of State," in *The Authentic Shakespeare: And Other Problems of the Early Modern Stage* (New York, 2002); for general accounts of the development of Elizabethan chivalry, see Roy Strong, *The Cult of Elizabeth* (London, 1977), and Frances Yates, *Astraea* (London, 1975).

2 The context of the painting is discussed in my "Shakespeare and the Cannibals," in *Cannibals, Witches and Divorce*, ed. Majorie Garber (Baltimore, MD, 1987), pp. 58–62. Roy Strong's indispensable discussion elucidates the contemporary political dimensions of the painting, which includes allusions to Sir Christopher Hatton and the English imperial ambitions, but he sees Elizabeth as a new Aeneas, and is apparently unaware of the tradition of the chaste Dido. See *Gloriana* (London, 1987), pp. 95–107.

3 John Harington, *Nugae Antiquae*, ed. Henry Harington and Thomas Park (London, 1804), 1:395; the passage, with an enlightening discussion, is cited in Jonathan Goldberg, *James I and the Politics of Literature* (Baltimore, MD, 1983), pp. 28ff.

4 Harington, *Nugae Antiquae*, p. 360.

5 Queen Anne formally converted in 1598 or 1599 – the documentation was discovered in the Vatican archives only in 1999 by Peter Davidson and Thomas McCoog, SJ (see "Father Robert's Convert – the private Catholicism of Anne of Denmark," *TLS*, November 24, 2000, pp. 16–17). The conversion naturally was kept very quiet, but her sympathies were always well known, and she refused to take the Anglican communion when she came to London as queen in 1603.

6 Lines 9–12; quotations are from *Ben Jonson: The Complete Masques*, ed. Stephen Orgel (Cambridge, MA, 1969).

7 Gloss on l. 36 (Jonson, *Complete Masques*, p. 526).

8 Her name appears once as Agnis Sampson, apparently a misprint, though the association of witchcraft with the hero whose downfall came from his attraction to heathen and emasculating women is worth remarking.

9 Bodley Head Quarto (also including *Daemonologie*), ed. G. B. Harrison (London, 1924), p. 15; the text has been modernized.

10 For a discussion of James's attacks on women as an index both to his relations with his mother and his sense of himself, see Goldberg, *James I*, pp. 24–5.

11 Cited in G. P. Akrigg, *Jacobean Pageant* (Cambridge, MA, 1963), p. 13.

12 *Newes from Scotland*, p. 17.

13 Ibid., p. 15.

14 Goldberg, *James I*, p. 16.

15 *Political Works of James I*, ed. C. H. McIlwain (Cambridge, MA, 1918), p. 272.

16 Ibid., p. 15.

17 Gloss on 1. 346.

18 These were the three most influential iconologies and mythographies of the period; they are sometimes cited by Jonson, but were more often used by him simply as reference works, without acknowledgment. Cesare Ripa's *Iconologia* was first published in 1593 without illustrations; the first illustrated edition appeared in 1603. It appeared in innumerable editions and mutations thereafter, and was an essential resource until well into the eighteenth century. The *Mythologia* of Natalis Comes (or Conti) was issued first in 1551, in an enlarged edition in 1581, and frequently thereafter. Vincenzo Cartari's *Imagini*, the most popular of the Renaissance mythographies, appeared first in 1556, and in two dozen editions by the late seventeenth century.

19 Ripa, *Iconologia* (Padua, 1611), pp. 537–40.

20 The story of Perseus appears in book 7, chapters 11 and 12: Comes, *Mythologia* (Padua, 1616), pp. 390–5.

21 Cartari, *Imagini* (Padua, 1571), pp. 383ff.

22 Ibid., pp. 383–4.

23 The point is made in John Freccero, "Medusa: the Letter and the Spirit," *Yearbook of Italian Studies*, vol. 2 (1972): 1–18; see esp. p. 7.

24 G. P. Valeriano, *Hieroglyphica* 16.32 (Lyons, 1610), p. 165.

25 Nancy Vickers, "'The blazon of sweet beauty's best': Shakespeare's *Lucrece*," in *Shakespeare and the Question of Theory*, ed. Patricia Parker and Geoffrey Hartman (London, 1985), p. 110. John Freccero's detailed and enlightening discussion of the figure in "Medusa: The Letter and the Spirit" has already been cited; see also Jonathan Goldberg's powerful and suggestive remarks in *Voice Terminal Echo* (London, 1986), pp. 150–1, and Tobin Sievers, *The Mirror of Medusa* (Berkley, CA, 1983), passim.

26 "Conversations with Drummond," in C. H. Herford and P. Simpson, *Ben Jonson* (Oxford, 1925) 1:140, 139.

27 Ben Jonson, *Epigrams*, in *Poems*, ed. Ian Donaldson (London, 1975), 83, 84.

28 The documentary evidence is analyzed in Mark Eccles, "Jonson's Marriage," *Review of English Studies*, vol. 12, no. 47 (July 1936): 268.

29 Ben Jonson, *The Forest*, in *Poems*, ed. Ian Donaldson (London, 1975), 1.

30 This is the earliest usage cited in the *Oxford English Dictionary*; "tribadree" appears in a manuscript poem addressed to Donne by "T. W." (Thomas Woodward?) dating from the mid-1590s (not recorded in the *Oxford English Dictionary*), printed in Milgate's edition of Donne's *Satires, Epigrams and Verse Letters* (Oxford, 1967), p. 212.

31 *The Forest* 10, lines 17, 25–9.

32 A classic version of this fantasy may be the source of Perseus's claim to be Fame's parent, "When Virtue cut off Terror he gat Fame." The mother of Fama in Virgil is *Terra*, the earth, who conceives Fama (i.e., rumor, spreading truth and falsehood indiscriminately), "monstrum horrendum, ingens," a horrible huge monster, in anger at the gods (*Aeneid* 4.174ff.).

33 Jonson, *Complete Masques*, p. 547.

Part II

Drama

4

Othello and the end of comedy

Othello begins at the moment when comedies end, with a happy marriage. It begins, too, where *The Merchant of Venice* and *Twelfth Night* leave off, with the question of ethnic or social outsiders – Shylock, Malvolio – as the catalysts for the destructive elements within society. It might seem that here the terms are reversed, with the dangerous alien now the hero, while the mysterious, incomprehensibly malicious, diabolical villain is the insider, one of us. But in fact, the insider/ outsider dichotomy is really a false one, because just as Shylock is essential to Bassanio's wooing, and Malvolio is essential to both Olivia's household and ultimately even to the marriage of Viola and Orsino, so is Othello essential to the safety and prosperity of the Venetian state. The tragedy is not that Othello is essential to Venice, but that Iago is essential to Othello.

We have, historically, focused on the interracial marriage as the crucial source of tension and tragedy in the play. But the larger issue in *Othello* has to do with the tragic implications not of miscegenation but of patriarchy on the one hand, and patronage or gender bonding (not limited to males in this case) on the other. I begin with the first: patriarchy is an issue that often provides both the principal motivation of comedy and a strong tragic element within it – as in the cases of Celia's villainous father in *As You Like It* and the obdurate Egeus in *A Midsummer Night's Dream*. It is on the defeat of these fathers that the comedy depends. In a strikingly ambiguous example, the death of the Princess of France's father, announced by a messenger appropriately named Mercadé ("mar-Arcady"), produces a tragic moment interrupting the comic wooing of *Love's Labour's Lost*: "The king your father – " "Dead, for my life!" … "Worthies, away; the scene begins to cloud" (V.2.710–11).[1] This could conclude the comedy, but it does not. It is, in fact, an enabling comic event, which permits the heroine to make her own decisions. Significantly, she exercises her new authority by refusing to allow the play to conclude with the marriages of comedy, implying thereby that perhaps marriage is not such a happy ending after all.

The patriarchal imperatives are powerfully present and shrewdly finessed in *The Merchant of Venice*, where daughters are all but equated with ducats, and the triumph of romance is engineered by Portia both adhering to the letter of her dead father's will and betraying its spirit – and not incidentally turning the patriarchal tables by reducing both her father and Jessica's to their ducats. Patriarchy is specifically sidestepped in *Twelfth Night*, in which all the fathers are safely dead and their estates safely settled before the play even begins. Viola and Olivia make their own decisions about marriage, and Sir Toby's avuncular attempt to stand in the place of Olivia's father is as firmly rejected as the authority of Brabantio is in *Othello*. Indeed, there is a significant link between the two plays in the relation of Iago and Roderigo, a very sinister refiguring of Sir Toby and Sir Andrew, with Iago keeping up Roderigo's interest in Desdemona merely because it means a constant supply of ready cash for the go-between. Even here, the woman is easily convertible into a source of ducats.

If *Othello* is the next step after comedy, it is also an obvious next step after the tragedy of *Romeo and Juliet*. However admirable Romeo and Othello are (and both are presented as, in themselves, highly suitable marriage material), the question of Juliet's and Desdemona's elopement would have been a real one for Shakespeare's audience: daughters in this society *are* ducats, and the daughter was, in effect, disposing of a valuable piece of her father's property without his consent. Legally either of the women would have been perfectly entitled to make the match, since both are of age. The age of consent was twelve for women, fourteen for men. In the Canons of 1604 it was raised to twenty-one for both, but Parliament failed to pass the necessary legislation, and the age remained statutorily unchanged until the eighteenth century. It is perhaps relevant that 1604 was also the year *Othello* was first performed: the issue of parental control over marriage was being actively debated at the time. Such a marriage, therefore, raised ethical and moral issues that would have had nothing to do with the fact that Othello was black. The point here is not that daughters are at fault if they disobey or fail to consult their fathers' wishes; it is that the patriarchal system inevitably involves divided loyalties, irreconcilable, and sometimes tragic, demands. As Desdemona points out when she is summoned to account for herself before the Duke and her father, she has a double duty; the patriarchy of her father conflicts with the patriarchy of her husband. One way to view the play, as with *Romeo and Juliet*, is certainly as a moral tale about the consequences of not listening to your father. This does not imply that father always knows best; what it implies is that right or wrong, he is still your father – being wrong does not undo his authority. Inherent in patriarchy, in other words, is always a divided loyalty, a potentially tragic element. Similarly, Shakespeare plays are full of bad kings, but they are not therefore arguments in favor of democracy: the point – often a tragic point – is that a bad king is still the king.

Nevertheless, the father is rarely simply rejected or ignored. Even in *Twelfth Night*, Viola, in determining to serve Orsino (determining in effect to fall in love with him) recalls her father talking of him with praise – she implicitly claims her father's posthumous approval for her pursuit of him. And though at the beginning of *Othello* Brabantio insists that he never had any romantic intentions for Othello and his daughter, it is nevertheless clear that Desdemona's love for the heroic Moor is an outgrowth, even an extension, of her father's – "Her father loved me," Othello says, "oft invited me" (I.3.128). Brabantio to the contrary notwithstanding, the marriage is presented as the logical climax to a patronage relationship, the traditional confirmation of masculine friendship – traditionally a happy ending, certainly, but one that also often constitutes the beginning of tragedy, as the comedy of Hercules's gift to Theseus of his prize, Hippolyta, leads not only to *A Midsummer Night's Dream*, but also, inexorably, to the tragedy of their offspring Hippolytus and Hippolyta's successor in Theseus's bed, Phaedra.

Consider *Othello* as a comedy. Suppose I said that this is a play about a jealous husband driven wild by the fear of being a cuckold, though his wife is in fact perfectly innocent; that the central action involves a trick played on him by a clever, malicious servant; that the crucial – and indeed, the only – piece of evidence is a missing handkerchief; and that at the end of the play the wife's innocence and the servant's trickery are both revealed to the repentant husband. I have not misrepresented the play's action at all, yet this sounds like a subject for comedy: the final sentence could very well be, "husband and wife are reconciled, and Othello promises not to be jealous any more."

In fact, the play tempts us with comic possibilities all the time. As with that other love tragedy *Romeo and Juliet*, nothing about it suggests the inevitability that we normally associate with tragedy. If they had only talked about it, we want to say; if Emilia had revealed the theft of the handkerchief a little sooner; if the momentary recovery of Desdemona had lasted (I am told that this is a physiological impossibility anyway – that is, it is already a miracle; but the miracle is simply another tease) ... and so forth. As with *Romeo and Juliet*, a significant part of the power of the play comes from how infuriatingly close it gets to not being a tragedy. We can derive a critical precept from this: what distinguishes comedy from tragedy is not the problems it deals with, but what it is willing to accept as solutions to its problems, what kind of satisfaction it is willing to deliver.

If marriage is the ultimate satisfaction of comedy, what happens next? What kind of tragic satisfaction does *Othello* deliver? Despite the fact that it opens with an elopement, it quite explicitly deprives us of the satisfaction of marriage, since on the only two nights Desdemona and Othello manage to get to bed together before he murders her on their wedding sheets, their lovemaking is relentlessly interrupted – it is not, in fact, even clear that the marriage has actually been consummated. Orson Welles's extraordinary film version, released in 1952, opens well after the play's conclusion, with the definitive end of the marriage, the funeral of Othello and Desdemona, in progress. Even this is interrupted, by a figure in chains being dragged to a wooden cage, into which he is thrust and which then, slowly, is hoisted up the sides of the castle wall, to hang from its tower as the funeral procession continues. All this takes place before even the title and credits. If we know the play, we will be aware that Iago's punishment has been meted out already. We will also be aware that, as far as poetic justice is concerned, this is all the satisfaction we will get, and that it is a satisfaction the play specifically refuses us.

But frustration clearly constitutes a good part of *Othello*'s dramatic force, and the play was from the very beginning extraordinarily popular – especially so after the Restoration, when it served as a powerful model for tragedy. The fact aroused the indignation of Thomas Rymer, who in a notorious attack published in 1693 declared that *Othello* "impiously assumes the sacred name of tragedy,"[2] but was, on the contrary, nothing but "a bloody farce" (p. 146). Rymer supports his judgment with one of the most detailed, and certainly the most thoroughly vituperative, analyses of the play ever undertaken. Though critics including Dryden treated it with respect, Rymer's indictment had little effect on either the theatrical repertory or the practice of criticism (far less effect, for example, than the equally moralistic arraignment of the stage by Jeremy Collier published five years later, which really did instigate certain reforms), and Rymer's attack survives in the critical literature primarily as a curiosity. However, T. S. Eliot claimed to have been convinced by it, asserting that he had "never … seen a cogent refutation of Thomas Rymer's objections to *Othello*," and that "Rymer makes out a very good case."[3] Rymer's case is worth looking at: everyone remembers the famous bit about the moral being that wives should look well to their linen, but there is a great deal more in it than that (it goes on for sixty pages), and one wonders how much of it Eliot actually read.

Rymer ridicules Shakespeare from the outset for having a black hero: it is preposterous to suppose that the Venetians would "set a Negro to be their General; or trust a *Moor* to defend them against the Turk," he says. "With us," he continues, "a Black-a-moor might rise to be a Trumpeter," but Shakespeare makes him a Lieutenant-General. "With us a *Moor* might marry some little drab," but Shakespeare gives him an aristocrat's daughter (pp. 91–2). The blatant racism of this is not at all historically determined, if we think of the popularity of Oroonoko in both Aphra Behn's novel and Thomas Southern's drama – Rymer is proud of being out of step with his society, and his point is precisely that the popularity of *Othello* indicates a significant deficiency in public morality and taste, a disregard of orthodoxy, an insufficient concern throughout the culture for principles, for correctness. This is surely one of the things Eliot must have liked about the essay – its underlying thesis is that of *After Strange Gods*, and if he did read beyond the handkerchief bit, both his passion for orthodoxy and his distaste for "free-thinking Jews" would have found in Rymer a sympathetic ancestor.

There is obviously for this critic no way for the play to compensate for the ethnicity of its hero, and though Rymer is genuinely, often brilliantly, observant, much of the analysis is simply vulgar invective. The plot is declared at the outset "intolerable and absurd" (p. 92), and it is all downhill from there. "Nothing is more odious in Nature than an improbable lye; And, certainly, never was any Play fraught, like this of *Othello*, with improbabilities" (pp. 95–6). The latter part of this observation is quite correct – the play's deployment of improbabilities, and indeed of impossibilities, is one of its dramaturgical strokes of genius, and Rymer is the first critic to catch on to the double time scheme in the play, but it provokes only rage, not admiration.

The rage testifies to the fact, however, that the improbabilities are all too credible. Much of the time it is not Shakespeare who is being berated, but the fictional Othello, for allowing himself to be duped so easily. When Othello says "Her name that was as fresh/ As Dian's visage is now begrimed and black/ As mine own face," Rymer furiously scolds the hero: "There is not a Monky but understands Nature better; not a Pug in *Barbary* that has not a truer taste of things" (p. 124) – in other words, you fool, can't you see she's innocent! Some of the discussion is clearly irrelevant, some is positively loony – Shakespeare is attacked for making Iago "a close, dissembling, false, insinuating rascal, instead of an open-hearted, frank, plain-dealing Souldier" because that is what soldiers are really like (p. 94). (Did Eliot really read this far?) Othello's "Farewell the tranquil mind, farewell content" speech is dismissed as having nothing poetical in it "besides the sound," and is invidiously compared with the blankest of blank verse speeches from *Gorboduc* (pp. 124–5). There had been no edition of *Gorboduc* since 1590, and it is doubtful that more than a handful of readers even knew what Rymer was talking about; but it cannot be coincidental that *Gorboduc* is the only English tragedy that Sidney, in the *Defence of Poesie*, could find to praise. It is difficult to imagine what Eliot would have considered a "cogent refutation" of so incoherent a performance (it is quite clear why he had never seen one), but obviously all that matters is that Rymer's indignant heart was in the right place.

Rymer is interesting for my purposes precisely because of his incoherences, because he notices everything and gets the point of nothing. His sixty-page tirade is sufficient witness to the fact that, for all the claims of ineptitude and incompetence, he finds the play utterly, indeed infuriatingly, compelling; and essential to his outraged fascination is a specifically generic claim, that *Othello* is not tragedy but farce. Buried beneath all the rant and rage there *is* a critical point, and something about it seems to me correct. Let us consider the famous bits (it should be emphasized that these passages consititute an infinitesimal part of the essay):

> The moral, sure, [he writes,] is very instructive. First, this may be a caution to all maidens of quality how, without their parents' consent they run away with blackamoors ... Secondly, this may be a warning to all good wives that they look well to their linen. Thirdly, this may be a lesson to husbands that before their jealousy be tragical the proofs may be mathematical [i. e., absolutely conclusive, like a proof in math]. (p. 89)

So here are the morals: 1) don't marry blacks unless your parents approve; 2) count your handkerchiefs; 3) don't murder your wife unless you're sure that she is unfaithful. This comes near the beginning of the essay. By the middle, Shakespeare is being indicted for learning his craft not from the classics (or from *Gorboduc*) but from the popular theater of his own time, mysteries and morality plays written by "carpenters, cobblers, and illiterate fellows," who interlarded their plots with "drolls and fooleries" to bring in the rabble (p. 111);

> And it is then no wonder that we find so much farce and apocryphal matter in his tragedies. Thereby un-hallowing the theater, profaning the name of tragedy; and instead of representing men and manners, turning all morality, good sense and humanity into mockery and derision. (pp. 111–12)

Here is the conclusion, thirty pages later:

> What can remain with the audience to carry home with them from this sort of poetry for their use and edification? How can it work, unless (instead of settling the mind and purging our passions) to delude our senses, disorder our thoughts, addle our brain, pervert our affections, hare our imaginations [i.e., frighten us, or make us hare-brained], corrupt

our appetite, and fill our head with vanity, confusion, *tintamarre*, and jingle-jangle...?

and so on in this vein for ten more lines – the invective is self-generating. The problem now is conceived in Aristotelian and Horatian terms: that *Othello* does not include the catharsis necessary to tragedy, and does not edify us, and therefore is worthless, or even vicious.

But then oddly, as the essay concludes, it turns out to be the comic elements that are all right:

> There is in this play some burlesque, some humor and ramble of comical wit, some show, and some mimicry to divert the spectators; but the tragical part is plainly none other than a bloody farce, without salt or savor. (p. 146)

It is the pretensions to tragedy that are so pernicious, unhallowing the theater, contributing to the general decay of the arts and morality, and debasing the nobility of the very category of tragedy.

What becomes clear here is that *Othello* is *the* quintessential drama for this hostile critic; it embodies everything that is trivial, dishonest, dangerous and immoral about theater itself, and its popularity is particularly frightening because the play, as Rymer sees it, is totally irrational and should therefore be both repellant and incomprehensible. There is actually something in this, but we would want to add that a good deal of the play's power derives precisely from that deep irrationality – that deep understanding of the profoundly irrational elements in our nature – an understanding which operates not only on the characters but, through the dramaturgy, on the audience as well.

Relabeling the play, declaring it farce rather than tragedy, is the *coup de grâce* here, but why does the genre matter? Why can it not simply be a bad tragedy?[4] A century earlier Sidney, in the first real classic of English literary criticism, had had equal contempt for the improbabilities of the tragedies of his time, but these defects only make the tragedies defective; they do not banish the plays from the category: though tragedy was assumed to be the noblest of the dramatic genres, there were better tragedies and worse ones, and the bad ones were still tragedies. For Renaissance critics generally, the genres were basically a filing system, and in the most detailed and compendious of the anatomies, the *Poetics* of Julius Caesar Scaliger, many plays appear under a variety of genres. Here is a characteristic passage. He begins by observing that many comedies end unhappily for some of the characters, and continues:

In the same way, there are a number of happy tragedies: in Euripides' *Electra*, despite the death of Aegisthus, many people are joyful; *Ion* has a happy ending as does *Helen*. Then too, although Aeschylus's *Eumenides* contains tragic elements (such as murders and the Furies), its structure is more like that of a comedy: the beginning [in *Agamemnon*] is joyful for the guard, though troubling for Clytemnestra because of her husband's arrival; then comes the murder [of Clytemnestra], and Electra and Orestes are happy; the ending is happy for everyone – Apollo, Orestes, the populace, Pallas, the Eumenides. Thus it is by no means true, as we have always been taught, that tragedy must have an unhappy ending: it need only include terrible things.[5]

There would have been no problem for Scaliger about farcical elements in *Othello*, clearly. For Rymer a century later, however, tragedy is not merely a category, it is a sacred name, and the genres constitute a hierarchy, with tragedy not simply at the top, but a divinely anointed king – there can be, in this taxonomy, no bad tragedies (in the sense that a bad tragedy is disposed of by being declared not to be a tragedy). It logically follows, however, that if tragedy is king it is always in danger of usurpation, and that is what Rymer perceives here: *Othello* not only profanes the sacred name of tragedy, it "impiously assumes" the name – usurps it. The trouble with thinking of dramatic genres this way, of course, is that a usurping king, like a wicked or tyrannical one, is no less the king, and the effort to dethrone *Othello* is doomed merely by definition.

What Rymer noticed, shrewdly and accurately, however, was something that for Scaliger was largely unproblematic in drama: that *Othello* works more like a comedy than like a tragedy. This is somewhat different from a point that has been observed occasionally by critics of the last century, that the play is partly indebted in its character types and situations to the *commedia dell'arte*; Rymer's invocation of the comic is structural and moral. The play is declared a farce rather than a comedy because comedy too has its civic virtues and social utility, and, perhaps most important, because farce has no classical precedent; but the distinction between comedy and farce in this context is nugatory: the essential point is to remove *Othello* from the sacred category by calling it something else, and that something is comic.

Rymer's lessons

Let us return to Rymer's three sarcastic lessons derived from the play: don't elope with a black unless your parents approve, keep track of your linens, don't kill your wife unless you're sure you're being cuckolded. What is wrong with this as a summary of the action? In fact, the only essential element of the drama that is omitted is Iago, and one of the most interesting things about Rymer's account of the play is that Iago really does not figure very significantly in it. Othello is a fool, Desdemona is a slattern and largely responsible for what happens to her, everyone is insufficiently dignified, the plot is crazy; but Iago's scheming is not a major factor in the tragedy – or farce. All the scheming, in this view of the play, is Shakespeare's. Once again, this seems to me basically correct, and I now turn to Iago.

In the most straightforward view of the plot, Iago is the agent of all the play's destructiveness and bad faith, the source of all the tragic energy – in short, the villain. A little less straightforwardly, he is certainly still the villain, but perhaps nevertheless not the agent and source at all, but merely the catalyst, externalizing and articulating the destructive chaos that lies just beneath Othello's love and rationality, the chaos that he himself says is kept in check only by his love for Desdemona – rather like the witches in *Macbeth*, or, indeed, Lady Macbeth herself, who, however evil, are not the culprits. A lot depends on how far you want to see Iago as a classic machiavel on the one hand, or as an extension of Othello on the other. The latter might seem to be a post-Renaissance conception, but in fact the play itself questions the simple view of Iago's malign responsibility for Othello's behavior when Emilia remarks that jealous souls "are not ever jealous for the cause,/ But jealous for they are jealous" – Othello's jealousy is not, then, simply the creation of Iago's scheming. There is a good deal of self-interest in this piece of wisdom, of course, since Emilia herself has provided the trigger of Othello's jealousy, the handkerchief, and is covering for both herself and her husband long after she understands quite clearly the mischief she has caused; but the observation is, nevertheless, also self-evidently true, and it is a truth around which Iago designs his scheme. Villain and victim, in fact, have much more in common, understand each other much better, than husband and wife: it is clear that Iago's cynical view of women as lustful, untrustworthy and characteristically unfaithful is, when the chips are down, Othello's view also, and therefore Othello instinctively believes in Iago's honesty, not in his wife's – this is true from the first moment Desdemona's fidelity is questioned; all Iago has to say is "I think Cassio's an honest man." One could argue, indeed, that the source of the tragedy is precisely in that gender bonding – in the fact that Othello's primary loyalty is to his friend, not his wife; in the fact that Emilia chooses to betray her mistress, not her husband. But it is also possible to imagine this play without Iago: certainly all those elements of jealousy, self-dramatization, rage and barely controlled chaos that Iago elicits are aspects of Othello's character clearly articulated from the outset.

In staging the play, to make Iago a sort of allegorical extension of Othello would, of course, make for a much more complex Othello than we are used to, one that would continually raise the question of how far the play's claim that the tragedy is all Iago's fault, which is essentially a claim that jealousy is explicable and reasonable – that men get jealous because villains steal handkerchiefs and tell lies – is borne out by the action. There are two ways of reading "In following him I follow but myself": as Iago's assertion of total self-interest in his relation to Othello, or alternatively, as an acknowledgment that, in a much deeper sense, they are inseparable – the bond can be construed as a love relationship, with Iago's resentment that of a scorned lover, rejected in favor of Cassio on the one hand and Desdemona on the other, a rejection all the more painful because it has been so casual. The jealousy, then, in the first instance would be Iago's. He presents himself again as a scorned lover when he accuses both Cassio and Othello of sleeping with his wife Emilia. This is basically the situation dramatized in the Sonnets, and if we take that sequence to be in any sense autobiographical, Shakespeare is depicting himself in Iago – Stephen Greenblatt long ago suggested, in *Renaissance Self-Fashioning*, that Iago, as the amoral manipulator and endlessly fertile improvisor of plots was a figure for Shakespeare,[6] but I am suggesting something much more psychologically and emotionally specific.

If we are thinking of Shakespeare's dramaturgy in terms of autobiography, here is another proposition: we know that Burbage played Othello, but in Shakespeare's company who played the much larger role of Iago? Iago is one of the longest roles in Shakespeare – 1,020 lines, almost 250 lines longer than Othello (250 lines is the length of the entire role of Caliban). Only Hamlet, the longest role by far, and Richard III are longer; these three are the only roles that are over a thousand lines (though Henry V almost makes it, at 999). For comparison, the whole of *The Comedy of Errors* is only 1,750 lines long, and *Macbeth* just over 2,000. Iago is a third of his play. Could it be a part that Shakespeare the actor wrote for himself?

Probably the answer is no; the one Shakespearian role we think we know Shakespeare played was Adam in *As You Like It*, and a much more apocryphal tradition has him as the Ghost in *Hamlet*. These stories at least suggest that the roles he took in his own plays were small ones; and John Lowin, who we know played the villainous Bosola in *The Duchess of Malfi* and the ill-tempered Morose in *Epicoene*, had joined the company in 1603, and would therefore have been available. Nevertheless the Sonnets provide an inescapable gloss on all the painful ramifications of the assumption that

"My friend and I are one." The identity, the interchangeability, of Othello and Iago has been a significant part of stage history for centuries, perhaps always. If the original Iago was not Shakespeare, and even if it was Lowin, did Burbage nevertheless – like Garrick, Edmund Kean, Kemble, Macready, Fechter, Irving, Edwin Booth, Olivier; even, unlikely as it sounds, Gielgud – play both roles, and were the roles, from the beginning, interchangeable; did the great actor always want to be both?[7] Virtuoso performers, starting with Edmund Kean and Charles Mayne Young, and including Macready and Samuel Phelps, Edwin Booth and Henry Irving, Richard Burton and John Neville, have even alternated the roles, sometimes from night to night, playing out, in the most literal way, "Were I the Moor, I would not be Iago." In fact, Kean, as Iago, refused to switch after he saw the first night of Young's Othello, convinced he could never equal it – Iago's envy was in this case the very essence of performance itself. The other roles that historically have been alternated are much less explosive: Richard and Bolingbroke, Hal and Hotspur, and most famously, in 1935, Gielgud and Olivier switching back and forth as Romeo and Mercutio. (Bernhardt, as a footnote, played both Ophelia and Hamlet, though decades apart.)

Throughout the eighteenth and much of the nineteenth centuries, the machiavellian Iago, innately evil and an obvious extension of Richard III, often outfitted, in the absence of a hunchback, with diabolically bushy eyebrows and black wig, was stardard; but from the time of Fechter and Irving, Iago has tended to be the really complex character in the play. A good deal of the cumulative effect of the drama depends on how you decide to play him. Most productions have made him complex but unattractive, saturnine, insinuating, crude, graceless – most of all, not a gentleman. In such performances, the real energy of the role goes into the villainy – it is a melodramatic energy, undeniably effective, but it simplifies the play, makes him a villain like Richard III, where his villainy is in every sense his defining characteristic. In the case of Richard III, his success is represented first as a political phenomenon, where he is supported by people who are either naively trusting or think he is horrible but will do them some good, and second – notoriously, in the wooing of Lady Anne – as a kind of mesmeric magic, because he is so obviously villainous. The problem with treating Iago this way is that such a reading does not make enough distinction between the public and the private Iago – Richard is always a villain, but until the final scene we know much more about Iago than any of the characters do, and there has to be some reason established dramatically for why everyone finds him so implicitly trustworthy. Dramatically, making him unattractive and graceless accounts for his hostility and resentment, but does nothing to explain his extraordinary persuasiveness.

As I stage the play in my own mind, he is attractive and very charming. The only performance I have ever seen that was anything like this was Kenneth Branagh's, in the film with Laurence Fishburne as Othello. There were lots of problems with this film – Fishburne looked great, but didn't do much with the verse; Irene Jacob's English was so heavily accented that she might have been in some other play – but the Iago was a revelation: easygoing, affable, good looking, affectionate, an instant best friend, somebody you wanted to confide in and have around. In this performance, the melodrama is saved for the soliloquies, so that Iago is completely different in public and in private. Branagh gives the film the sense of a stage performance by talking directly to the camera (rather than "thinking" his soliloquies); he plays with the audience, taking them into his confidence, making them his accomplices, charming them, flirting with them, just as he does with Roderigo and Cassio, not so much persuading as wooing them.

I would even take this a step farther, and take the analogy of the Sonnets into account, making Iago an attractive gay man seriously in love with Othello, and Othello a narcissist, not at all averse to being adored, fully trusting Iago because he trusts his own attractiveness; knowing, moreover, that he does not have to promote Iago, because he is perfectly aware of his sexual power over his subordinate. (My use of the shorthand term 'gay' is anachronistic only in the sense that the term is modern; there have always been men who fell in love with other men.) The sexual dynamic here would be a two-way affair, and when, in this production of mine, Othello elicits from Iago the words of the marriage vow, "I am your own forever," he is quite conscious of what he is doing. After all, throughout the play Othello is under the impression that he is using Iago, not the other way round. The fantasy of replacing Desdemona with Iago as his wife is in my production parallel to Iago's fantasy of lying awake in bed with Cassio asleep – or pretending to be – and sexually excited, taking Iago for Desdemona – or pretending to. Is Othello's fury at this solely at the idea of Cassio imagining he is in bed with Desdemona? Is the idea of Cassio actually making love to Iago no part of it? Quite possibly the answer is an indignant no, no part of it at all; quite possibly my Othello would at the very suggestion stalk off the rehearsal stage (*but why is he so angry?*); nevertheless, it is obvious that the crucial relationships in both these episodes are between the men. As in the Sonnets, who knows how much is implied by "My friend and I are one," "I am your own forever"?

Two friends to whom I have proposed this haven't liked it; both objected that making Iago gay explains too much, that the malignity ought to be left motiveless. I am surprised that love is assumed to constitute more of an explanation than hatred; but, in any case, Iago does explain at some length why he hates Othello – the problem is really that he offers too many motives, not too few. Cassio has a daily beauty in his life that makes Iago's ugly, Othello has preferred Cassio to him, Othello and Cassio have been to bed with his wife – all the explanations boil down to envy and jealousy; and as Romeo (that is, Shakespeare) says, "Here's much to do with hate, but more with love." Coleridge's point was surely that the explanations didn't really explain anything, didn't produce a *rational* motive, produced only jealousy, or hatred (or love), not that they weren't there. Romeo cites not only the inseparability of love and hate, but the motivelessness of both as well: "Why then, O brawling love, O loving hate,/ O anything of nothing first create!" (I.i.174–6).

Some productions have in fact accounted for Iago's behavior by suggesting that he was gay. Tyrone Guthrie in 1938 had Olivier as a homosexual Iago furtively longing for Ralph Richardson's Othello. Since the interpretation was based on Freud's view of homosexuality via Ernest Jones, there was more repression and neurotic angst than flirting, and very little satisfaction of any kind. Here is Olivier's account in his autobiography:

> Tony Guthrie and I were swept away by ... Jones's contention that Iago was subconsciously in love with Othello and had to destroy him. Unfortunately, there was not the slightest chance that Ralph would entertain this idea. I was, however, determined ... ; we constantly watched for occasions when our diagnosis might be made apparent ... . In a reckless moment during rehearsals I threw my arms around Ralph and kissed him full on the lips. He coolly disengaged himself from my embrace, patted me gently on the back of the neck and, more in sorrow than in anger, murmured, "There, there now, dear boy; *good* boy ... ."

In performance when Othello fell to the ground in his fit, Iago fell beside him, simulating an orgasm – Olivier considered this "terrifically daring." But a trusted friend later told him she had "*no* idea what you were up to when you threw yourself on the ground," and none of the critics seemed to catch on to the fact that Iago was supposed to be queer. So they abandoned the whole theory, deciding that "Iago just hated Othello because he was black and his superior officer." This perfectly straightforward, perfectly straight, interpretation, however, did not work either, despite a great cast including Anthony Quayle as Cassio and Martita Hunt as Emilia. Olivier declared the production a disaster – the queer Iago was obviously not the culprit.[8] Disaster was a term that was often used of Guthrie productions, sometimes even by Guthrie.

In Terry Hands's 1985 RSC production with Ben Kingsley as Othello and David Suchet as Iago, Iago *was* widely perceived as gay, and the performance was well received, not least because by 1985 it was permissable to acknowledge that someone was gay. Hands apparently did not intend Iago to be gay, and was surprised at the reviews. David Suchet, however, in a thoughtful interview about the performance in one of the *Players of Shakespeare* volumes, says that he considered the possibility at some length. He decided that the account of the night spent with Cassio is a lie, though a significant one. He thought it quite conceivable that Iago and Cassio may in fact have been lovers, and that Othello may well be jealous of the idea that they have been to bed together – Suchet was, in short, on to my idea long before it occurred to me, and I am interested to see that an intelligent and thoughtful actor seriously considered it as a way of making the character work psychologically.[9] (Ben Kingsley, in the same volume, says nothing about any of this, and claims to have had his mind entirely on his parents' marriage, accounts of performances by Edmund Kean and Salvini, and the philosophy of Albert Camus.)

My native informant, Lois Potter, who saw the production and has total recall, has written me a wonderful note about it which I can do no better than quote:

> I did see the Kingsley–Suchet *Othello* and I think that some idea of gayness crossed my mind, mainly because of Suchet's horrified grief when Othello finally committed suicide. But this was a surprise to me, which is why it is the thing I remember best from the production; in other words, he had not come across as being in love with Othello. It was more like a cat feeling upset that the toy it is been playing with (a live mouse) has stopped moving. Or perhaps like someone suddenly realizing that there's no longer any purpose to his life. Both actors said they weren't playing the character as gay, but that reviewers did tend to think that there was a gay subtext. It also struck me that no one was remotely interested in the Desdemona (Niamh Cusack).

That last bit seems to me very much to the point. Potter then goes on with a comment on the Olivier Iago, about which she has written:

> My suggestion was that audiences weren't used to seeing gay behavior depicted onstage before 1968 except in a comic context, and thus actors didn't have a shorthand by which to communicate it.[10]

By the end of the twentieth century, we have had an openly gay Mercutio who goes partying in drag in Baz Luhrman's 1996 *Romeo and Juliet*. My students like this, and when I asked what they liked about it one young woman explained that "cool gay guys are really neat." Apparently more than half the audience of the American version of *Queer as Folk* is straight, or, at least, identifies itself as such to telephone interviewers. I want my Iago to be a really cool gay guy, a Iago who is all the more dangerous because both Othello and more than half the audience find him attractive.

The villain

Iago is the play's villainous schemer, but the principal, enabling scheme is not his. Credit for discovering the double time scheme in *Othello* is always accorded to two ingenious Victorian critics, Nicholas Halpin and John Wilson, writing in *Blackwood's* in 1849; but they were merely the first critics to treat it systematically and consider it a good idea. It is all in Rymer, and drives him into a frenzy.

Here, briefly, is the point.[11] Time in the play goes very fast; the action, in fact, is almost uninterrupted. Act I covers the night of the elopement and the Council scene. Othello and Cassio go to Cyprus the next morning, and Desdemona, Iago and Emilia follow in however long you want to imagine it takes them to get ready and make the voyage – this would be a minimum of a couple of weeks (Cassio says they have come unusually fast, a week earlier than they were expected). So there is that one gap, two weeks or so, when Othello and Cassio are on Cyprus, and Desdemona, Iago and Emilia are on their way. From the time they reach Cyprus the action again is continuous, through the night of Desdemona's arrival, the next day, and that night, which is the night of the murder (the usual estimate is thirty-three hours). The momentum is important because the whole credibility of Iago's plot depends on speed – clearly if Othello ever gets a chance to compare notes with anyone, the scheme will fall apart, as it does as soon as the literal notes are produced from the slain Roderigo's pocket.[12]

But: if you take that aspect of the play seriously, the play as a whole will be a mass of impossibilities, just as Rymer says it is. When, in this thirty-three hours, was the adultery supposed to have taken place? Othello left Venice on his wedding night, taking Cassio with him – this is the man he believes has been cuckolding him. When? In order to prevent the audience from noticing this, Shakespeare uses some brilliant sleight of hand, compelling our belief in the plot through references to action that there is no time for in the time of the play. For example, Iago's story about the night that he spent in bed with Cassio, when Cassio took him for Desdemona – during the whole time of the marriage Cassio has been in Cyprus with Othello, and Desdemona has been with Iago in Venice or on a ship; there was no night Cassio and Iago could have spent together. Or Cassio talking about how Bianca runs after him, and threw herself at him "the other day," and Othello overhearing this thinks he is talking about Desdemona – *what* other day? The only other day was yesterday, which is the day she arrived. Or the whole opening of Act IV, Scene 2, where Othello questions Emilia about whether she has seen Desdemona and Cassio together, and a long period and a number of occasions are alluded to. The reason this works is that we are treated just the way Othello is, persuaded parenthetically, not given time to ask any questions or compare notes. Not, of course, entirely without resistance: I have already alluded to the famous story of the man leaping up during the death scene shouting "You fool, can't you see she's innocent?" The story is no doubt apocryphal, but it is unique to this play. There are no parallel stories of audience members trying to stop the blinding of Gloucester or reminding Albany that he has forgotten about Lear and Cordelia.

This treatment of time is not at all unique to this play. There is a similar instance in *Love's Labour's Lost*, for example, where Jaquenetta is declared to be pregnant by Armado two days after their first meeting; but it is generally a comic dramaturgy, and the audience is in on the joke – nobody ever leaps up from the stalls to explain to Armado that he cannot be the father. But comedy in *Othello* is the device of villainy, and, to my knowledge, nowhere else is it

4.1 The Mediterranean in 1595. Detail of the map of Europe in the Mercator–Hondius atlas of 1623. Venice at the upper left and Cyprus at the lower right are circled.

employed so systematically. There is an especially subtle example of the device in the scene where Othello is recalled to Venice because the Turks have been defeated, and Cassio is appointed in his place. The defeat took place only the day before – Othello arrives victorious from the battle just after Desdemona and Iago land. How long does it take for the news of the victory to travel from Cyprus to Venice, and then for the Venetian emissaries to travel back to Cyprus? Figure 4.1 is a detail of Mercator's map of the Mediterranean, drawn in 1595. Venice is at the upper left, Cyprus is the large island at the lower right. Traveling by ship, the distance is about 1,600 miles each way. A really fast ship of the period (I am informed by a sailing expert friend) had a maximum speed of 7 knots, a little more than 8 miles an hour – this is with everything working out right, good winds from the right direction, calm sea, perfect sailing conditions for the whole voyage in both directions. The absolute minimum time for this voyage in one direction would be nine days; the round trip would take almost three weeks, allowing for time in Venice to deliver the news, get new instructions, replenish the ship. We are taught by the history of theater not to question such conventions; and this is one of the moments that make us think there is much more time in the play than there really is. The distance represented on this map, the space of this geography, is precisely the period of time when Desdemona and Cassio are supposed to be carrying on together, the time between Desdemona's arrival and Othello's recall to Venice. This is the time of, the space for, Iago's scheming. But the deception is not being practiced on Othello by Iago, it is being practiced on us by Shakespeare. Shakespeare is the *real* villain in this play, and we are the willing dupes.

Note: For information and suggestions I am indebted to John Russell Brown, Jonathan Crewe, Suzanne Gossett, David Halperin, Peter Holland, Adrian Kiernander, Lois Potter, B. J. Sokol and John Stokes.

Notes

1 Shakespeare quotations are from the *New Pelican Shakespeare*, eds. Stephen Orgel and A. R. Braunmuller (New York, 2002).

2 Thomas Rymer, *A Short View of Tragedy* (London, 1693), p. 164. Subsequent page references are in the text.

3 T. S. Eliot, "Four Elizabethan Dramatists" and "Hamlet," in *Selected Essays* (New York, 1950), pp. 97, 121.

4 The account here summarizes the more extensive treatment of the subject in my essay "Shakespeare and the Kinds of Drama," in my collection *The Authentic Shakespeare* (Routledge, 2002).

5 Julius Caesar Scaliger, *Poetices Libri Septem* (Lyons, 1581), 367; my translation.

6 Stephen Greenblatt, *Renaissance Self-Fashioning* (Chicago, 1984), p. 252.

7 Gielgud initially saw himself as Iago, and played the role in his first *Othello*. He did not play it again, and did not play Othello until thirty years later.

8 Laurence Olivier, *Confessions of an Actor* (New York, 1982), pp. 105–6.

9 Russell Jackson and Robert Smallwood, *Players of Shakespeare 2* (Cambridge, 1988), pp. 192–4.

10 See Lois Potter, *Shakespeare in Performance: Othello* (Manchester and New York, 2002), p. 92.

11 I am in part summarizing my own account in the Introduction to John Sutherland and Cedric Watts, *Henry V, War Criminal?* (Oxford, 2000).

12 Or perhaps not slain, another tease: at V.2.309 he is "the slain Roderigo," but at V.2.327–8 "even but now he spake,/ After long seeming dead."

5

King Lear and the art of forgetting

Memory has been recognized since ancient times as a basic element of artistic creativity, but I propose here a counter-argument: that forgetting, or the suppression or subversion of memory, is an equally essential creative principle – we memorize in order to forget. My primary example is Shakespeare, but Shakespeare in this can hardly be unique. I have in mind both really big creative acts like forgetting that the Lear story has a happy ending, or forgetting the deaths of Mamillius and Antigonus in constructing the transcendently happy ending of *The Winter's Tale*; and really small but even more baffling creative acts such as in *As You Like It* introducing a character named Jaques and forgetting that there is already a character named Jaques in the play, or in the second part of *Henry IV* introducing a character named Lord Bardolph when there is already a character named Bardolph in the play, or in *The Comedy of Errors* calling Adriana's servant Luce the first time she appears, and in the next scene calling her Nell, or at the beginning of *Othello* describing Cassio as "almost damned in a fair wife" and then having him unmarried for the rest of the play, or in *The Tempest* listing Antonio's son as one of the shipwreck victims and then never mentioning him again – there are many more such examples in Shakespeare. And (how could it be otherwise?) the process of constructing the Shakespeare we want has for the most part also been a process of forgetting about these elements of Shakespeare's creative process. Such examples, however, are surely keys to the act of creation – this is the essential Shakespeare, the essence of drama itself. Anthropology tells us that drama begins as ritual, but ritual is an act of memory; it only becomes drama when it forgets and revises, when plots become unexpected, when the end forgets the beginning, when every performance forgets the previous one, and forgets the text it purports to follow, when every text emends the last, hoping to consign to oblivion all except the forgotten but endlessly restored original.

My main example will be the case of *King Lear*, but I begin with a famous emendation, which is particularly germane because it depends on a case of memorial reconstruction – a case, that is, in which it would appear that Shakespeare's genius was both materialized through an act of memory, and at the same time obscured or even vitiated by it. Here is the account of Falstaff's death given by Mistress Quickly in *Henry V*: "His nose was as sharp as a pen, and a table of green fields … ." This was the text from 1623 until 1733, when the editor Lewis Theobald decided that Shakespeare's manuscript had been misread: that "a table of green fields," had nothing to do with the matter, but that rather, in dying, "'a [he] babbled of green fields." This emendation, indisputably a stroke of editorial genius, seemed to have restored what Shakespeare must actually have written. Bibliography here communicated with Shakespeare himself – or at least, with Shakespeare's manuscript before it reached the printer.

But let us pause over this editorial watershed. If we agree that Theobald was correct, and that a compositor setting the type in the printing house was misreading Shakespeare's handwriting, what happened before the play got to the compositor? "Table" is the 1623 folio's reading; so the folio's printer is the culprit. But the only other substantive text, the 1600 quarto, in a passage that bears little resemblance to the folio text, at this point reads not "babbled" but "talk," and it is apparent that the folio was not set up from this very garbled quarto, but directly from Shakespeare's manuscript. So neither of our two primary sources reads "babbled": "babbled," even if it is impeccably correct, is all Theobald. The quarto seems to be a reported text provided by two actors – the creativeness of the *ars memoriae* in this case is only an index to its radical fallibility – but if the folio's "table" is a misreading resulting from a visual error in deciphering Shakespeare's handwriting, so would the quarto's "talk" seem to be. In a reported text, however, the error ought to be an auditory one. If the quarto is really a reported text, then, the counter-argument here would have to be that the reporters heard "babbled" but remembered it as the simpler concept "talk" (or "talkd," as it's usually emended). This argument would be more persuasive if "talkd" looked less like "table." Moreover, even if we agree that "babbled" was what Shakespeare wrote, it might also be the case that Shakespeare's handwriting was hard to read for everyone, and was misread not only by the folio compositor but by the scribe who prepared the promptbook, who also would have been working from Shakespeare's manuscript – and the promptbook, after all, would have been the source of the actors' scripts too, and thereby of what the reporters heard, or misremembered. Maybe the actors were (incorrectly) saying "table" or "talkd" all along. For Theobald's purposes, however, what the actors said, what the reporters recalled, what all the audiences from 1599 to 1733 heard, was irrelevant; his communication was with Shakespeare's mind – or at least, with Shakespeare's putative bad handwriting. Theobald's intuition here effectively abolished the performing tradition, the play's collective memory.

Perhaps the oddest thing about this sort of puzzle is to decide where the playwright fits into it. In 1599, Shakespeare was on the spot to see that the promptbook and the actors got it right – how could "table" (or "talkd") be wrong? But in fact this isn't a very persuasive argument: as I've indicated, there are numerous perfectly obvious muddles in the Shakespeare texts. The examples of Cassio's fair wife, Antonio's shipwrecked son, and Adriana's servant Luce/Nell are evidence, no doubt, that Shakespeare sometimes changed his mind during the process of composition, the only puzzling aspect of which is why they remained a permanent feature of the texts. Didn't the actors playing Cassio and Antonio wonder about their missing families? Didn't the boy cast as Luce or Nell demand to know, as soon as he got his part, what his name was? Didn't Shakespeare thunder "'babbled,' not 'table,' idiots!"; and why didn't the embarrassed prompter then immediately correct the error? How did the confusion survive the first rehearsal, to remain a permanent part of the play's memory?

Here is a different kind of example, involving a complex interplay of memory and forgetting. The first quarto of *Hamlet*, published in 1603, purports, on its title page, to be the text of the play as it was performed everywhere: on the London stage, at Oxford and Cambridge, "and elsewhere" – the text as all the audiences who wanted a reading copy of this popular drama would have remembered it. But two years later Shakespeare's company issued a second quarto of the play, this time, according to the title page, "enlarged to almost as much again as it was, according to the true and perfect copy" – the claim here is that the true and perfect copy includes a great deal that you couldn't see in performance, and that in effect your memory of the performance, even if it was perfect, was misrepresenting the true and perfect copy. In fact, it is clear that the first quarto itself is an act of memory, a version of the play put together on the road, in the absence of the playhouse copy, by a group of actors at least two of whom had been in the original production, playing Marcellus and Voltimand. And they did produce something that is certainly more like what a Shakespeare play must have been on the stage than all but a couple of other surviving texts are, a play that really can be performed in the two hours that we know was the standard performing time for plays of the period. Here is their version of the most memorable and memorized passage in the play, perhaps the crucial document in the whole of the Shakespearean memorial archive:

> To be, or not to be, ay there's the point,
> To die, to sleep, is that all? ay all –

No, to sleep, to dream; ay marry there it goes,
For in that dream of death, when we awake,
And borne before an everlasting judge,
From whence no passenger ever returned,
The undiscovered country, at whose sight
The happy smile, and the accursèd damned.
But for this, the joyful hope of this,
Who'd bear the scorns and flattery of the world,
Scorned by the right rich, the rich cursed of the poor,
The widow being oppressed, the orphan wronged,
The taste of hunger, or a tyrant's reign,
And thousand more calamities besides,
To grunt and sweat under this weary life,
When that he may his full quietus make
With a bare bodkin, who would this endure,
But for a hope of something after death?
Which puzzles the brain and doth confound the sense,
Which makes us rather bear those evils we have
Than fly to others that we know not of.
Ay, O this conscience makes cowards of us all.
Lady, in thy orisons be all my sins remembered.

It's an odd version of the speech, but there are some things right about it: it's faster, more direct, and significantly shorter than the familiar version – more like a play, less like a meditation. It also comes earlier in the action than it does in the standard texts, and thus involves Hamlet in less emotional backtracking. But it also misses the point of the speech as we know it: for this Hamlet, the undiscovered country from whose bourn no traveler returns is a joyful hope, not the dread that keeps us from suicide – is this merely a lapse of the reporter's memory? Of course, even "the true and perfect copy" is strikingly forgetful in this instance, since the play's whole action has been precipitated by a traveler returning from that undiscovered country, the ghost of Hamlet's father. How has Hamlet – or Shakespeare, or the rest of us – forgotten this? Indeed, the whole force of the speech depends on this act of forgetting, because the conviction that we can never know what happens after death, which "puzzles the will/ And makes us rather bear those ills we have/ Than fly to others that we know not of," is the measure of what Hamlet has forgotten: what happens after death is precisely what his father's ghost has told him.

I turn now to the famous case of the ending of *King Lear*. In every other version of the Lear story, both in the chronicles of early British history and in the earlier play *The True Chronicle History of King Leir and his Three Daughters* (published in 1605, a year before the first recorded performance of Shakespeare's play), Cordelia's forces are victorious, Lear's throne is restored to him, he dies in peace, and she rules after him, presumably to be succeeded by her heirs. Nahum Tate notoriously returned to this ending in his Restoration adaptation of the play, a change of which Dr. Johnson notoriously approved. According to the chronicles Cordelia was some years later deposed and imprisoned by her nephews (the sons of Goneril and Regan, whom Shakespeare also killed off childless), and committed suicide, but that is part of another story; she has been succeeded by her legitimate heirs, and both the continuity of Lear's line and the facts of early British history are assured. To kill off Cordelia without heirs and bestow the kingdom on Edgar, as Shakespeare does, was both historically perverse and a significant defeat for any early audience's expectations, as well as for their historical memory. It is not even clear in the play why Edgar should have any claim to the throne at all, to say nothing of Kent, whom Albany designates as co-ruler with Edgar, though Kent declines the honor. Of the characters left alive, Albany himself would seem to have the best claim to succeed Lear, being his son-in-law; but instead he ends the play by dividing up the kingdom as Lear had done, this time between two people who have no right to it whatever.

Shakespeare is not especially faithful to history elsewhere, but this is surely an extreme example, analogous to making Henry V lose the battle of Agincourt, and installing somebody – anybody – else as king. Modern views of the play typically ignore, or forget about, the historical absurdity; but is there really nothing here for critical commentary to take account of? From Tate to Johnson, a standard element in the defense of the happy ending was that it was true: it was Shakespeare who had changed the ending, not Tate. The question of why (and how) Shakespeare changed the ending is not, for us, a serious one – Tate's ending, we argue, trivializes the suffering, and therefore must be wrong; though the subtext of this argument is surely that if Shakespeare did it, it must be right. But there is nothing normative, even within Shakespeare's own work, that dictated the ending. What he added to a very mixed plot was a degree of abjectness and cruelty unmatched in his drama since *Titus Andronicus*. It is precisely those elements that we do not take seriously – Johnson takes them seriously, when he says that "I was many years ago so shocked by Cordelia's death, that I know not whether I ever endured to read again the last scenes of the play till I undertook to revise them as an editor."[1] Surely it is worth asking what, in a dramaturgy that could produce tragicomedy like *Measure for Measure, Cymbeline, Pericles, The Winter's Tale*, all plays whose sufferings are redeemed in a reversal of fortune that we might even call characteristically

Shakespearean, seemed to require so radical an act of forgetting to produce an outcome at once so bleak and so unexpected.

Forgetting is crucial within the play's action, too: it is a radical act of forgetting that precipitates Shakespeare's catastrophe. After the final battle and the imprisonment of Lear and Cordelia, Kent appears, no longer in disguise, seeking a reconciliation with his master. The virtuous Albany has finally taken charge and the villains have disposed of each other. All the elements of a happy ending are in place; but Kent has to remind the victorious Duke of the absence of his royal prisoner – "Is he not here?" (V.3.234).[2] Albany's telling reply, "Great thing of us forgot," might be a motto for the play as a whole, which begins with Cordelia's "nothing" and ends with Lear's five "never"s. Forgetting a great thing makes it a nothing; losing track of time reduces the critical moment to a never. It is in the space of Albany's failed memory that the dead Edmund's order to execute the prisoners is carried out.

What possessed Shakespeare? The answer to this question may well be biographical, and therefore beyond the limits of our evidence. Nevertheless, it is worth recognizing as an issue, and insisting that the ending is not one that is determined by the plot (as, for example, the very bleak endings of *Coriolanus* and *Timon of Athens* are). This is a play in which Shakespeare goes out of his way to raise expectations only to – perhaps in order to – defeat them.

Possibly, however, we judge the general tone of the play, its exceptional bleakness, by an anachronistic standard, and this is why the ending seems right to us. For us, Lear starts out with a spectacular display of bad judgment, and it's all downhill from there. Notice, however, that though it's Kent who initially objects to Lear's bad judgment, only the villains believe that it renders him unfit to rule. In fact, elsewhere he's referred to in the play not as blind, foolish, irascible, self-centered, mad, incompetent (or as we would sum it up, senile), but as *kind* – Kent deplores "the hard rein which both of them have borne/ Against the old kind king ..." (III.1.28). Lear in Act I calling himself "So kind a father" (I.5.34) is presumably to be taken ironically, but his later protest, "Your old kind father, whose frank heart gave all" (III.4.20), is, objectively, true, though of course it's not the whole truth. When Shakespeare's leading man Richard Burbage died in 1618, his elegy lists the roles that made him famous:

> No more young Hamlet, old Hieronymo,
> Kind Lear, the grievèd Moor...[3]

Kind Lear. All these examples insist on Lear's essential goodness; but the play's largest point would surely be a firmly monarchical one: that even a bad king is still the king. This is no doubt why King James liked this play about a monarch destroyed by his heirs enough to have it performed for him at court in 1606 – this is the first recorded performance, and the only one recorded in Shakespeare's lifetime. For us, in so far as Shakespeare's play is about kingship, it concerns the responsibilities of the office, not its prerogatives; but we tend to view the play less as political than as deeply personal. It is about how thoughtless small acts can have formidably terrible effects, about how little we understand even the people who are closest to us, above all, about our capacity for suffering, about the fact that however bad things are, they can always be worse. To Jacobean audiences, however, the play would have said something deeply admonitory about hierarchy and history: that ignoring the patriarchal imperatives – whether in the royal family or in any other – brought chaos to the kingdom, abolished the line of succession; indeed, consigned history itself, Cordelia's forgotten heirs, to oblivion. The failure of deference is a failure of historical memory, with incalculable, unthought-of consequences. Shakespeare's ending was a surprise, but it was also a warning. Perhaps our objections to the sentimentalization of the play that Tate's version represents are anachronistic. It was already quite a sentimental play, deploring the failure to preserve an incompetent king from the effects of his own bad judgment: in blaming Lear, we have adopted the point of view of the villains. Tate's version is sentimental in a different way, but he does understand something about the play in Shakespeare's time that we have forgotten.

In this reading, the play anticipates *The Winter's Tale* in its focus on the preservation of the monarch, however perverse or irrational, as the essential element in the integrity and continuity of the commonwealth. Shakespeare sets up a powerful tragic momentum reminiscent of *Lear* in the opening three acts, only to disarm it at the conclusion with fantasy and magic. Why does Shakespeare preserve Leontes and ultimately exonerate him – why is he not treated in the fashion of all those other foolish, headstrong, misguided, tyrannical Shakespearian kings, who go to their deaths even in those cases where it is acknowledged that they are more sinned against than sinning? Shakespeare's source was a novel by Robert Greene called *Pandosto*, which actually gave him a strikingly dramatic model: at the conclusion, the repentant king falls in love with his still unidentified daughter; and, when he learns who she is, he kills himself, to be succeeded on the throne by the unsullied next generation, his daughter and son-in-law. This is an ending that would be perfectly consistent with the tragedy of royalty as Shakespeare practiced it, and the preservation of Leontes is as unique in his drama as is the mode by which it is effected, a statue coming to life. Even the miraculous happy ending involves as significant a lapse of memory as Albany's forgetting about Lear and

Cordelia: Mamillius, Leontes' son and heir, who died of grief at the height of his mother's ordeal, and Antigonus, the faithful servant who died preserving the infant Perdita from Leontes's threats to burn her, are forgotten among the general wonder and rejoicing – no statue of Mamillius comes to life; Antigonus does not reappear in a bear skin. Losses are restored by forgetting them.

This ending is as much a surprise as the ending of *King Lear*, but what is most striking in the resolution of *The Winter's Tale* is the intensity of its focus on Leontes, the play's unwillingness to move beyond him, as if grace and wonder require and inhere only in kingship. If we think about Shakespeare's attitude toward kings in his plays of the 1590s, we'll see this as a specifically Jacobean vision, and one that, moreover, involves many major acts of forgetting on Shakespeare's part. Throughout his history plays, bad kings, weak kings, usurping kings, are always found invoking the divinity that protects the monarchy, just before they are assassinated – divine right is a doctrine that the young Shakespeare treats with considerable irony. As did Queen Elizabeth. But it was a central tenet of James I's political philosophy. *King Lear* is its negative version, and *The Winter's Tale* anatomizes what kind of forgetfulness is required of the playwright and the commonwealth to produce a happy ending.

Notes

1 Samuel Johnson, *Preface to Shakespeare: King Lear*. Quotations are from the online text of the University of Adelaide, http://etext.library.adelaide. edu.au/j/johnson/samuel/preface/lear.html.

2 Quotations are from the New Pelican text, ed. Stephen Orgel (Penguin, 2002).

3 C. M. Ingleby et al., *The Shakespeare Allusion Book*, revised edition (London, 1932), vol. 1, p. 272.

6

The case for Comus

When Milton was commissioned to write the text for the work we call *Comus*, he was twenty-four and unknown as a poet. The only thing he had published was a commendatory poem on Shakespeare included anonymously in the introductory matter to the second folio, which had appeared two years before in 1632. The commission for a masque almost certainly came his way through the musician Henry Lawes, who composed the music for *Comus*, and was a friend of Milton's father. Lawes was the house musician to the Earl of Bridgewater, before whom the masque was presented at Ludlow Castle, on the Welsh border, in September, 1634 – Milton had several years earlier composed the brief entertainment *Arcades*, also with music by Lawes, for the same family. *Comus* exists in two quite different early states: the performing text – the script – that Milton initially provided his employers with, and the revised and greatly elaborated version that he subsequently prepared for publication.

A good deal of critical energy has been expended over the question of whether this work is really a masque or not. Milton seems to me to have settled this matter quite conclusively by titling it *A Maske Presented at Ludlow Castle*. The title *Comus* was devised for an eighteenth-century theatrical adaptation, in an attempt to transform it from an occasional work into a drama by focusing on its most memorable character. To start, then, with a definition, a masque, in the period, was most simply an entertainment including masked performers, primarily dancers. In its most characteristic form, it was a private entertainment that related to its audience in a manner significantly different from drama: it was basically celebratory; it was about the group it entertained, and always ended by including them in the fiction. In court masques the usual way of bringing this about was to conclude the work with a grand dance, in which the masquers descended from the stage and took partners from among the spectators, so that what the audience began by watching they ended by becoming. It was more of a game than a show, an expression of aristocratic identity and privilege, with the masks providing a degree of freedom, even if only notional, from the constraints of place, office and self.

Comus is, obviously, a very scaled-down version of the form, but Milton called the work a masque and clearly thought of it as one. Part of the reason it looks so unlike those classics of the genre composed by Jonson, Campion and Davenant is that when we use those as the norms we are comparing it with masques for the royal court at Whitehall, designed for the participation of a significant segment of aristocratic society, whereas Milton's masque is designed to be performed by three children and their music teacher before the children's parents and their friends; it is very much a family affair. This is not to say that Milton is not taking a critical and even revisionist look at the masque genre, but it is the same sort of look he took at everything he turned his hand to – to argue that *Comus* is not "really" a masque is like saying that *Paradise Lost* is not really an epic because it does not look enough like *The Iliad* or *The Aeneid*.

The three child stars were children of the Earl of Bridgewater – he had fifteen children in all, and these three were already experienced masquers, having performed at Whitehall in two of the most splendid Caroline productions, *Tempe Restored* (1632), with a text by Aurelian Townshend and costumes and settings by Inigo Jones, and the greatest of the Stuart masques *Coelum Britannicum* (1634), by Thomas Carew and Jones. Bridgewater was Lord President of Wales: this is equivalent to governor, except that it is not an elective office; the incumbent is appointed by the Crown in London, and the Bridgewater family home was near London – the family name was Egerton. He and his children therefore are outsiders at Ludlow. The natives in the masque are Comus and his animal minions, a bit of Miltonic plotting that reflects the general English attitude to the place: Wales in Milton's time was considered wild and uncivilized, and was very far from the center of both power and culture. The eldest of the three performing children was Lady Alice Egerton, aged fifteen, who played the Lady; the boys were John, aged eleven and Thomas aged nine – John ultimately succeeded his father as the next Earl; Thomas died young; Alice eventually married a local landowner and settled in Wales, and her history is part of my subject. Henry Lawes, the composer and their music teacher, played the Attendant Spirit, who in the manuscript is called a Guardian Spirit or, in Greek, Daemon, a classical figure similar to the Christian Guardian Angel, but much less effective as an agent.

Most discussions of *Comus* focus on its political or religious implications, and its status as a precursor to Milton's ethical and revolutionary thinking in his prose pamphlets and major poems. I am concerned here, on the contrary, with its implications specifically as a private work, a family affair; these are what seem to me most significantly Miltonic. I focus on three questions:

Why is Milton's ethical masque about three lost children trying to get home? What is wrong with Comus – why is he a villain? How happy is the happy ending?

I begin with the question of the masque's subject. It is usually claimed that the work was composed to celebrate the Earl of Bridgewater's installation as President of the Council and Lord Lieutenant of Wales, but a look at both the relevant dates and the text itself make it obvious that this cannot be the case, at least in any simple way: the masque was performed on Michaelmas Night, September 29, 1634; Bridgewater had succeeded to his Welsh offices more than three years earlier, in June and July, 1631, though he did not take up residence at Ludlow Castle until three years later, in May 1634. The Attendant Spirit does seem to link the action of the masque to the Earl's installation when he describes the Lady and her brothers as "coming to attend their father's state/ And new entrusted sceptre"; nevertheless, the masque was not presented until a further four months had passed – the sceptre was hardly new. The selection of Michaelmas for the date of the performance was doubtless significant: the provincial courts began their sessions at Michaelmas, and the holy day would therefore have marked the beginning of the viceregal administration *in situ*. But the masque does not have the look of a public celebration: on the contrary, performed by the family children, organized and composed by their music teacher, who also played in it, it is very much a family affair. Definitively so, in fact: had it been a public celebration, the aristocratic young masquers would not have taken speaking parts – masquers can dance in public because dancing is the prerogative of every lady and gentleman, but acting is a profession, hence the continuing outcry throughout the Caroline period against Queen Henrietta Maria's court theatricals.

So the masque we call *Comus* was a family matter: this is not, of course, to say that it may not have been other things as well. Patron, composer and poet all had their political views; moreover, the wildness of the Welsh as a danger to "good order" (the standard euphemism justifying control by a government several hundred miles away in London) was an old theme – a theme almost built into the very idea of Wales for the English – hence the identification of Comus and his rout as the natives. Leah Marcus has also made a persuasive case for explicitly anti-Laudian elements in the masque, though these, of course, may have more to do with Milton's interests at the time than with the Earl's.[1] I find attempts by Marcus and others to link the masque's concern with chastity to the Castlehaven scandal less persuasive, not least because, thanks to the work of Cynthia Herrup, the notorious case looks rather different now from the way it looked forty years ago when the suggestion was first made.[2]

Castlehaven (who was convicted of a complicated set of charges including orchestrating the rape of his own wife and committing sodomy with his servants) was Bridgewater's brother-in-law, married to Bridgewater's wife's sister, and the case was both genuinely sensational and a legal landmark: he was the first nobleman in over a century to be executed on a charge other than treason. But, as Herrup shows, the capital crime had more to do with subverting the concept of patriarchal authority than with kinky sex, and it is not clear to me that either Milton or his Egerton patrons were concerned in the masque with cleansing the family name. If Castlehaven had been the subtext, the masque would surely have been about what a good husband and father Bridgewater was, not about how highminded the children were.

Castlehaven was executed in 1631, a few months before Bridgewater's accession to his high office; and though the case was certainly a skeleton in the family closet, the closet was long closed. Here, again, both the age of the children for whom the masque was written and Milton's own perennial concerns about personal integrity and the dangers represented by temptation seem more direct sources for the focus on militant and inviolable innocence. But even if we decide that the work is indeed about viceregal politics and the errors of Laudian Anglicanism, or alternatively is designed as an antidote to spousal rape and routine domestic buggery, what has any of that to do with three lost children trying to get home? I shall return to the work's cultural implications, but for the moment I am interested in the lost children, who strike me as the peculiarly Miltonic element. What keeps you from getting home? And where is home? And what happens when you do get there?

To begin with, to say that the children are going home is to occlude an important issue: Ludlow is home only in the sense that it is where their parents are to be found. Ludlow Castle was a crown property, the seat of whoever was Lord President of Wales, and as far as the natives are concerned, the inhabitants of the place are definitively outsiders (some would even say invaders): they are not at all at home. More to the point, then, is where the children are coming from. In one sense, they are coming from nowhere (or anywhere, or everywhere): they find themselves, like Dante, like everyone, in the middle of a journey in a dark wood where the right way is lost. But in another sense, they are coming *from* home, or moving from one home to another, from the court at Whitehall to the court at Ludlow, and from *Tempe Restored* and *Coelum Britannicum* – the royal masques in which they danced at Whitehall – to this masque with no name for the viceregal court. Innocents they may be, but they are thoroughly experienced masquers, and they are moving from the most central of courts to the most peripheral, and (they may have felt) from the most civilized to the wildest.

On such a journey, what keeps you from arriving at your destination? Questions that might seem prior to this – what are these children doing alone in the woods in the first place; questions that raise precisely the issue of parental care and adult responsibility – are clearly not to the point: in these woods, we are all children alone. You lose your way in the woods in part simply through the exigencies of travel – or travail, the same word in Milton's time: uncertainty, confusion, fog, "envious darkness" (as the Lady puts it), the natural malevolence of night, to say nothing of bad maps and unmarked trails. When life is construed as woods, that's just life. But you also lose your way through deliberate misdirection, the misrepresentations of the villain Comus, who presents himself as a harmless shepherd offering help and hospitality but is nothing of the sort.

Nor is this the whole story: there is yet another kind of misdirection and misrepresentation as well, in a way even more insidious than that of Comus: that of the Attendant Spirit, unquestionably good, divinely sent, who, however, also presents himself as a shepherd and isn't (why the disguise?), and is supposed to be your guardian angel but actually is remarkably inattentive to your needs. He is not around when you get lost, has difficulty finding you himself, warns the boys about Comus but not their sister (who is the one who needs the warning and could profit by it); and though he is in charge of the rescue operation, he is unaccountably not there when it happens, so the boys muff it by driving Comus and his minions off but not seizing his wand. The Lady still is not free, and the Attendant Spirit blames the boys – he *told* them to seize the wand – and they are too well-mannered to ask him where he was when the action started. In this context, all the insistence on the absolute self-sufficiency of virtue sounds relentlessly upbeat, but what it really means is that you are completely on your own: there is no father, no guiding star; even your Attendant Spirit has lost you. What keeps you from getting home, then, is partly inexperience and partly misdirection, but mostly a degree of complexity in the journey that no amount of experience would prepare you to resolve: the difficulty, in this case the impossibility, of knowing good from evil. Both Comus and the Attendant Spirit look like innocent shepherds, both tell lies that sound like truth. How can you know the good lies from the bad ones?

Comus is, nevertheless, obviously the villain – though part of the point is surely that the fact is *not* obvious, until it's too late, or until someone who already knows explains it to you. It is made obvious only to the audience, and this is really significant, because for the audience Comus is the most attractive figure in the masque. Why is he a villain, then? What is bad about him, and how bad is he? Very bad, certainly: he turns people into animals,

"Into some brutish form of wolf or bear,/ Or ounce, or tiger, hog, or bearded goat" (ll. 70–1).³ The issue is complicated, however, by the clear implication that the transformation is their own fault – he is turning them into the animals "they really are." He engages their passions and plays on their affections, but the passions and affections are theirs. Moreover, nobody can be transformed unwillingly; and, once they are transformed, "so perfect is their misery,/ Not once perceive their foul disfigurement,/ But boast themselves more comely than before/ And all their friends and native home forget/ To roll with pleasure in a sensual sty" (ll. 72–6). The sensual sty is construed here, by the Attendant Spirit himself, as a perfect form of pleasure; this is a bad thing, "misery," and the worst part of it is that it pre-empts home, thereby subverting the whole point of the masque – getting home, for these happy travelers, is no longer the point of the journey. Even in the Attendant Spirit's terms, the problem is not saving travelers from Comus, it is saving them from themselves; and the biggest part of the problem is that they do not want to be saved. The argument in favor of home, after all, has to be an argument against "perfect … pleasure," pleasure that only the Attendant Spirit conceives as misery. So another way of looking at Comus is to say that he enables people to be what and where they want to be – and that is construed as a bad thing.

Comus in fact is a pleasure principle. We watch him at work, first as he responds to the Lady's song:

> Can any mortal mixture of earth's mould
> Breathe such divine enchanting ravishment?
> Sure something holy lodges in that breast,
> And with these raptures moves the vocal air
> To testify his hidden residence;
> How sweetly did they float upon the wings
> Of silence … (ll. 244–50)

We notice his receptiveness to the experience – for a villain, he is a remarkably appreciative audience. His command of metaphor and poetic language, too, is striking – he has the most individual voice in the masque. As he continues, to locate himself within a world of classical allusion, we are clearly being given a double signal by this verse.

> I have oft heard
> My mother Circe with the Sirens three,
> Amidst the flowery-kirtled naiades,
> Culling their potent herbs and baleful drugs,

Who as they sung would take the prisoned soul
And lap it in Elysium; Scylla wept,
And chid her barking waves into attention,
And fell Charybdis murmured soft applause;
Yet they in pleasing slumber lulled the sense,
And in sweet madness robbed it of itself ... (ll. 252–61)

Circe and the Sirens are destructive figures, but they are not being presented as such here – the song is ravishing (a significantly double-edged word). Even in the small details, negative images are balanced by positive ones: baleful drugs with potent herbs, the prisoned soul with Elysium, fell Charybdis/ soft applause, sweet/madness; and, indeed, the virtuous Lady's song is being compared to the dangerous and destructive song of the sirens. When a little later Comus says "I'll speak to her/ And she shall be my queen. Hail, foreign wonder ..." (ll. 264–5) he is proposing a very subversive version of the meeting of Ferdinand and Miranda in *The Tempest* ("O you wonder! ... I'll make you/ The queen of Naples" [I.2.427–50][4]) – subversive because it so perfectly realizes Prospero's fears: that admiration leads inevitably to seduction, to ravishment. Only here Comus is the victim, seduced and ravished.

What he offers, however, is not what is in his heart – adoration, marriage, a crown, regal power – but simple hospitality, the simplest, and therefore the most persuasive, of lies. The Lady is tricked by what she is most familiar with, the civilized virtues of the courtly world she has just left, grace, charm, generosity; tricked by everything her experience tells her to trust. What she has not heard in Comus's voice is what he has addressed only to us, his courtly poetry, notoriously the medium of hypocrisy and seduction. Trapped by his hospitality, paralyzed on his throne, she nevertheless insists that she is not in his power (and perhaps more to the point, she does not understand the ways in which he might be in hers). She regards the lie as crucial: she has been deceived, therefore she has not really, willingly, accepted him. Her will, she insists, remains free, armed with the cardinal virtues Faith, Hope and Chastity (a more specific virtue than the more familiar Charity, but equally canonical): these have not enabled her to see through him, but they nevertheless render her impervious to him – or, to put it another way, render her unable to love him. They are, just as much as his magic, what paralyzes her.

The end of this romance is of course predetermined, and there is little suspense at this point in the drama; but the debate that forms this scene is addressed to us, not to the participants – the battle is for our judgment. Comus's argument is a variant on the familiar 'gather ye rosebuds while ye may' theme: make good use of time; pleasures are there to be enjoyed. But it has a larger ethical argument as well: that nature's riches are here for use, and that not to enjoy them is rejecting God's bounty; is, in effect, blasphemous. This argument has its specious elements, but (or perhaps therefore) it produces some of the best poetry in the masque. It seems to have engaged Milton's poetic sensibility far more powerfully than anything in the Lady's role, perhaps precisely because, as Shakespeare put it, the truest poetry is the most feigning.

The Lady's answer is a firm argument in favor of moderation and temperance, but she also insists that Comus is misrepresenting nature: that it is not simply a treasure to be plundered, but has ethical rules of its own. Behind this debate are, obviously, two antithetical views of nature. Comus assumes that nature is something *other* than us, and is therefore properly subject to us, ours to use, enjoy or plunder; whereas the Lady assumes that nature is part of us, an aspect or extension of ourselves, that we must treat it and care for it as we treat our own bodies. This argument looks a little different when we realize that it is a version of the standard English argument against the behavior of Spain in the New World – though it too has its specious elements, and would surely have looked quite different still had Ralegh ever succeeded in discovering any gold in Guiana, that country that, notoriously, "hath yet her maidenhead." [5] Maidenheads, as Ralegh and his English backers from the virgin queen and the pacific king on down assume, are there to be taken.

The allusion to *The Tempest* is significant too because the debate over our relation to nature is related to Prospero's implied debate with Caliban: what is our relation to newly discovered lands and their inhabitants – do they become ours, or have they an integrity that must be respected? Is the New World an extension of ourselves, or is it The Other? These are not simply literary questions, they are major legal issues in the age: what legal claim have Europeans to land in the New World; what claims do we have on nature? The standard argument is that natives can only be said to own the land if they work it, in other words farm it; hunters and fishermen live off it, give nothing back to it, do nothing that makes it theirs (this is an argument against Caliban, but it is also an argument against Prospero). The argument naturally had to be abandoned whenever the Europeans had to deal with farming Indians, but it indicates how far into European society these issues extended, because one thing the English were especially eager for the New World to provide was a large supply of great estates, a remedy to the problems of primogeniture; somewhere the younger sons of the gentry could go and be gentlemen and landowners in their own right, be as good as their fathers and eldest brothers. Shakespeare takes a darker and more complicated view of Prospero in his dealings with Caliban than Milton does of the Lady facing down Comus; but just as Shakespeare gives Caliban, through his astonishing verse, a larger presence in the play than Prospero's view of him will allow for, so Milton gives Comus more resonance than the Lady's arguments alone can dismiss. Caliban's poetry is a telling refutation of Prospero's view of him as an inarticulate savage; Comus's arguments can be argued away, but the rich, sensuous, wonderfully inventive, indeed Shakespearean, poetry is Milton at his best. In fact, it is tempting to think that as the Attendant Spirit was written for Lawes to play, Milton wrote Comus for himself. There is no evidence that this is the case, but for the first printed edition of the masque, Milton supplied an epigraph from Virgil's Second Eclogue, "Eheu quid volui misero mihi! floribus austrum/ Perditus – " ("Wretch, what have I longed for! The south wind, desperate, upon my flowers ..."). The desperate, lovelorn shepherd Corydon bewails the coldness of his beloved Alexis. Milton here speaks as Comus, in the grip of an impossible love.

I am not implying simply that Milton had divided loyalties. Milton's masque is precisely about how complicated the choice of virtue is as soon as it stops being treated as an abstract question. Few of us set out to be deliberately wicked, but if deception exists it doesn't do us much good to know our own minds. It is the deceptive Other we need to know, and, as the history of rhetoric amply demonstrates, false arguments are as persuasive as true ones. Both the Attendant Spirit and Comus present themselves as innocent shepherds; there is nothing to indicate that one is good and the other bad – and neither is the real thing, both are lying. We think we make free choices, but we don't. Indeed, to claim, as Milton wants to do here, that virtue is absolutely self-sufficient, he really has to load the case. The Attendant Spirit says that Comus offers "to every weary traveler/ His orient liquor in a crystal glass/ To quench the drought of Phoebus, which ... they taste/ (For most do taste through fond intemperate thirst) ..." (ll. 64–7), and that is what enables them to be turned into animals. But is *thirst* really fond – foolish – and intemperate? Are we at fault for being thirsty after a long journey in hot weather? Even in the Attendant Spirit's terms, there is no indication that the weary traveler commits any sin by drinking, that gluttony or greed is involved – it isn't that the traveler drinks too much, instead of taking only enough to quench the thirst, or covets the crystal glass. How would one know not to drink? Is the crystal glass a tipoff, as it is in a similar moment in Spenser, when Guyon is offered a drink at the entrance to the Bower of Bliss, and smashes the glass to the ground? But in *Paradise Lost*, what is good about the banquets the angels have in heaven is not the food, which Milton understandably doesn't try to imagine, but precisely the fact that it is served on gold plates. Would the Lady reject even a meal from God? What does the Attendant Spirit serve his drinks in? Is there any way of not falling for this temptation short of refusing to quench one's thirst? Total abstinence is not the same as temperance. Isn't this a claim that whatever evils we encounter are simply our own fault, a classic case of blaming the victim?

In revising the masque for publication, Milton produced a version about a third longer than the performing text, in which those arguments in favor of temperance and chastity get rewritten and elaborated, and grow even more doctrinaire. In particular, the Lady's peroration on "the sage and serious doctrine of Virginity" and the Attendant Spirit's long final speech about the absolute freedom of the virtuous mind were not part of the performance. The quality of innocence, unworldliness, abstraction, are things Milton wants to retain, elaborate and strengthen, not edit out; and they therefore cannot be accounted for by saying that the performers were children. The famous passage in *Areopagitica* about refusing to "praise a fugitive and cloistered virtue"[6] suggests that the primary virtue is experience, not innocence; but in fact there is a very strong desire, throughout Milton, to find ways to believe that whatever experience confronts us with, we really *can* hold on to our innocence, and that when we fail to do so, as we inevitably do, it's through our own fault. For all Milton's obvious emotional investment in the figure of Comus, it is surely not irrelevant that he was a fastidious and rather delicate young man, whose nickname when he was an undergraduate at Christ's College, Cambridge, was "the Lady of Christ's."

So let us consider the Lady now. I focus here on the way she is finally released from her bondage by the production of another version of herself, the nymph of the River Severn, Sabrina, another embattled virgin. This resolution through duplication interests me because the work, in fact, is full of duplication – even of duplicity. The Attendant Spirit and Comus are the image of each other; Comus's court is a parodic image of the court at Ludlow, which in turn is a miniature version of the court at Whitehall, with the Earl representing, refiguring, mirroring the King. Mirror images, repetitions and reversals are essential elements in the action. The Lady, when she first finds herself alone in the wood, invokes the nymph Echo, an auditory mirror image. Why invoke this figure? In a world that includes Attendant Spirits, to say nothing of the visible figures of Faith, Hope and Chastity, there are obviously many other tutelary figures to invoke. What assistance can your own echo give you?

And if we press on the allusion, it becomes even stranger, in this anti-sensualist work. In Ovid, Echo is a nymph who was Jove's confidante in his love affairs; but she was a bad confidante – she told everybody about them. She was so loquacious that she was punished by being condemned to speak only when spoken to, and then only to repeat what she heard. She fell in love with the youth Narcissus, who was in love only with himself, and killed himself when he found he could not possess the beautiful image of his own face, a visual echo – when he found that the self was not the Other. When Narcissus died, Echo too pined away, and was transformed into a rock, but she still retained the same power of repetitive speech. Is all this relevant, or not? If so, it is difficult to see it as anything but a subversive moment, introducing self-absorption and a dangerous vanity into the purity of the Lady's character. And if it is *not* relevant, what is Echo doing here?

One thing she might be doing is something musical. The Echo Song, in which the last part of the verse gets repeated as a refrain, or as an answer, was a popular form in the period. Jonson is fond of echo songs in his early masques, as, for example, in *The Masque of Beauty*: "It was for beauty that the world was made,/ And where she reigns Love's lights admit no shade./ – Love's lights admit no shade./ – Admit no shade."[7] That is surely what we are led to expect here, the young poet's exercise in this classic genre, with Milton imitating Jonson, and Lawes imitating Ferrabosco. Here is the song – and notice that the notion of echo being invoked is not simply an abstract one, but is quite specific about the Ovidian allusion:

> Sweet Echo, sweetest nymph that liv'st unseen
> Within thy airy shell
> By slow Meander's margent green,
> And in the violet-embroidered vale
> Where the love-lorn nightingale
> Nightly to thee her sad song mourneth well,
> Canst thou not tell me of a gentle pair
> That likest thy Narcissus are?
> O if thou have
> Hid them in some flowery cave,
> Tell me but where,
> Sweet queen of parley, daughter of the sphere,
> So mayst thou be translated to the skies,
> And give resounding grace to all heaven's harmonies. (ll. 230–44)

What is baffling about this is the fact that Echo does not answer – "Grace to all heaven's harmonies" would be the obvious refrain, seemingly an ideal text for Lawes's melisma; but, in fact, in Lawes's setting, there are no repetitions at all in the song. This is quite unlike Ferrabosco's settings of Jonson, or

Robert Johnson's of Shakespeare songs, or Dowland's of his own verse, or Lawes's brother William's settings of Shirley's masque songs in *The Triumph of Peace* in the same year. (This, in fact, seems to me one of the problems with it as a piece of music: it gives you no help; if you miss it the first time, you get no second chance.) Why does Milton go out of his way to defeat our expectations about this? Could it be part of the point, that the song is just as uncompromising and unresponsive as the Lady herself is? But, of course, even if there were a reply, what could it say? Echo would only be able to repeat the Lady's song – how would that help?

It does, certainly, emphasize the fact that the Lady has *only* herself to rely on. The Lady, singing to Echo, is literally singing to herself, and Comus therefore is, if not eavesdropping, at least overhearing the most private of communications. But it also means that she is surrounded with – or creates for herself – a world of versions of the self, of solipsism. It is not only Comus and the Attendant Spirit who are mirror images; she herself compares her brothers to Narcissus (and if they are like Narcissus, they are also mirror images of each other). She cannot be released from Comus's spell because her Narcissistic brothers forget to seize his magic wand; the wand is necessary because it needs to be reversed – "Without his rod reversed,/ And backward mutters of dissevering power,/ We cannot free the Lady" (ll. 815–17). Good magic is bad magic backwards, its mirror image. This is why she can only be rescued by the production of yet another embattled maiden, another version of herself. Undoing things can never free us from the things themselves. This is a vision in which freedom is a repetition, the mirror image, of bondage.

Comus is in its way a love poem, full of a sense of both the potential richness of sensuality and its dangers; and full of a more subversive sense, too, of the inhumanity of virtue, the destructiveness of unresponsiveness – the Lady's invocation of Echo does not even produce an echo. If we could imagine a version of *Comus* written from Comus's point of view, what would the Lady look like? Noble and virtuous, or cold, rigid and ultimately barren? I have often wondered whether Milton did not have the ambivalences of Shakespeare's Sonnet 94 somewhere at the back of his mind, the sonnet about those "that have power to hurt and will do none":

> Who moving others, are yet themselves as stone,
> Unmoved, cold, and to temptation slow,
> They rightly do inherit heaven's graces,
> And husband nature's riches from expense,
> They are the lords and owners of their faces … . (ll. 3–7)[8]

Owning one's own face is clearly being represented as an unambiguous virtue. But all Narcissus owned, and all he wanted, was his own face, and that might give us pause. The Lady, too, "moving others," is yet herself "as stone/ Unmoved, cold, and to temptation" – not slow, but utterly impervious. Is this an unambiguous virtue, a model for ethical behavior? No doubt – all the critics assure us that it is; but praising someone by declaring her cold as stone does not promise much in the way of human responsiveness, feeling or even decency. And of course perhaps the Lady is not the ethical model at all; perhaps the point is precisely how attractive temptation is – how attractive it has to be to tempt us. It is, after all, we, not the Lady, whom Comus tempts, we who find him attractive.

I want to look now at Comus in some other contexts. Shakespeare's version of Milton's masque is *Venus and Adonis*. The sexes are reversed, which makes for a rather misogynistic comedy instead of Milton's high ethical morality play; but it is also true that though Adonis preserves his virtue Shakespeare seems to have very little invested in his hero's chastity. Adonis denounces Venus much as the Lady denounces Comus, as the embodiment not of love but of "sweating lust," and Venus is certainly represented as gross and unattractive. Most readers, however, have found the case a little loaded and Adonis rather prissy – even in Shakespeare's moralizing culture, healthy adolescent males were not expected to turn down free sex with no consequences; the more so since, in the traditional story, Adonis is as eager for Venus as she is for him. The ethical issue is not the main one for Shakespeare; *Venus and Adonis* is all about subverting norms – the norms both of canonical classical stories and of love poetry.

In fact, the most powerful and characteristic English Renaissance love poetry is just the sort exemplified in Comus's speeches, the poetry of seduction. In Donne, Carew or Marvell we can see how much the age had invested precisely in figures like Comus winning. That is, there is a way in which Milton's battle of wills, with the virtuous Lady routing the charming seducer, is the really subversive conception. The age has a great deal invested in both the power of rhetoric and in men getting what they want. In such poetry, what they want is women, certainly; women, however, not simply as lovers, but as representatives or embodiments of something much larger, of new worlds, power, riches, a satisfaction that is a great deal more than sexual – "O my America, my newfound land!" [9] The idea of the woman as a site of incredible riches or fabulous new lands is not simply a poetic fantasy. What men married for in the period was money, or position, or alliances. The woman was the enabling figure in the advancement and consolidation of male authority – this is why fathers were given the legal power to arrange their children's marriages; it is also why women are provided with dowries: quite simply, no one will marry them otherwise. Children are legally their fathers' possessions, women are legally their husbands' possessions – it is to the point that the Lady is liberated from Comus only to be delivered into the keeping of her father: there is no imaginable alternative. The Lady is eloquent in her captivity about the freedom of her mind, but her mind is not free: far from it. In particular, she is not free to choose Comus, not because there is anything wrong with Comus but because the choice of her husband belongs to her father, not to her – she is free only to concur in his choice, and the situation would be no different if her suitor were the Attendant Spirit. What is wicked about Comus's transformed minions is precisely that they have assumed that their minds were their own, exercised the freedom of their wills, ignored their fathers, decided not to go home.

Suppose we did imagine the masque from Comus's point of view, as one can imagine *The Tempest* from Caliban's. The touchstone of Caliban's unregeneracy for Prospero is a more violent version of Comus's seductive imperialism, his attempt to rape Miranda. But if one takes Caliban's claim to be the king of the island seriously – and surely by any legal standard he has a good case – then that act looks rather different: it is, like the rape of the Sabine women, or the rape that enabled the establishment of Carthage, a foundational act. Miranda, Caliban says, would not merely have satisfied his lust, she would have founded a race, "peopled/ This isle with Calibans" (I.2.349–50). Rape is the originary myth of empire. And, in a different version of the story, Prospero, after all, might have decided not to bend his efforts toward a pointless revenge and the restoration of the dukedom he had no interest in ruling, but instead to make the most of his exile in this new world by allying himself with the island's ruler. In this scenario, Caliban, not Ferdinand, would have been the right husband for Miranda – and, no doubt, a romantic hero – and Miranda's feelings on the matter would have been irrelevant, just as irrelevant as those of Alonso's daughter Claribel, married off unwillingly to the king of Tunis.

Comus is more clearly the king of the woods than Caliban is king of the island, and Milton's allusion to *The Tempest* in the first encounter with the Lady, already cited, is in fact not to Caliban but to the charming and morally impeccable Ferdinand: "I'll speak to her,/ And she shall be my queen. Hail, foreign wonder ... ." Arguably, however, the real problem is that Comus is going about the seduction the wrong way. He wants to be attractive to the Lady, but he really needs to be attractive to her father. In fact, the Earl might well consider this a good alliance: Comus rules the woods, the Earl rules everything else. If Comus marries the Lady, the family rules everything. In this version of the plot, the Lady's virtue is taken care of by the fact that what is in question is a marriage, not a seduction; and, in any case, it is the father who is being seduced, not the Lady. Her wishes are not exactly irrelevant, but they are expected to coincide with her father's.

What is really wrong with Comus, then, is that he bothers with the Lady's feelings at all. In this respect, the Castlehaven case, that skeleton in the family closet, is actually very enlightening, not as a source, but as an index to the relevant social norms. The initial charge against Castlehaven had nothing to do with spousal rape or sodomy. Castlehaven had married his daughter to one of his favorite servants, on whom he had settled a large amount of money. His eldest son, apparently fearing that he would be disinherited, lodged a complaint against his father with the king. It was only then that Castlehaven's wife brought her own complaint about being forced to have sex with another servant, an event that had taken place several years before. In his defense, Castlehaven insisted that he could not be prosecuted on such charges. His wife's body and his daughter's hand in marriage belonged to him; he could do with them as he pleased. The reason this was a bad defense was not that it was incorrect. On the contrary, it was egregiously, blatantly, shockingly, dangerously true. What was wrong with it, and ultimately made it a capital offense, was precisely that it *was* correct, and thus exposed the basic flaw in the whole patriarchal system; hence the invocation of the buggery charge, which was unambiguously prosecutable (though according to the legal definition of buggery at the time, Castlehaven probably was not guilty of it).

So the Lady is rescued and delivered to her father – nothing subversive from Milton the revolutionary there. What happens next? What is the happy ending; what happens when she gets home? If we pursue Lady Alice Egerton's history a little further, the reading I am proposing will sound less eccentric. She was fifteen in 1634, when the masque was performed. She did not marry until 1650, at the age of thirty-one – a distinctly advanced age for marriage in aristocratic families. The groom was a prosperous Welsh landowner, Richard Vaughan, Earl of Carbery; the title is less grand than it sounds, since it was in the Irish peerage – as an English peer, he was a mere baron. He was twice widowed, fifty-two years old – twenty-one years older than she, literally old enough to be her father – with several grown children. Lady Alice was well beyond the age of consent at this point, and had not lived at Ludlow for more than ten years, but the match doubtless pleased her family well enough: Carbery was a royalist peer, and a man of substance, though not of unambiguous character: some of his wealth was said to have been acquired through extortion and embezzlement. Moreover, as commander of a section of the royal army in Wales in 1644, he had been decisively defeated and accused of cowardice, or even of deliberately losing the battle. It was only through his connections and the assiduous courting of influential people that he managed to escape the heavy fine that was levied on him. Despite his royalist politics, he managed to live comfortably under the Commonwealth – his second wife, who died in the same year he married Lady Alice, so impressed Cromwell with her piety that he rescinded his order to have Carbery arrested. Doubless the idea of Lady Alice as the third Countess of Carbery satisfied the Egertons; she was, after all, one of fifteen children, eleven of whom were daughters; how choosy could one be? By 1650, moreover, her father's approval was no longer an issue: the marriage took place a year after his death – did she wait until he died to marry? In one respect, at least, her husband replicated her father: at the Restoration Carbery succeeded to Bridgewater's former posts, the Lord Presidency of the Council and Lord Lieutenancy of Wales, offices he held until 1672, when he was removed, charged with malfeasance and exceptional cruelty to his servants and tenants. As one ambivalent eulogist put it at his death, he was ideally suited to high office, save for cowardice and a want of integrity.

Lady Alice, it will be observed, scarcely figures at all in this narrative. In a fulsomely adulatory poem addressed to her shortly after her marriage, variously entitled *To Alice Countess of Carbery, on her Enriching Wales with her Presence* and *To Alice Countess of Carbery, on her first coming into Wales*, the extraordinary Welsh poet Katherine Philips ("the matchless Orinda") extravagantly praises her for the most vague and abstract virtues: for bringing light to the obscurity and chaos of Wales, for civilizing the wilderness, mostly for condescending to be there at all – what, indeed, Philips seems to ask, *is* she doing there? It is the same question Comus asks on hearing the Lady's echoless echo song. The ode, hyperbolic and inscrutable, is a curious gloss on *Comus*, and suggests how little had changed in the way Alice Egerton was regarded, or presented herself, in the intervening twenty years. Whether the marriage was a happy one is not recorded; it may or may not be relevant that the couple had no children. Alice Egerton's story, like most women's stories throughout history, ends with marriage. In fact, for our purposes, it ends sixteen years before her marriage, with Milton's masque.

Notes

1 Leah Marcus, *The Politics of Mirth* (Chicago, 1986), pp. 169–212.
2 See Cynthia B. Herrup, *A House in Gross Disorder* (New York, 1999).
3 Quotations are from the text of the masque in *John Milton*, ed. Stephen Orgel and Jonathan Goldberg (Oxford, 1991).

4 Quotations from *The Tempest* are from the Oxford edition, ed. Stephen Orgel (Oxford, 1987).

5 *The Discovery of … Guiana*, ed. Sir R. Shombergk (London, 1848), p. 115.

6 *Milton*, p. 247.

7 Lines 243–6; text from the Yale Ben Jonson, *Complete Masques*, ed. Stephen Orgel (New Haven, CT, 1969).

8 The text used is that of the New Pelican Shakespeare, ed. Stephen Orgel (New York, 2001).

9 John Donne, Elegy xix: "To His Mistress Going to Bed," l. 27.

7

Completing *Hamlet*

Hamlet is probably the most famous play in literature, thoroughly international in its appeal, admired and imitated in Asian cultures as well as in the west. Its fame in its own time may be considered a matter of record, though the record has certainly been overstated; and that is a good place to begin. For a reading public, several Shakespeare plays were considerably more in demand during Shakespeare's lifetime: *Richard II, Richard III, Henry IV, Romeo and Juliet, Titus Andronicus, Pericles,* all went through many more editions than did *Hamlet,* and both *Venus and Adonis* and *Lucrece* were by a considerable margin Shakespeare's best known and most widely quoted works. It is true that there are far more allusions to *Hamlet* recorded in *The Shakspere Allusion Book* than to any other play, but many of these are dubious, merely bits of conventional wisdom, reflecting primarily a desire on the part of Shakespeare's nineteenth-century editors for a plethora of *Hamlet* allusions, but also revealing how full the play is of commonplaces. Still, there is no question of the play's popularity when it was new. Gabriel Harvey, apparently writing before the play was in print, said it pleased "the wiser sort," and Anthony Scoloker in 1604 praising "friendly Shakespeare's tragedies," adds that theater "should please all, like Prince Hamlet" – everybody liked the play.[1] If we scrutinize the 34 citations to *Hamlet* before 1623 in the *Allusion Book,* however, only six turn out to be unquestionably quotations from the play. Of these, three refer to the ghost beneath the stage crying "Swear," one refers to Hamlet mad and in shirt-sleeves, one quotes the Player's Pyrrhus speech, and one the Player Queen's "In second husband let me be accursed/ None wed the second but who killed the first." If we may take these few examples as indicative, the most memorable thing in the play in its own time was the ghost. The most substantial reference to the play during Shakespeare's lifetime, though not noted as such in *The Shakspere Allusion Book,* is Robert Armin's parody in *The Two Maids of More-clacke,* which, as a gloss on *Hamlet* written by the principal clown of Shakespeare's company, surely deserves more attention than it has received.

The seventeenth century found little fault with the play. Davenant revising it for the Restoration stage did not tinker with the plot, and confined his efforts to cutting – as both Shakespeare himself and his contemporaries must also have done. The greatest actor of the Restoration Thomas Betterton throughout his long career made the role particularly his own, and was hugely successful in it – Pepys saw the play four times in the ten years recorded in the diary, and admired it, though all his praise is specifically for Betterton. Dryden deplored the rhetorical excesses of the Player's speech ("What a pudder is here kept in raising the expression of trifling thoughts"[2]), but rescued the rest of the play by declaring the passage an interpolation by some other poet. Seriously negative criticism of the play began only in the eighteenth century. Voltaire notoriously called it "a crude and barbarous piece, … the outgrowth of the imagination of a drunken savage"[3] and had a great deal of fun summarizing its plot. The critique was widely ridiculed in England, but Johnson, the least bardolatrous of Shakespeare's editors, was scarcely less pejorative, and distinctly condescending. Declaring the play's chief merit to be variety, he finds it deficient in plausibility.

> Hamlet is, through the whole play, rather an instrument than an agent. After he has, by the stratagem of the play, convicted the King, he makes no attempt to punish him, and his death is at last effected by an incident which Hamlet has no part in producing.
>
> The catastrophe is not very happily produced; the exchange of weapons is rather an expedient of necessity than a stroke of art. A scheme might easily have been formed, to kill Hamlet with the dagger, and Laertes with the bowl.
>
> The poet is accused of having shewn little regard to poetical justice, and may be charged with equal neglect of poetical probability. The apparition left the regions of the dead to little purpose; the revenge which he demands is not obtained but by the death of him that was required to take it; and the gratification which would arise from the destruction of an usurper and a murderer is abated by the untimely death of Ophelia, the young, the beautiful, the harmless and the pious.[4]

Johnson exemplified a critical skepticism, increasingly strong throughout the century, regarding the play's seriousness. At the beginning of the next century Coleridge rejected such views with the voice of a revisionist; but he also did so with surprising vehemence, characterizing the critical consensus of the previous age not merely as misguided, but as shallow, stupid, arrogant, vulgar and indolent.

The seeming inconsistencies in the conduct and character of Hamlet have long exercised the conjectural ingenuity of critics; and, as we are always loth to suppose that the cause of defective apprehension is in ourselves, the mystery has been too commonly explained by the very easy process of setting it down as in fact inexplicable, and by resolving the phenomenon into a misgrowth or lusus of the capricious and irregular genius of Shakspere. The shallow and stupid arrogance of these vulgar and indolent decisions I would fain do my best to expose. I believe the character of Hamlet may be traced to Shakspere's deep and accurate science in mental philosophy. Indeed, that this character must have some connection with the common fundamental laws of our nature may be assumed from the fact, that Hamlet has been the darling of every country in which the literature of England has been fostered. In order to understand him, it is essential that we should reflect on the constitution of our own minds.[5]

The play's essential seriousness here has to do primarily with Shakespeare's delineation of Hamlet's mental state – the character is to be taken seriously because its psychology is realistic. But it is not really Hamlet's psychology that is the basic issue:

Now one of Shakspere's modes of creating characters is, to conceive any one intellectual or moral faculty in morbid excess, and then to place himself, Shakspere, thus mutilated or diseased, under given circumstances. In Hamlet he seems to have wished to exemplify the moral necessity of a due balance between our attention to the objects of our senses, and our meditation on the workings of our minds, an equilibrium between the real and the imaginary worlds.[6]

Hamlet's excellence here lies in the truth of its psychological insight; but, more particularly, the delineation of Hamlet's psychology is beyond criticism because the psychology is Shakespeare's own – the play shows "himself, Shakspere, thus mutilated or diseased," the playwright placed in Hamlet's circumstances. This is an odd critical move, quite unnecessary for the progress of the argument, but it helps to explain the vehemence with which any negative observations are rejected. Reservations about Hamlet impugn Shakespeare's knowledge of himself, and Coleridge the advocate speaks with the authority of Shakespeare.

By the twentieth century, however, there was more to Shakespeare than psychology and more to drama than character. The play's philosophical seriousness (as opposed to its truth to life) is a product of the late nineteenth and twentieth centuries, of the assumption that Hamlet's meditations and the revelations of the ghost imply a whole metaphysical system – is this why, according to Gabriel Harvey, *Hamlet* pleased "the wiser sort"? But T. S. Eliot was dissatisfied with the play, asserting that, despite the soliloquies with all their overt philosophizing, the action was insufficiently motivated, and Eliot introduced a term that has entered the critical language: Hamlet's emotional state lacked an 'objective correlative' – the phrase served to account less for Hamlet's problem, or for a perceived problem in Shakespeare's dramaturgy, than for our problems with the play, its failure to deliver what by the early twentieth century we had come to want from it, a solid anchor in a sea of doubt and alienation.[7] Half a century later the metaphysics and the prevailing sense of loss had become critical virtues, evidence in the move to historicize Shakespeare's own psychology and embed Hamlet's scepticism in his studies at Wittenberg and the intellectual movements of the Protestant reformation. In this reading the ghost of the murdered father emerging from Catholic purgatory was England's past returning to haunt the present.

Motivation and action

But in fact, Coleridge to the contrary notwithstanding, even for character-based criticism motivation has always been an issue in the play. If Hamlet's father is the problem, why is he so focused on his mother? Why does he delay avenging his father's murder? Why is he in such a funk? Why does he behave so badly to Ophelia? Ernest Jones, following a suggestion of Freud's, answered these questions by invoking the Oedipus Complex.[8] The argument as Jones presented it relied more heavily on generalizations about human nature than on textual analysis, but it did not misrepresent the play. It has, however, enabled any number of increasingly steamy sex scenes between Hamlet and his mother in modern productions. In the 1948 film, in their first scene together, Eileen Herlie's Gertrude gives Olivier's Hamlet a deep, wet kiss as the court watches; a generation later, in the BBC production, Derek Jacobi's Hamlet dry-humps Claire Bloom's Gertrude as he harangues her on her bed in her bedchamber. This presumably was not what Jones and Freud had in mind: the whole point about the Oedipus Complex is that it is repressed. There is, however, more evidence for its presence in the play than Jones or Freud were aware. Hamlet himself is quite explicit about it, berating himself in his final soliloquy for his inaction:

> How stand I then,
> That have a father killed, a mother stained... (IV.4.56–7)

Hamlet's ambiguous syntax accuses himself of his uncle's crimes; he is the parricide and the incestuous son. Freud perhaps had read the play only in German, in which the double syntax would not have been apparent; but how did an anglophone psychoanalyst looking for Oedipus miss this? Is there perhaps something more to the argument that is being repressed?

None of this bears on the more basic question, the first question students ask, of why Hamlet is not king to begin with. Why did he not he succeed his father? In a provocative recent reading of the play, Margreta de Grazia makes this the missing key: he has been disinherited, in violation of every expectation. This, not his father's death and his mother's o'er-hasty marriage, is the objective correlative that explains everything.[9]

The reading is tempting, but there is actually little in the play to support it. Such an argument makes more sense to us than it would have done for Shakespeare's audience; royal succession was not invariably determined by primogeniture (e.g. in Shakespeare's lifetime in the cases of the Holy Roman Emperor and the Elector Palatine), and King James himself was not the only or even the obvious claimant to succeed Queen Elizabeth. He became king because Elizabeth named him her heir, and he was supported by the people in power. Questions of succession were very much the stuff of melodrama. At the beginning of *Macbeth* Duncan seals his own fate by declaring his son Malcolm the heir to his throne, in violation of the Scottish practice at the time, which was determined not by primogeniture but by tanistry, or election from among the royal kinsmen. It is to the point that nobody in the play thereafter supports the claims of Malcolm until he returns at the head of an invading English army. Neither does anyone in *Hamlet* imply that Hamlet ought to be king, or that young Fortinbras should have succeeded his father on the throne of Norway.

It is certainly the case, however, that the dynastic plot as such is to be taken seriously. What does it mean to take the play seriously? Both Voltaire and Johnson intentionally trivialized *Hamlet* by reducing it to its plot, but there are, obviously, more ways than one of approaching the plot, some less reductive than others. The real problem, since it is a Shakespeare tragedy we are dealing with, is that no version of the action seems sufficiently heroic to fulfil our expectations of the genre. The hero is a romantic student. He is told he must become an avenger; he says over and over that he is not fit for the task. The play is about his effort to convert himself into the son his father's ghost demands; it is not until the final scene of the play that he mentions that he ever wished to be king, that Claudius "popped in between th'election and my hopes" (V.2.64) – this is something new, and unexpected; it comes as part of his transformation into the good son. His desire to be king indicates that he is prepared at last to be the avenging hero, which he does, more or less, succeed in doing; and Fortinbras, ascending the Danish throne himself, acknowledges Hamlet's transformation in an ironically contrafactual eulogy: "he was likely, had he been put on,/ To have proved most royal."

How exactly Hamlet reaches this point, however, is left unclear. How does the neurasthenic youth to whom "this goodly frame the earth seems ... a sterile promontory, ... a foul and pestilent congregation of vapors" (II.2.269–73) become the hero for whom "there is a special providence in the fall of a sparrow," for whom "the readiness is all" (V.2.198–200)? *Hamlet* is a play, we might say, that from moment to moment wants completion, calls out for us to fill in the blanks. We undertake to do this through critical readings, complex editorial projects, commentary and massive elucidation; but historically we have also done it more directly, through rewriting and restaging, a strategy that has always been part of the performing tradition, and continues to the present day.

Ducis's *Hamlet*

I focus now on two major examples, alternative approaches to the problem of filling in the blanks. In 1769 Jean-François Ducis produced a French *Hamlet*, the first theatrical version of a Shakespeare play in France. It was in effect a response to Voltaire's critique, a *Hamlet* imbued with the principles of French classical drama. Ducis passionately admired Shakespeare, though he knew no English; he read the play in the truncated version of Pierre Antoine de la Place. In fact, Ducis's *Hamlet* has little in common with Shakespeare's beyond the basic situation, but – or perhaps therefore – it was hugely successful, especially after a radical revision for Talma in 1803 (there were at least four versions of the script).[10] The play was rendered thoroughly decorous, losing much of the variety for which Johnson had admired it; but it gained a real Racinian intensity. In the earliest of Ducis's versions, the ghost made several brief appearances; but within a year, by the time the text was published in 1770, he was eliminated as a character, communicating with Hamlet only in dreams and visions. Rosencrantz and Guildenstern, Laertes and Fortinbras were gone, as were the Players and the play within the play and all the problems with Norway. There was no voyage to England or encounter with the pirates or suicide of Ophelia, and hence no gravediggers or memories of Yorick. Hamlet has, from the beginning, succeeded to his father's throne, though because of his *pénible ennui* Gertrude is ruling in his place, until he regains his equilibrium. Claudius is *premier prince du sang*, and he and Gertrude are not married – their relationship therefore is adulterous but not incestuous, and possibly therefore more acceptable to French audiences. Ophelia is the daughter of Claudius, not Polonius, who is a minor character, and Gertrude has a confidante named Elvire, the only totally invented character in the play. The principal figures are Hamlet, Gertrude, Claudius and Horatio, who has been renamed Norceste. In the earlier versions of the plot, Hamlet tells Norceste of the ghost's revelation of his murder at the hands of Claudius and Gertrude – this Gertrude is fully implicated; indeed, it was she who administered the poison, though the plot was Claudius's. Norceste and Hamlet resolve to test the truth of the ghost's story by having Hamlet confront the queen with the urn containing her husband's ashes, and demanding that she swear on it that she is innocent. She avoids adding perjury to murder by fainting, which Hamlet interprets correctly as a confession; but when she revives, Hamlet immediately forgives her:

> Ah, revenez à vous,
> Voyez un Fils en pleurs embrasser vos genoux:
> Ne désespérez point de la bonté céleste.
> Rien n'est perdu pour vous si le remord vous reste.
> Votre crime est énorme, exécrable, odieux;
> Mais il n'est pas plus grand que la bonté des Dieux.

[Ah revive; see, your son in tears embraces your knees. You have lost nothing if you still have remorse. Your crime is tremendous, execrable, hateful, but it is not greater than the gods' goodness.]

Retribution nevertheless comes quickly: Claudius enters at the beginning of Act V to say that during the night he has killed the now dangerously remorseful queen. His daughter Ophelia enters and denounces him. She is escorted out under guard. Polonius urges swift action against Hamlet and Norceste, and goes off to martial Claudius's supporters. Hamlet appears, saying that he has been led to Claudius by his father's ghost. Claudius throws open a door to reveal the body of Gertrude, and summons his followers, but as they rush in Hamlet stabs Claudius, and dares the others to attack him. They hold off, and Hamlet declares "Mon père est satisfait." To conclude the play, Ophelia enters with Norceste, and is shown the body of her father – "Ah! Qu'as tu fait, barbare?", to which Hamlet replies "Mon devoir," my duty; "Mais je suis homme et Roi": he has at last become a man and the king.

In the revision for Talma, done in 1803, an ingenious adaptation of Shakespeare's play-within-the-play scene precedes Hamlet's confrontation of the queen with the urn. Norceste has recently returned from England, where the king has been poisoned. He and Hamlet decide to test the ghost's revelations by reporting the story of the murder, which they adapt to the present circumstances by ascribing the crime to motives of ambition and "une flamme adultère," and seeing whether Claudius and Gertrude display any incriminating reactions. Claudius is unmoved as Hamlet tells the story, but the queen is clearly troubled. In this version of Ducis's play Claudius does not kill Gertrude, but accuses Hamlet of the murder of the old king, and in the final act arrives with soldiers to arrest him. He is forestalled by Norceste leading a mob of Hamlet's supporters, shouting, in the best revolutionary fashion, "Peuple, sauvez Hamlet!" Claudius is promptly dispatched, and the queen resolves her own problems by committing suicide – or at least trying to do so, since in at least one of the later versions of the play she is still alive to speak the final lines. In all versions, Hamlet survives to rule over the Danes.

This *Hamlet*, however eccentric in relation to Shakespeare's original, addresses a number of genuine critical issues, and not only those relating to French classical decorum. Hamlet here is king from the beginning (solving the problem that occupies de Grazia), and most of the delay in the execution of the revenge, which has troubled critics since the eighteenth century, results from the difficulties of eliciting a confession from Gertrude – the confession here really is necessary, since Ducis's ghost, as far as Hamlet is aware, is simply a dream. But the confrontation of the queen with the urn does more than confirm the reliability of the dream. It addresses a real problem in Shakespeare, adding to the play a scene that, even in Shakespeare's own time, was felt to be missing, a scene that would provide an answer to the question of the queen's complicity in her husband's murder. In Shakespeare's play, when Hamlet goes to the queen's bedchamber after the play scene, he still lacks two essential pieces of information: whether Gertrude was committing adultery with Claudius before his father died and, more important, whether the queen was implicated in the murder, or even knew about it. These issues have been left ambiguous in the Ghost's account – the Ghost refers to Claudius as "that adulterate beast," which can mean either adulterous or simply foul; and he tells Hamlet to ignore the question of Gertrude's guilt, to "leave her to heaven." How guilty is Gertrude, and what is she guilty of? But Hamlet raises neither question, and it turns out that what he really wants from his mother is not an assurance of her innocence but only her promise not to sleep with her husband any more.

Within a year or two of the play's first performances, something was felt to be lacking here. The first quarto, a shortened and somewhat rationalized version of the play apparently assembled from memory by a group of actors on tour, and published in 1603, adds a bit to the bedchamber scene in which Gertrude unequivocally asserts her innocence – of the murder at least; the

question of adultery is again left to heaven. In a later scene with no parallel in
Q2 or F, Horatio tells her of Hamlet's return from England, and she agrees
to join in the plot against the king.[11] All this still leaves open the question of
Hamlet's singleminded focus on his mother instead of his uncle, but in Ducis
that is simply enough accounted for: she, not Claudius, was the murderer.

Ducis provides a version of the story with much less for critics to complain
about, infinitely fewer puzzles and loose ends. The French *Hamlet* offers,
in its way, a satisfying sense of completeness, not least in allowing the hero
his ultimate triumph. To indignant critics who deplore Ducis' presumptuousness in rewriting Shakespeare, one can only point to Talma's success in
the role, and observe that adapters have been at work on *Hamlet* from its very
inception – the first quarto itself is an adaptation. Modern commentators have,
on the whole, preferred to deal with the play's puzzles through elucidation
and commentary, rather than through theatrical revision – we tend now to
prefer bibliographical explanations (and revisions) to narrative ones, thereby
moving the play increasingly away from the stage and toward the book and
the putative manuscript behind it. But given the immense length of its text,
Hamlet in performance has always been incomplete, and to provide a sense of
completeness, at least for a satisfactory evening at theater, has always required
not only major cuts but often discreet additions as well.

Hamlet is often claimed to be the first dramatic character with an inner life,
a genuine psychology; and he certainly claims, in his soliloquies, to have one.
Nevertheless, we have argued for centuries about his motivations: that crucial
bit of his psychology is missing. To provide motivation became increasingly
the task of the actor in search of a psychologically credible character; and
since the psychologically credible changes from age to age, Hamlet has been
the most mercurial of figures. Garrick notoriously employed a pneumatic wig
for his first sight of the ghost, so that his hair could stand on end. The lines,
for Garrick, required this additional bit of business, which was considered
sensationally realistic at the time – today, it would be a joke. In contrast,
Olivier's beautiful 1948 film presented a melancholy and contemplative Hamlet
in his first scene at court, a psychologically consistent and entirely persuasive
character. The persuasiveness depended, however, on the excision of about a
third of Hamlet's lines from the scene, including all the sarcasm and wit –
completeness here was the enemy of credibility.

The Cranach Press *Hamlet*

Hamlet the book then. It is only as a text that we can have the complete play;
but what text of *Hamlet* can be said to be complete? Surely the impulse to

conflate quarto and folio texts of *Hamlet* (as of *King Lear* and *Romeo and Juliet*) springs from a conviction that none of the individual texts is complete: the second quarto includes 230 lines not in the folio; the folio includes 70 lines not in the quarto. Scholarly editions aspire to completeness through their inclusion of alternatives and textual variants (as if a textual history of Shakespeare were anything more than a history of departures from a lost original); but in the case of *Hamlet* we want more than any of the surviving texts can supply, and not only more text – explanations for his psychology, what he studied at Wittenberg, what he really felt about Ophelia, whether he was really mad, why he was still at university at the age of 30 ... the questions are endless.

It is no surprise, then, that *Hamlet* was refigured through an idea of comprehensiveness into the most monumental book of the twentieth century. Count Harry Kessler's Cranach Press *Hamlet* was published in a German edition in 1929 and in an English edition in 1930.[12] For this tremendously ambitious project, Kessler commissioned a new type based on a font used in the Mainz Psalter of 1457. Edward Gordon Craig was engaged to produce illustrative woodcuts; the book was printed in a strictly limited edition on handmade paper, with a few copies also on vellum. In 1910, Craig had collaborated with Stanislavski on a *Hamlet* for the Moscow Art Theatre. For this, he designed a nonrealistic stage, the central element of which was a set of complex, moveable screens. The collaboration was, from the outset, not a success – Craig's abstract theater was the wrong vehicle for Stanislavski's intensely psychologized, character-centered view of drama; moreover, the screens could not be got to work properly and kept falling down. But the concept remained with him, and the stage he could not create for Stanislavski he realized in large measure for Kessler.

Kessler's conception was to present *Hamlet* in a Renaissance setting; the book would be a reflection of the historical *Hamlet* – not, however, the *Hamlet* of the quartos, the Shakespeare folio, or (least of all) the putative "real" *Hamlet*, but a bibliographic embodiment of the towering monument to Renaissance culture that *Hamlet* had become. It would complete the idea of *Hamlet*. So the models for the book were the masterpieces of the great fifteenth- and sixteenth-century presses – the *Nuremberg Chronicle*, the *Hypnerotomachia Poliphili*, the Gutenberg and Koberger bibles, the great Estienne and Plantin editions of the classics. It is significant that Kessler's typeface was based not on a font from Shakespeare's age, but on the grandest of the early German models: this Hamlet was the German intellectual, the Wittenberg student, the humanist philosopher and scholar. The design of the book was that of a very grand late fifteenth- or early sixteenth-century scholarly edition: the text was in the center of the page, and in the margins around it, in smaller type, related material was placed. In sixteenth-century editions, the marginal material would have consisted of commentary and notes; Kessler's marginalia were the play's main sources, the *Hamlet* story in the Latin chronicle of Saxo Grammaticus and the *Histoires tragiques* of François de Belleforest – these were printed in both the original languages and in translation. For the German edition, the text was the standard translation of Schlegel, embellished by Gerhardt Hauptmann, who supplied several additional scenes (such as the confrontation of Claudius's emissaries Voltemand and Cornelius with the Norwegian king) to fill in what he conceived to be gaps in the plot, and thereby render the play more "complete" than Shakespeare. Kessler records in his diary for 1927 that Hauptmann had explained to him that the play was not at all as Shakespeare intended:

> In his view copyists were responsible for utterly distorting the fourth and fifth acts of the play as originally conceived by Shakespeare. He proceeded to describe to me the alterations he has undertaken … . The key-point, he said, is that he makes Hamlet, not Laertes, responsible for the uprising against Claudius. It is Hamlet, not Laertes, who speaks the words, "Oh thou vile king, give to me my father." Hamlet has struck up an alliance with Fortinbras and returns with him to Denmark to avenge his parent and reconquer his inheritance. This is the only way to render the last two acts intelligible and it frees Hamlet from the appearance of being no more than a spineless procrastinator and argumentative dabbler. Goethe came close to appreciating the switch which occurred in the roles of Laertes and Hamlet, but he did not take the point to its logical conclusion. I was much impressed by Hauptmann's arguments and I believe that he may well be right.[13]

On more mature consideration, Kessler stopped short of including Hauptmann's most radical revisions; the fourth and fifth acts are relatively undisturbed, and the German Hamlet remains as spineless a procrastinator as he is in English. (Schlegel's version itself, however, was not unproblematic: it moves the "To be or not to be" soliloquy to the fifth act.) For the English edition, J. Dover Wilson prepared a more straightforward text based on the second quarto – not, significantly, a conflation of the quarto and folio, which regularly constituted the "complete" English text in the period.

Craig provided seventy-two woodcuts for the German edition and five additional ones for the English version. The deployment of these on the page resembles more the format of the *Nuremberg Chronicle* than any illustrated scholarly edition of drama: the images are not contained by the typography, but are in full partnership with it, and sometimes seem even in control (figures 7.1–7.2). Hamlet and Horatio await the ghost, dwarfed by a setting composed of a combination of Craig's woodcut screens, Shakespeare's text and Saxo's chronicle. Throughout the book, Craig's images are superbly attuned to the play's changes of mood. Several of the woodcuts had to be printed in two stages, to register lighter and darker blacks. For the play scene, a cast of *commedia dell'arte* characters in black silhouette appears in various formats – free-standing across the bottom margin, within whole scenes incised with white on black and gray backgrounds, in a tiny roundel in the center of a page, and, most startling, for the Dumb Show, two elaborately masked and costumed silhouettes replacing the central text on facing pages, with the description of

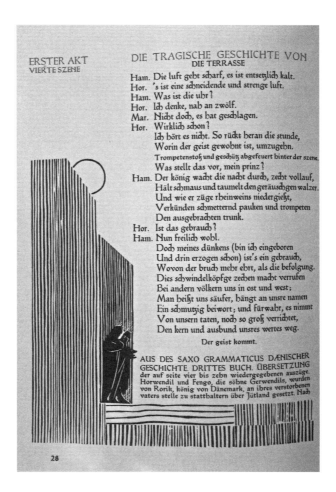

7.1 Hamlet and Horatio await the Ghost. Cranach Press *Hamlet*, 1927, p. 28.

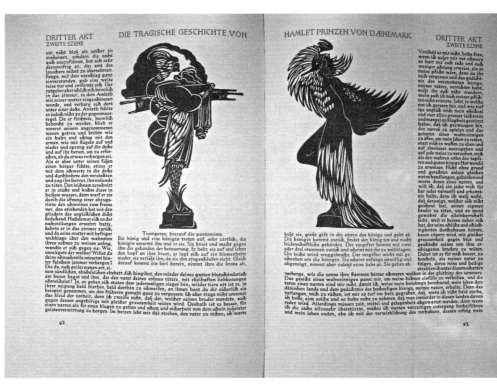

7.2 The Dumb Show. Cranach Press *Hamlet*, pp. 92–3.

the pantomime printed in red beneath them. Ophelia's last appearance is as a
tiny white waiflike form within a grid of pale blue, flanked by two of Craig's
massive black woodcut screens, with a silhouetted mob beyond them – this is
the only use of color in the woodcuts, and it is tremendously affecting. There
is no illustrated Shakespeare in which the images are so thoroughly integrated
with the typography, and in which text, book and performance are conceived
so completely as a whole. The Cranach Press *Hamlet* undertakes to rethink
the relation of drama, book and image – in short, the nature of dramatic
representation on the page – from the beginning; it reconceives the book of
the play as a performance and completes the play as a book.

But of course there can always be more. Kenneth Branagh's 1996 film was
gigantic in every way. It ran more than four hours and filled the screen with
sumptuously costumed extras, and in addition to including all the dialogue
of a conflated text, filled in blanks that even Hauptmann had not noticed.
Battles that are merely referred to are staged in full; court scenes seem to be

attended by the entire population of Lichtenstein. When Polonius instructs Ophelia to return Hamlet's love letters, there are intercut scenes of Hamlet and Ophelia naked in bed making love – it is unclear whether these are flashbacks, or represent Polonius's unfounded fears or Ophelia's unrealized desires: more unanswered questions. During the Player's speech about the rugged Pyrrhus, roles are written in for Priam and Hecuba (cameo appearances by Gielgud and Dench); we see both Old Norway and Yorick ... there can always be more. And, of course, there can also always be less: Zeffirelli's *Hamlet*, with Mel Gibson cast as an action hero, wonderfully cut "To be or not to be...," the one thing you thought you could be sure of.

Notes

1 C. M. Ingelby et al., *The Shakespere Allusion Book*, revised edition (London, 1932), vol. 1, pp. 56, 133.

2 John Dryden, from the preface to his adaptation of *Troilus and Cressida* (1679), b2v.

3 Helen Phelps Bailey, *Hamlet in France* (Geneva, 1964), p. 12.

4 Samuel Johnson, *Johnson on Shakespeare, ed. Walter Raleigh* (London, 1929), p. 196.

5 Samuel Johnson, *Lectures and Notes on Shakspere and Other English Poets* (London, 1904), p. 343.

6 Ibid., p. 344.

7 See T. S. Eliot, "Hamlet and His Problems," in *The Sacred Wood* (London, 1920). The term was first used by Washington Allston in the 1840s to describe the relation of the mind to external reality; see the Introductory Discourse to his *Lectures on Art* (New York, 1850).

8 Originally published as Ernest Jones, "The Oedipus-Complex as An Explanation of Hamlet's Mystery: A Study in Motive," *The American Journal of Psychology*, vol. 21, no. 1 (January, 1910): 72–113; subsequently expanded as *Hamlet and Oedipus* (London, 1949).

9 Margreta de Grazia, *Hamlet Without Hamlet* (Cambridge, 2007).

10 There are two editions recording the four versions: *Hamlet*, Paris, 1770, and the collected *Oeuvres*, 3 vols. Paris, 1812 (*Hamlet* is in vol. 1).

11 In the Arden 3 *Hamlet, The Texts of 1603 and 1623* (ed. Ann Thompson and Neil Taylor, Thomson, 2006), scene 11, lines 85–6 (p. 134). The added scene between Horatio and Gertrude is scene 14.

12 Shakespeare, *Hamlet* (Weimar: Cranach Presse, 1929 and 1930).

13 Harry Kessler, *Berlin in Lights, The Diaries of Count Harry Kessler*, trans. and ed. Charles Kessler (New York, 1999), pp. 318–20.

Part III

Books

8

Open secrets

I begin with some bits of household advice from the sixteenth century. The first group comes from a volume called *A Thousand Notable things, of sundry sortes. Whereof some are wonderfull, some straunge, some pleasant, divers necessary, a great sort profitable and many very precious*, collected by Thomas Lupton, published in London in 1579, and many times thereafter.

> The root of peony, which is the herb of the sun, being pulled out of the earth on a Sunday, in the hour of the sun, the sun then being in Leo, called the Lion: and the Moon increasing in light (which is from her change to the full) delivereth them of the falling sickness that bear it upon them. (pp. 85–6)

The authority cited is Ficino. Many writers in the period ascribe similar properties to the peony – Joshua Sylvester agrees with Ficino that it cures epilepsy, Sir Thomas Elyot says it purges choler. It is generally claimed to have a calmative effect. What is notable in Lupton's account, however, are the calendrical and astrological imperatives: these are essential to the herb's medicinal potency.

Here is another remedy involving the peony:

> The professors of natural magic affirm that vervein (=verbena) being taken up or gathered when the sun is in Aries, the Ram, and stamped with the seeds of peony, and strained with white wine, and drunk, doth marvelously heal them that have the falling sickness. (p. 84)

Verbena had many uses in early modern pharmacology; as a styptic, an eye balm, even a snake repellent. Its effectiveness against epilepsy here would seem to derive from its decoction in combination with peony. A crucial element, however, is once again the astrological moment. The authority cited this time is Mizaldus, or Antoine Mizault, the contemporary French astronomer and physician: "Oftentimes proved, saith Mizaldus." The combined practice of astronomy and medicine would seem to constitute sufficient authority in such a matter; however, it is not Mizaldus's practical expertise that is critical here, but his own reliance on prior authority – Lupton's account concludes, "Which he had out of a very old book of the seven herbs of the planets, written to Hermes." What is expert about Mizaldus's testimony to the remedy's effectiveness, "oftentimes proved," is the antiquity of his reference book, and its association with the magical name of Hermes Trismegistus.

In Lupton's remedies, the utility of astrology in the treatment of sickness is exceedingly broad. On the one hand, it determines the critical juncture, from the very moment of gathering the herbs, on which success depends. On the other, it renders all the efforts of skill or magic pointless:

> If at the time of the first falling sick of one, or at the time of a question for the sick, if the moon be in the fourth house with Mars, and good planets be cadent, it is sign of death. (p. 86)

This disheartening piece of expertise comes from Johannus Ganivetus's fifteenth-century *Amicus Medicorum* – friendly advice to the physician, presumably, not even to bother treating the patient.

If astrology offered a universal guide, witchcraft was a universal danger. My next citation comes from the *Secreti d'Alessio*, a very popular handbook of domestic economy by Giralomo Ruscelli, first published in Venice in 1538, and in many subsequent editions; and in English translation in various partial versions starting in 1558 as *The Secrets of Alexis*. A collected edition appeared in 1595; my quotation comes from what is claimed as the first complete English edition, published in London in 1615.

> To be assured and safe from all sorcery and enchantment.
> Take squilla [a bulb of the onion family], and tie it upon the principal gate or door of your house, and you shall assure all the inhabitants in it from sorcery and enchantments: and this squilla assureth and keepeth all plants and trees that are about the house where it is planted or set from all noisomeness and infection of the air. (Fol. 145r)

An all-purpose prophylactic, to be sure, rather like what is claimed for *feng shui* now. Still, *feng shui* is said to require a certain expertise. What is striking about Alexis's secret is how simple it is to keep oneself safe from the universal threat of witchcraft. On the other hand, in case the preventative fails, or hasn't

Yſ one be bewytched of any, put quyckſpluer into a 4
qupll and ſtoppe it, oꝛ els into a hollowe Nut ſhel,
encloſed faſt with wace : and lape the ſame vnder
the pyllowe of the partpe bewytched ; oꝛ vnder the
thꝛeſhold of the dooꝛe where he enters into the houſe
oꝛ Chamber. Iohannes Weckerus.

.1 "To put away witcheries," Thomas Lupton's *A Thousand Notable Things*, 1579, p. 163.

been installed in time, Lupton's *Thousand Notable Things* has a remedy for
the effects of sorcery (Figure 8.1).

> If one be bewitched of any, put quicksilver into a quill and stop it, or else
> into a hollow nutshell enclosed fast with wax, and lay the same under
> the pillow of the party bewitched, or under the threshold of the door
> where he enters the house or chamber. (p. 163)

An early owner of my copy of the book found this item especially useful,
glossing it "To put away witcheries," and marking it "Nota," suggesting that
the effects of witchcraft were a constant problem.

The reason I am starting with these recipes is to indicate the utter
commonplaceness of magic in the period. This is a point that has been made
exhaustively by Keith Thomas in his magisterial, essential, *Religion and the
Decline of Magic*; but I want here to offer some qualifications to Thomas's
account, and to examine some of its implications that cast a number of familiar
literary texts in an unfamiliar light. To begin with, it is important to note that
none of my examples supports Thomas's general contention that magic always
worked in tandem with a good deal of religious apparatus – that in gathering
the herbs one made the sign of the cross, or recited the Paternoster or the
Ave Maria, or that the practitioner hung an amulet with prayers or Christian
symbols (or with these backward or in anagrams) around the patient's neck;
and that this was the essential element in the supposed potency of the cure.
Thomas claims, for example, that vervein had to be crossed and blessed
when it was gathered; but, as we have seen, this is not the case in Lupton's
pharmacopeia. What is most striking, in fact, about both my early modern
compilations is how overwhelmingly secular a system they imply – this despite

the fact that Lupton even includes a number of ways of determining whether somebody is possessed with devils: dealing with this issue does not even involve making the sign of the cross to protect oneself. *Secrets of Alexis*, to be sure, in a preface makes much of the omnipotence of God and the necessity of faith; but thereafter God and faith do not figure at all in the operation of the protections and cures. And Lupton's *Thousand Notable Things* does not make so much as a gesture toward the idea that its cures are faith-based: even in its dedication and introduction it presents itself as operating completely within the world of natural forces. A few times Lupton asserts the operation of God's providence in human affairs, but always as a way of affirming the truth of predictive astrology and the folly of trying to avoid the fate determined through it – prayer is recommended only as a means of reconciling oneself to one's horoscope.

The magical practice Keith Thomas describes also depends heavily on specialists – village wizards, cunning women, parallels and anti-types to priests or ministers on the one hand, who promised little, and the dubiously effective physicians on the other, who were, in any case, extremely scarce. Once again, Ruscelli and Lupton present quite a different picture. No specially endowed practitioner is required; the expertise involves no mystical component, whether religious or occult; and, perhaps most striking, the magical power, the secret knowledge, is transmitted simply by reading a commercially available book. To judge from the volumes' printing history and from individual copies, moreover, the claim was not an idle one. My copy of Lupton is heavily annotated throughout by a contemporary owner, with remedies he found particularly effective signalled (as the antidote to sorcery, cited above, is) with a marginal "Nota," or a pointing hand, and occasionally with some addition to the recipe – the book clearly got a great deal of use. And it continued to do so: it was reprinted numerous times throughout the sixteenth, seventeenth and eighteenth centuries, with three editions in the 1790s, and one published in Manchester as late as 1800. Ruscelli was translated into every European language; seventy-nine editions are known.

Part of the explanation for Ruscelli's and Lupton's effectiveness, of course, must lie in the difficulty of determining what constitutes a cure for the myriad ailments these works address. The remedy for the bewitched depends on being able to decide what constitutes being bewitched – no examples are offered. An extremely elaborate cure for headaches involves making a complex plaster and applying it to the sufferer for nine consecutive nights – the entry concludes, "This medicine never fails" (p. 166), and a marginal "Nota" presumably indicates the owner-sufferer's satisfaction even with so long a course of treatment. Similarly, an earache cure takes nine nights, and is declared "proved" (p. 228) – the mystical number nine is doubtless significant, though both cures are said sometimes to work sooner. Toothache cures, on the other hand, of which there are many, are all said to be immediate, which suggests a certain ambiguity in the concept of pain relief.

Magic in these compilations is about getting through ordinary life: keeping the house secure, knowing what to expect, doing something to make the distress of everyday existence more bearable. There are also, of course, much grander claims for magic in the period: the miraculous transformations of the enchanters in Ariosto, Tasso and Spenser, Prospero's power over the elements, John Dee's conversations with angels, Paracelsus's ability to produce life itself. But even stories like these have their mundane subtexts. The search for the philosopher's stone, for all its recondite implications about the unity of matter and its promise of the development of particle physics, is basically a search for a steady source of income; the fabled erotic sorcery of the multitude of Circe figures, Alcina, Armida, Acrasia, has in view not true love, but merely a steady supply of compliant sexual objects, and the outcome, even in the world of poetic romance, is generally unsatisfactory. This, however, is the view from outside; the practitioners, no matter how modest their successes, are always believers. John Dee was unable to understand a word his angelic messengers told him, but this had no effect on his faith in his art. Even in our sceptical age Stephen Greenblatt's similarly audacious project of speaking with the dead has eventuated only in a series of books on Shakespeare – which doubtless, for the author at least, have been validation enough.

Magic is always a disappointment, and always irresistible. In an essay on Marlowe called "Tobacco and Boys" I observed that, for all its admonitory aspects, *Doctor Faustus* would have functioned much more as a temptation than as a warning. Every audience, every reader, of this immensely popular morality play has felt that Faustus isn't ambitious enough, doesn't ask for the right things, doesn't really know what to ask for; that the play is under-imagined, and that any of us could do better, make the pact with the devil and get more out of it – or even get away with it, repent at the last minute. My colleague David Riggs, having resisted this claim of mine for many years, in his biography of Marlowe finally concurred: he observes of Faustus that "instead of scaring people away from magic, he drew them in," and cites the wonderful case of a medical student in Tübingen who used incantations from Johann Spies's *Faustbuch*, published in 1587 and Marlowe's immediate source, in an attempt to make a pact with the devil to pay off his debts. The mundane aspects of this dangerous transaction are especially striking. Or they ought to be; however, the only real danger in such cases came not from any diabolical visitors, but from the ecclesiastical authorities, since sorcerers like the impecunious medical student were bound to discover that the devil did not come when you called him, and it was only a small step beyond that to concluding that he did not exist at all. The Faust story, when used in this way, was more likely to produce atheists than believers.[1]

Nevertheless, considering the perilous quality of early modern life, Faustus's fantastic bargain is not an unattractive one. It is not about the promise of riches and power (which produce intoxicating fantasies in the play, but are really incidental); what it offers is control over one's own destiny for twenty-four years. Even for people with less hazardous careers than Marlowe's, the gamble – Pascal's wager in reverse – might have seemed well worth taking. Here is what I said about *Doctor Faustus* in "Tobacco and Boys": if Marlowe had made Faustus's deal he would have lived another twenty-four years, and died in 1617, the year after Shakespeare. Consider the life expectancy in this period: if you were male and made it past adolescence without succumbing to childhood diseases, plague and the multitude of perils incident to everyday living, you had a chance of reaching a reasonable age, which in the early seventeenth century was not the threescore and ten stipulated by the Word of God but anything over forty-five – Marlowe would have died at fifty-three, a year older than Shakespeare. Obviously it would have helped a lot if you could make a deal with the devil; it was clear you couldn't make one with God.

Faustus's ambitions are a good index to how far the promise of magic extended. Marlowe starts with a fantasy of unlimited desire and unlimited power to satisfy it. When Faustus summons Mephistophilis, he articulates a megalomaniac dream: to live in all voluptuousness, to be the emperor of the world, to control nature and the supernatural. This is what the diabolical deal promises him. But four scenes later, when his bad angel urges him to think on the wealth he can have, his eager reply is "The seignory of Emden shall be mine!" (A II.1.23)[2] – Emden is a rich commercial port; the dream is already a good deal less ambitious than ruling the world, and he hasn't even signed the bond yet. By the end of the same scene his voluptuousness has diminished significantly too: "let me have a wife, the fairest maid in Germany, for I am wanton and lascivious, and cannot live without a wife" (143–5). But Mephistophilis will not supply a wife – marriage is a sacrament. He instead proposes to bring Faustus the fairest courtesans in the world to sleep with. For a truly wanton and lascivious voluptuary this sounds like a much more attractive proposition than marriage, but Faustus doesn't even comment on it, and Mephistophilis effortlessly moves him on to what it turns out he really wants, books. The books are of incantations, astronomy and natural history: universal power is epitomized in the written word – the power is literacy; the pact with the devil is an allegory of Marlowe's own humanistic education, the search for the right books, Aristotle, Pliny, Hermes Trismegistus – or, for the less ambitious and educated, *The Secrets of Alexis*, *A Thousand Notable Things*.

If magic is power, what do you do with power in Marlowe's world? Faustus's initial instincts are altruistic. A good deal of the play's appeal is to English anti-Catholic sentiments. All the horseplay with the Pope is the other side of the ambition to build a wall of brass around Protestant Germany. The real English fear of the danger of Catholic power is disarmed by magic's ability to make fools of its audience. Faustus is, for a little while, a version of the Protestant hero. But where do the real ambitions lie? At the play's center, after all, is a confrontation with Catholic power itself in the person of the Holy Roman Emperor. The visit to Charles V ought to be a triumphant entry: Faustus has humiliated the Pope; he is more powerful than any earthly monarch. Why isn't this a scene of two emperors, either paying homage to each other or threatening each other? But Faustus appears instead as an entertainer, "The wonder of the world for magic art" (B IV.i.11), and from the sorcery materializes not a promise of infinite power but simply the phantom figures of Alexander the Great and his paramour – Marlowe's heroic drama reduced to a miniature pantomime.

Underlying all this is a striking sense of the limits of fantasy, of what, we might say, magic really can be expected to accomplish. Faustus comes to Charles V as John Dee came to the emperor of Hungary, not in triumph but as a petitioner, a supplicant. What he seeks is what Dee sought, a job in the Emperor's service – the dream of glory and power is finally only an upwardly mobile middle-class Elizabethan dream: Spenser's dream of a good civil service job or a place at court; Jonson's dream of the Mastership of the Revels; Donne's dream of a secretaryship to somebody, anybody, rich and important; not even Sidney's dream of political influence and independence.

Here then is the progression of fantasies: imperial power is almost immediately abandoned for money, and not even for what we would call "real money," all the gold in the New World or the riches of Asia, but something much more modest and localized, the commercial revenues of Emden. Women get short-circuited as soon as it turns out marriage is impossible – if marriage is impossible, so is sex: Faustus turns out to have the most conventional middle-class morals. There is no megalomaniac fantasy in this magic, nothing irregular or transgressive, not even Marlowe's interest in boys. The desire for books certainly shouldn't be a problem, but this too doesn't satisfy him; obviously there's got to be more to life than books. So the play starts over again, with less material ambitions: he wants to fly, to go to Rome, to be invisible, to humiliate the Pope. And then he wants, not to be emperor, but to *impress* the emperor, to get secure employment, to be noticed, successful, admired – by the middle of the play, at the point where, after all, Faustus is at the height of his powers, this is what magic can do for you: on the one hand not a great deal, but on the other hand (to be realistic) everything you could reasonably ask for.

It also, however, puts you in mortal danger, not for your soul but for your life. The greatest danger isn't damnation, it's human envy, the other upwardly mobile young men who are your competitors and resent your success. Running parallel with the dream of success, therefore, is necessarily a dream of invulnerability: the magic that damns you is also the only thing that can save you. You literally can't live without it. If it gets you damned, it nevertheless preserves you until you get there. But does it even necessarily lead to damnation? Faustus's friends Valdes and Cornelius, experienced conjurors who train him in the art, seem in no danger from the infernal powers. Is Faustus damned because he is the play's only believer?

Of course the essential point about Faustus's magic is that it is not really Faustus's. It depends on having Mephistophilis as his servant; and one way of accounting for the intense attractions of magic in early modern society is probably as the ultimate image of the servant class under complete control. This is certainly what magic is for Prospero in *The Tempest*: the storms and apparitions and spectacular transformations through which Shakespeare's magician brings his designs to fruition are, properly speaking, the work of Ariel, acting on his master's orders. What Prospero has is not magical power, but education, the liberal arts (literally, arts appropriate to a free man or gentleman); in short, the knowledge of how to keep Ariel and his army of spirits in servitude. It is a knowledge that works much less successfully on Prospero's other servant, Caliban, no doubt because he deals with the more prosaic daily tasks of providing food, keeping the fire going and washing up. Even magic has trouble getting this sort of work done – what any householder would recognize as "real" work. Jonson brilliantly deconstructs the assumptions behind such magical fantasies in *The Alchemist*, when the servants, left to their own devices, set themselves up precisely as magicians, and are implicitly believed, and duly con the neighborhood.

It is not accidental that the only thing Jonson's alchemists actually produce is a rich widow for the returning master to marry: the area of life in which claims of magic are most routinely invoked is love. "I must from this enchanting queen break off" – Antony's construction implies no actual sorcery on Cleopatra's part, but only that enchantment is the natural condition of erotic relationships, at least of those outside of marriage. For Pompey, however, it is precisely Cleopatra's magic that can be counted on to keep Antony out of the way:

all the charms of love,
Salt Cleopatra, soften thy waned lip!
Let witchcraft join with beauty, lust with both!
Tie up the libertine in a field of feasts,
Keep his brain fuming. (II.1.20–4)

The operation of witchcraft in love is here clearly a reciprocal matter, with Antony's lust the critical third term. As for breaking love's fetters, the antidotes to love are few, and tend to be ineffective. It is probably significant that, in love plots, it is almost always the woman whose magic is operative – Cleopatra is clearly as captivated by Antony as he is by her, but nobody proposes that she break his spell and get back to the business of ruling Egypt. Among male lovers, Othello is quite unusual in claiming to be in possession of some love magic himself, the "magic in the web" of the handkerchief that would – or as it turns out would not – bind him to his love (significantly, not bind her to him) forever. Spenser's enchanter Busirane, like Milton's Comus, can torture the objects of his passion, but seduction is beyond the power of masculine witchcraft. The Don Juans of the early modern world operate not with charms, but with charm, and testosterone, and they have, in addition, a great many very eager women to work with.

When love is literally represented as enchantment, the magic is generally treated allegorically or symbolically – as, for example, in the case of Isolde's love potion. Would she and Tristan not be in love without it? Why, indeed, is it there at all? If we take it literally, does it not cast doubt on the reality of the love, suggest that it's not "true" love? The case appears even more obvious in *A Midsummer Night's Dream*, where the juice of Oberon's "little western flower" produces instant infatuation with absolutely anyone, "the next live creature that it sees." But here the anti-literalist argument seems misguided. Both these plots imply that love can indeed be induced by magic, and that the love so induced is no less love than the love that arrives unassisted. Both are a part of nature; love itself is a kind of witchcraft. The case seems, oddly, especially clear in *A Midsummer Night's Dream*, despite the obvious triviality of the love plot: Puck's misapplication of the magical juice does certainly put the wrong Athenian lovers together; but, as we see at the play's opening, Demetrius has already transferred his affections from the right girl, Helena, to the wrong one, Hermia, who loves Lysander. Moreover, Titania has in the past been Theseus's lover, and Oberon has been Hippolyta's. With or without the magic flower, people change their affections, break their vows, fall in love with the wrong people or with people who don't love them. Titania's compelled passion for Bottom is only an extreme example of the normal situation. There is no difference whatever between the love induced by Isolde's potion and real love, just as there is no implication that when Demetrius is finally, through another application of the magic juice, induced to return to his first love Helena, this does not constitute a happy ending. Questions like what would have happened if Isolde had been given the potion on behalf of King Mark, the original plan, instead of sharing it with Tristan, are not exactly beside the point; they simply indicate the difference between tragedy and comedy, and the possibility of either as the culmination of any love plot.

There are no love potions in *Secrets of Alexis* or *A Thousand Notable Things*, though both books imply a relationship between men and women that would certainly render such a nostrum credible, especially given what constitutes evidence of success in, say, toothache and earache cures. A number of the recipes do relate to the problems of love, however. Remedies are given for impotence, including the impotence caused by witchcraft, a sufficiently attested condition to qualify as one of the very few legally acceptable grounds for divorce – in, for example, the notorious case of the Earl and Countess of Essex in 1613. Lupton's prescription is surprisingly simple: "If a married man be let or hindered through enchantment, sorcery or witchcraft from the act of generation, let him make water through his marriage ring, and he shall be loosed from the same ..." – my contemporary reader considers this useful enough to gloss it "to stay witchcraft" (p. 20). For the most part, however, Ruscelli and Lupton concern themselves with sexual failure as a general failure of the loins, whether from a lack of energy or from kidney problems. Ruscelli's remedy, a surprisingly simple one, is parsnips boiled with sugar, honey and various spices, and is said to produce "a marvelous effect" (fol. 336v).

Lupton has recipes for both assuaging and inducing lust, among them the following curious double-acting powder:

> If the piss of a bull that is all red be made in powder, and a dram thereof ... be given to a woman in a draught of wine, it will make her loath to have to do with a man .... And the same powder given in meet medicines to a man, doth contrary stir and make him have lust therein. (p. 19)

The puzzling practical applications of this potion are probably less its point than the evidence it purports to provide that women and men are opposites, and function by contraries. A significant number of the recipes in both books are concerned specifically with controlling women's appetites, sometimes, as in this one from Ruscelli, apparently quite pointlessly:

To make that a woman shall eat of nothing that is set upon the table.

Take a little green basil, and when men bring the dishes to the table, put it underneath them, that the woman perceive it not: for men say that she will eat of none of that which is in the dish whereunder the basil lieth. (Fol. 131r)

Men here are completely in control, not only bringing the food but giving the essential testimony to the effectiveness of the trick, the only purpose of which appears to be precisely to demonstrate control. Given the emphasis on control throughout both books, it is especially interesting how few of the remedies address the affective life. There are cures for melancholy, to be sure, but none to make a woman love you, or to keep your wife faithful, or to keep your husband from straying – none even to ensure that when you take any of the various lust-inducing potions the object of your passion will be receptive. These are very unromantic handbooks, concerned not with wish fulfillment, and certainly not with the art of the possible, but, within the social and cultural norms, with the art of the conceivable.

Even theatrical magic, as we have seen, had its mundane subtexts; but for the spectacular effects of sorcery one certainly went to theater. Love magic, indeed, figured prominently in attacks on the stage, which was regularly compared to Circe in its allure and danger. The fictions of playwrights, Stephen Gosson warned his readers in *The School of Abuse*, were the cups of Circe. The magical power of Renaissance theater, its ability not merely to compel wonder in its audiences but to change them, whether for good or evil, by persuasion or seduction, is assumed by both attackers and defenders of the art, and Gosson's warning fully acknowledges both the danger of the stage and its irresistible attractiveness. When Prospero, near the end of *The Tempest*, renounces his magic with a speech adapted almost verbatim from Ovid's Medea, the evocation of witchcraft through the classic exemplar of a dangerously beautiful woman encapsulates the full range of Renaissance attitudes to the theatrical magician's powers. For John Rainoldes, "men are made adulterers and enemies of all chastity by coming to such plays,"[3] and Philip Stubbes notoriously particularized the erotic danger of theater:

Then these goodly pageants being ended, every mate sorts to his mate, every one brings another homeward of their way very friendly, and in their secret conclaves covertly they play the sodomites, or worse.[4]

If the vice worse than sodomy has no name, it is clear that for such observers there was no erotic possibility, not even the nameless ones, that theater did not encompass and promote. Perhaps this is why love potions were unnecessary, at least when the actors came to town.

Most magic plays, however, are in fact not concerned with love, but with power, subversion, mischief; above all, with the evocation of wonder. The wonder for the most part depended more on the imaginative complicity of the spectators than on the ingenuity of the performers – Philip Henslowe's theatrical properties included "a robe for to go invisible" that was obviously quite visible – but mysterious visions, ascents and descents, flying machines and transformation devices had been staples of theater almost from the beginning, and only the most naive would have been unaware that the magic in these was mechanics and sleight of hand. Nevertheless, the involvement of theater with diabolical sorcery – the assumption that it was real and dangerous magic – was a staple of anti-theatrical polemics. The fact is exemplified by a group of stories about *Doctor Faustus*. In one version, during a performance in Exeter, as Faustus was conjuring surrounded by a group of devils, the actors became aware that there was one devil too many, and stopped the play and fled from the town in fear for their lives and souls. In other less stylish versions of the story, Satan himself actually appeared during a performance. Such stories are part of the mythology of anti-theatricalism, intended to demonstrate how inherently profane and dangerous an amusement theater is; but they also indicate the extent to which theater was acknowledged to be in touch with an aspect of reality that was beyond rational control. They are stories that construe theater as magic, with *Doctor Faustus* as the paradigmatic instance.

By the early seventeenth century, doubtless largely in response to the new king's interests, witchcraft and the diabolical were especially good theater business. The magic plays that seem to have been prompted by *Macbeth* – a play about James's ancestry in which James himself is summoned up in a vision – give a good sense of what was commercially viable in theatrical magic at this time: Barnabe Barnes's *The Devil's Charter* was at the Globe in the same season as *Macbeth*, 1606, and Marston's *The Wonder of Women*, with its sorcery scenes, was at the Blackfriars. Jonson's antimasque of witches in *The Masque of Queens*, performed at court in 1609, inaugurated a decade of sorcery plays and masques, including *The Tempest*, *The Alchemist*, *The Witch*, *The Witch of Edmonton*, *The Devil is an Ass*, and the revived and revised *Doctor Faustus*. What was most attractive on the stage, evidently, was diabolical magic: only *The Tempest* and *The Alchemist* present secular magicians.

I have written about the intimate connection in King James's mind between kingship and witchcraft. Here I am summarizing material discussed in my book *Imagining Shakespeare*, in connection with *A Midsummer Night's Dream*. The king was convinced that from his earliest childhood a systematic conspiracy of witches directed by the devil had been at work against him. He attended witch trials, and conducted interrogations of the accused himself whenever possible. The outcomes, not surprisingly, always confirmed his belief. He made himself an expert on witchcraft, and when he came to the English throne the two works he published to introduce himself to his new subjects were the *Basilicon Doron*, his philosophy of kingship, and his dialogue *Daemonology*, a treatise on witchcraft. He is what might be called sceptically credulous: though he found the practice of witchcraft widespread, he argued that those who thought themselves witches were deceived. Their mischief and marvels were the work not of their spells, but of the devil, a means of persuading them to give him their souls – this is essentially Marlowe's version of sorcery in *Doctor Faustus*.

English readers had already learned of the king's involvement in the subject through a pamphlet called *Newes From Scotland*, published in 1592. Three cases of witchcraft are described, all highly theatrical. In one, a servant girl is found to possess miraculous healing powers. Though the magic seems entirely benign, her master fears her abilities are unlawful, and under torture she confesses to being a witch, and to prove the point performs a witches' dance for the investigators, "playing … upon a small trump." (One of the most striking aspects of all these cases is the insistence of the defendants on demonstrating their guilt.) The case was duly reported to King James:

> These confessions made the king in a wonderful admiration, and sent for the said Geillis Duncane, who upon the like trump did play the said dance before the king's majesty, who in respect of the strangeness of these matters, took great delight.[5]

The association of witchcraft with theater is all but explicit here.

The second case is summarized in *Jonson and the Amazons* (see pages 65–6): the witch Agnis Tompson claimed that she had been commanded by the devil to kill the king and had raised the storms that had prevented James's bride Anne of Denmark from coming to Scotland. Tompson's schemes had failed only because of the king's invincible faith. Figure 8.2 is the illustration that accompanies the account of this case: at the left, the devil dictates instructions for a group of witches to a scribe; the two incapacitated gentlemen at the lower and middle right have been bewitched; above right, the witches stir a cauldron, which causes the sinking of the ship at the upper left. The king was an active participant in this trial: the witch, faced with the royal skepticism, whispered to the king the secrets of his wedding night, and he authenticated her testimony. Like Henry VIII insisting on his own cuckoldry, James became the witness to the vitiation of his marriage. I have observed that James's fascination with witchcraft is obviously related to his general distrust of women, and his very public attachment to young men – the domestication, in his psychic drama, of Oberon's compulsive pursuit, in *A Midsummer Night's Dream*, of the lovely Indian boy.

The third, and most theatrical, case concerns a schoolmaster named John Cunningham, also called Dr. Fian, under which name he was "a notable sorcerer." Cunningham took a fancy to a girl who, however, rejected his advances. He undertook to make her love him through sorcery, and persuaded her brother to "obtain for him three hairs of his sister's privities." But as the boy was attempting to fulfill his promise on the sleeping girl, she awoke. The scheme was revealed to their mother, who was a witch herself, and she substituted for her daughter's hair three hairs from the udder of a young cow. These were brought to the sorcerer, who then "wrought his art upon them," and immediately

8.2 Witchcraft in action. *Newes from Scotland*, 1592.

8.3 Dr. Fian and the devil. *Newes from Scotland*, 1592.

the cow whose hairs they were indeed came unto the door of the church wherein the schoolmaster was, ... and made towards the schoolmaster, leaping and dancing upon him, and following him forth of the church and to what place soever he went, to the great admiration of all the townsmen ... . (pp. 21–3)

In the illustration in Figure 8.3, Fian conjures with a magic circle above, and is approached by the cow; below he rides behind the devil on a black horse. The trope of Oberon's little western flower is domesticated, naturalized, and explicitly sexualized here – the magic of irresistible erotic attraction now lies in the female "privities." But except for the reversal of the sexes, the fantasy remains that of Oberon, Titania and Bottom: the witch mother punishes the lascivious Fian by inventing a preposterous love affair with an animal, and the spectacle of the bestial romance provides the town with a piece of popular theater parallelling the courtly love of the Fairy Queen and an ass.

The perennial question of what kind of magic Prospero practices – black or white, neoplatonic philosophy, Baconian science – is misguided. The model for what he practices is theater. His resources and repertoire include a troupe of actors, flying machines, thunder and lightning, disappearing banquets, mysterious music, ascents and descents, a masque of goddesses, even a closet full of costumes, the glittering apparel that proves so fatally attractive to Stephano and Trinculo. Prospero the magician has been, historically, one of Shakespeare's most compelling creations, a figure who, like Hamlet and Falstaff, seems to have a life outside the confines of his play. The play itself prompts this, as Prospero, in his epilogue, entreats us to send him back to Italy through the help of our applause so that he may continue his story without us. Through his agency we have become the magicians, and the crucial act of magic is to bring the play to a successful conclusion. Since the early nineteenth century, when Edmond Malone declared *The Tempest* to be Shakespeare's last play, our applause has also brought Shakespeare's career to an end, and thereby turned Prospero into a piece of Shakespearean autobiography, the playwright's farewell to the stage, with Prospero's magic an allegory for the playwright's craft, Shakespeare's summary of and commentary on his theatrical career.

But magic in *The Tempest* is a profoundly ambivalent art. If it is empiricism, knowledge, science, the liberal arts, it is also dangerously narcissistic – Prospero himself blames his philosophical pursuits for his dereliction of duty as a ruler. In this view, magic is not a source of power but a retreat from it; and the return to Milan and the reassumption of his dukedom require the renunciation of the art. The darkest view of magic is also to be found in the play, in the figure of Sycorax, that ghostly memory of Ariel's recounted to Prospero, which remains so intensely present in Prospero's mind, so vividly summoned up in his rage against Caliban and Antonio, the perverse, irrational, violent, malicious, vindictive principle in nature, progenitor of monsters, lover and agent of the devil on earth. The theatrical is also the anti-theatrical; illusion is both pleasure and deception, delight and danger; the masque, the culminating display of the magician at the height of his powers, is also merely "some vanity of mine art." But in fact the drowning of the book and the breaking of the staff at the play's end do not consign Prospero and us to a world without magic. They return us to the world of *A Thousand Notable Things* and *Secrets of Alexis*, in which magic is everywhere, and everyone practices it.

Notes

1   David Riggs, *The World of Christopher Marlowe* (London, 2004), p. 235.

2   Quotations are from the parallel texts edited by W.W. Greg, *Marlowe's Doctor Faustus 1604–1616* (Oxford, 1950). In citations, A is the 1604 text, B the 1616 text.

3   John Rainoldes, *Th'Overthrow of Stage Plays* (Middleburgh, 1599), p. 18.

4   Philip Stubbes, *The Anatomy of Abuses*, ed. Margaret Jane Kidnie (Tempe, AZ, 2002), p. 204.

5   James I, *Daemonologie and Newes from Scotland*, ed. G. B. Harrison (London, 1924), p. 14. Quotations from this text are modernized.

9

Textual icons: reading early modern illustrations

My essay is about certain problems with the metaphor of books as early modern computers, as ways of storing, accessing and processing information. I focus on a particular kind of evidence, illustrations, and ask what kind of information they contribute to or encode in books, and what is revealed when we turn our early modern search engines on them. Illustrations in early modern books serve a wide variety of functions, and none of these are simple. Sometimes, as in scientific texts, they are essential explanatory devices; but even in these cases the pictures are rarely merely explanatory. They share with the imagery of narrative and discursive works a dimension that ranges from the decorative to the dramatic and symbolic – they are one way of making the Renaissance computer appear user-friendly. The practice of book illustration has been most fruitfully treated in the context of the history of printing, but it is an aspect of the history of reading too, and that is what I will be considering here. I am concerned not with cases in which pictures and text complement and elucidate each other – these have been frequently discussed – but with a number of counter-examples, which strike me as equally characteristic: a group of cases in which the pictures are clearly designed to constitute an address to the purchaser and reader, an attraction, whether as embellishment or elucidation, but in which they seem, nevertheless, entirely dysfunctional – illogical, inappropriate or simply wrong.

Early modern book illustration is rarely straightforward. Even the early iconologies – of Vincenzo Cartari, Cesare Ripa, Pierio Valeriano, the Hieroglyphs of Horapollo – were, in their earliest editions, not illustrated. Here pictures would seem to be of the essence; but printed iconology was initially conceived as an ekphrastic enterprise. On the other hand, in the history of printing, the illustrated book is as old as the book itself. Woodblock books, such as the *Biblia Pauperum*, employed pictures to epitomize, recall and even control the interpretation of the scriptural histories. In this context, the image is not an adjunct to anything; but neither is it the primary mode of communication. In a characteristic example, the Crucifixion will be flanked by the betrayal of Joseph by his brothers, and Jonah being thrown overboard in the storm. The disposition and juxtaposition of imagery provide a critical commentary on the matter of sacred history, but the pictures will make no sense to a viewer unfamiliar with the biblical stories, and even for that reader the relation of the images to each other must be explained – the pictures, that is, depend on narration and explication. It has been claimed that block books were designed for illiterate or unsophisticated readers, but exactly the opposite must be true: they require the most detailed knowledge not only of the scriptures, but of the principles of biblical exegesis.

The emblem provides an analogous case: emblem books are often cited as examples of the primacy of the image, or at least of the indivisibility of the image and the word. But historically this is not correct: Andrea Alciato, the inventor of the form, defined the emblem as a visual epigram; the book as he conceived it was not intended to include pictures, and the first emblems circulated in manuscript were not illustrated. The pictures were added by the German publisher of the first printed edition, who thought they would make the book more attractive; and even in later years, when emblems were invariably illustrated, the form was always conceived to be ekphrastic. The image, that is, always requires elucidation. In iconologies the crucial innovation, then, would be the invention of the caption, whereby the image stands by itself, an epitome of the text but also independent of it: to understand the mysterious image in figure 9.1, from a 1571 Cartari, one has to search quite a lot of text; whereas the same imagery in the edition of 1616 (figure 9.2) has been made self-explanatory by the caption – but even here the text cannot be read while viewing the picture: the page is designed so that the caption is upright; to compare the image the book must be turned.

I am not concerned here with images that primarily convey information – in herbals, treatises on fortification, anatomies and the like (and even these often turn out to be less simply informative than they appear) – but with imagery as part of the rhetoric of the book, those graphics that will, even when nothing is wrong with them, only confuse our computer's search engine. I begin where books have begun since late incunabular times, with title pages, and with a straightforward example, which does seem to work the way we would expect it to do. Figure 9.3, the famous title page to Jonson's *Workes*, 1616, constitutes a genuine collaboration between William Hole, the artist, and Jonson, the author. A triumphal arch frames the title, in Roman capitals, and the author's name, in a calligraphic italic. On either side stand

9.1 Hercules, from Vincenzo Cartari, *Imagini de i Dei de gli Antichi*, Venice, 1571.

9.2 Hercules, from Vincenzo Cartari, *Vere e Nove Imagini*, Padua, 1616.

the figures of Tragedy and Comedy; above, the third of the classic genres, the satiric or pastoral is anatomized into the figures of satyr and shepherd. Between them is a Roman theater; above this stands Tragicomedy, flanked by the tiny figures of Bacchus and Apollo, patrons of ecstatic and rational theater respectively. On the base of the arch are two scenes illustrating the ancient sources of drama, the *plaustrum*, or cart of Thespis, with the sacrificial goat, the tragedian's prize, tethered to it, and an amphitheater with a choric dance in progress. The figures participating in both these originary scenes, however, in contrast to the classic figures above, are in modern dress – they are Jonson himself and his contemporaries.

This is a title page that is specifically designed for this book, a visual summary of Jonson's sense of his art, defining drama in relation to its history and its kinds, and postulating a set of generic possibilities. Visually, this is how Jonson presents himself, not with his own image – the book does not include a portrait. Figure 9.4, Robert Vaughan's engraved portrait of Jonson, issued

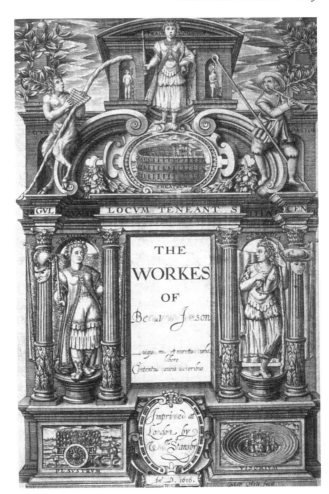

9.3 William Hole, title page to Ben Jonson, *Workes*, 1616.

in 1626, was first included in the posthumous 1640 edition of *An Execration against Vulcan* and in the first volume of the 1640 collected Jonson; it was re-engraved for the third folio of 1692. It was not until the late eighteenth century that bibliophiles began adding it to the 1616 folio, usually as a way of completing an elaborate rebinding: there are no early bindings that include the portrait, and these copies of the first folio are therefore essentially imitating the posthumous second and third folios. In 1623, when Jonson introduced the Shakespeare folio with its title-page portrait, he significantly urged the reader to 'looke/ Not on his picture, but his Booke.'

The Jonson title page is is a case where the Renaissance computer in its graphics mode really does tell us things we need to know about the text. The

9.4 Robert Vaughan, engraved portrait of Ben Jonson, c. 1626, frontispiece to Volume I of the 1640 *Workes*.

engraving would make no sense in any other book. It was not even used in the posthumous second volume, published in 1640, where it would certainly still have been appropriate. I turn now to an equally straightforward case in figure 9.5, the title page of William Cunningham's *The Cosmographical Glasse*, 1559. This is a book about cosmography, cartography and navigation, and the design both epitomizes and historicizes the work. At the top are three symbolic representations of time in relation to human life: Saturn, as Kronos/Chronos, personifies Time (the goat legs have never been explained, and are apparently unparalleled: I suggest that they constitute the same sort of etymological pun as Kronos/Chronos, fancifully etymologizing Saturn from satyr); he leads the progression of mankind from childhood to maturity to old age. He is flanked on either side by sun and moon, day and night, including figures of youth

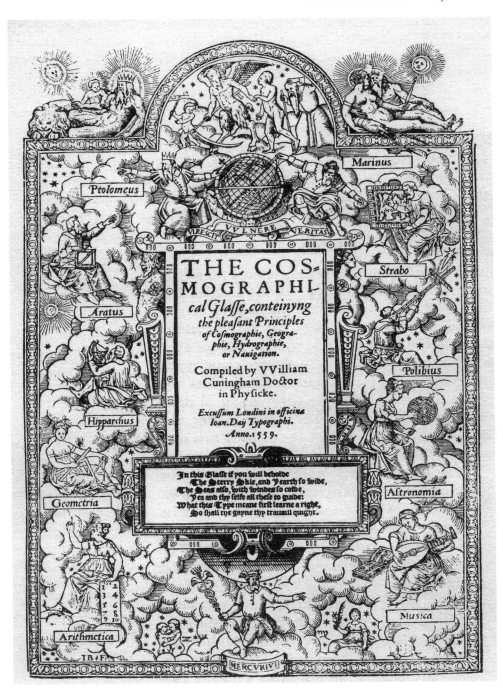

9.5 I. B., title page to William Cunningham, *The Cosmographical Glasse*, 1559.

and age, earth and sea. Below these are depicted famous ancient geographers and astronomers. At the bottom, around Mercury, patron of scholars, the quadrivium is anatomized in the figures of Geometry, Astronomy, Arithmetic and Music.

This title page was designed for John Day, the publisher, possibly by the woodcut artist John Bettes (it is signed I. B.). It is comprehensive and specific, quite as specific to this book as William Hole's title page is to Jonson's, and equally difficult to imagine in any other context. And yet over the next sixty years it reappears as the title page to an astonishing variety of other books. Day himself used it again only a year later, in 1560, for the *Works* of Thomas Becon, the Protestant divine, to which it has no conceivable relevance. Thereafter he used it in 1564 for a commentary on the book of Judges, in 1570 for a Euclid, in 1572 for a volume on British ecclesiastical antiquities and in 1574 for the Acts of King Alfred. The woodcut then migrated to the printing house of Peter Short, who between 1597 and 1603 used it for books of airs by Dowland and Rosseter, and for Morley's *Introduction to Practical Music* – the woodcut does, at least, have the tiny figure of Musica personified in the lower right-hand corner. It was then owned by Matthew Lownes, Short's son-in-law and heir, who used it in 1605 for the fourth edition of Sidney's *Arcadia* (figure 9.6), and again in the same year for Sternhold and Hopkins's *Psalms*. Between 1606 and 1613 Matthew's brother Humphrey Lownes used it three times for new editions of Dowland and Morley.

What does this mean – does it, indeed, mean anything? To begin with, the technology is a factor. As a woodcut, Day's cartouche is easily adaptable to the changing typography of new titles because woodcuts are printed on the press with the type. Engraved title pages like Jonson's must be printed separately, and changing their lettering involves re-engraving the plate. But all this means is that re-using a woodcut title page is technically simpler than re-using an engraved one: why did Day *want* to use this title for Becon, and the commentary on Judges, and the Acts of King Alfred; why did Lownes want it for Dowland, Morley, the psalms and Sidney? The term for this use of illustration is "disjunctive" – that is, unrelated to the text – and it is generally taken to reflect the quality of the printing house. Since it is obviously a way of saving money, it is argued, bad printers will tend to do it and good printers will not. This explanation begs all sorts of questions (why are irrelevant illustrations a way of selling badly printed books?), but it really will not explain this case at all: nobody has ever claimed that Day and Short and the Lowneses were bad printers. The basic point in all these instances seems to be simply that large expensive books need to have elaborate title pages, and these were on hand. The iconography is not critical, the elegance is. But then

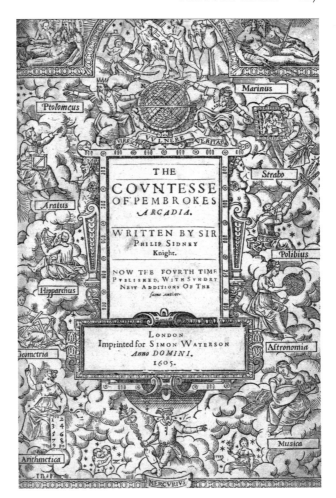

9.6 Philip Sidney, *The Countesse of Pembrokes Arcadia*, fourth edition, 1605, title page.

why commission symbolically specific title pages in the first place? Why not simply have a stock of decorative compartments? And did a 1559 title page not look awkwardly old-fashioned in 1613?

But on the other hand, is iconography really irrelevant? Here is another case, which appears to be a significant counter-example. Figure 9.7 is the title page for the second and third editions of Sidney's *Arcadia*, 1593 and 1598, the first folio editions. Its iconography relates it specifically both to the narrative and to Sidney himself. A shepherd and an Amazon flank the title: these are the heroes Mucidorus and Pyrocles in their romantic disguises as Dorus and Zelmane. Above them is a porcupine, the heraldic animal of Sidney's coat of arms. On either side are the lion and bear that, in an episode from Book 2, threaten the heroines Pamela and Philoclea, and from which the disguised heroes rescue them (the lion also figures in the Sidney arms, as the bear does in that of Sidney's uncle Leicester). The emblem below, a marjoram bush announcing to an approaching pig "Non tibi spiro", my scent is not for you, gives warning that the book is addressed only to readers of refinement.

Ponsonby used this title page twice for *Arcadia*, and three decades later, long after Ponsonby's death in 1603, it resurfaced in the seventh and ninth editions of the book – in the fourth edition, 1605, we have seen that Matthew Lownes was using the *Cosmographical Glasse* title page for *Arcadia*. In 1611 and 1617, however, Lownes used Ponsonby's title for the first folio editions of Spenser's works (figure 9.8); and here the association of Spenser with Sidney certainly makes sense: *The Shepherd's Calender* had been dedicated to Sidney; *The Faerie Queene* is the poem that responds most clearly to Sidney's precepts in *The Defence of Poesie*, and if we think of Colin Clout and Britomart, shepherds and martial women are as relevant to Spenser's epic as to Sidney's

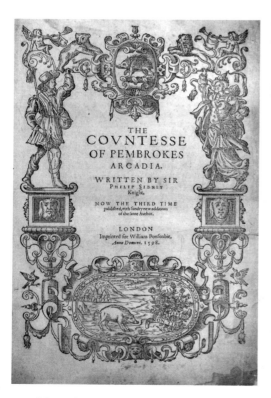

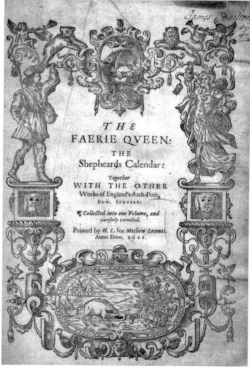

9.7 Philip Sidney, *The Countesse of Pembrokes Arcadia*, 1598, title page.

9.8 Edmund Spenser, *The Faerie Queen* and other works, 1611, title page.

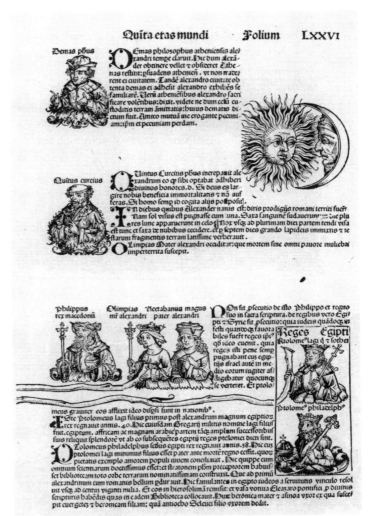

9.9 Hartmann Schedel, *Liber Cronicarum* (the Nuremburg Chronicle), 1493, portraits of ancient rulers.

romance. Sidney's coat of arms presides over Spenser's work as Sidney's writing was a model for the poet's endeavor.

But can we really conclude that the use of the title page here was deliberate? In 1595, between the second and third *Arcadia*s, Ponsonby himself used the title page for a translation of Machiavelli's *Florentine Historie*, and in 1625 Lownes was using it for an English Boccaccio. Ten years later Humphrey Moseley attached it to a translation of Giovanni Francesco Biondi's romance *La Donzella Desterrada, or the Banished Virgin*. Is the woodcut's relevance to Spenser perhaps mere coincidence? And even if Lownes intended it to relate Spenser to Sidney, did any readers make the connection? In short, how did readers read title pages? Given the arbitrary nature of so many examples, did they ever regard them as anything other than decorative? And what was the status of that very small number of title pages that really did supply information? Since I have no answers to these questions, I now move on into the body of the illustrated book, to the famous case of the Nuremberg Chronicle, the *Liber Cronicarum* of 1493. Every account of a city in this lavishly designed work has its accompanying woodcut, but, as has often been noted, many of these are simply generic cityscapes, some repeated up to eleven times. Critical attention since the late nineteenth century has focused almost exclusively on the cityscapes, but the book is not merely topographical. It also includes hundreds of portraits of famous people, mostly fanciful, such as those in figure 9.9, and of mythological figures, and scenes of legendary and historical events, and famous buildings; in all, 645 blocks are used 1809 times. The book is acknowledged to be a landmark in the history of printing, but the generic cityscapes have been a stumbling block, a touchstone for how different the early modern reader was from us. The original readers of the book, we are told, did not expect topographical verisimilitude, and would not have been bothered by the undifferentiated woodcuts, but would have interpreted them simply to mean, as A. Hyatt Mayor puts it, "here you can read of a city."[1]

The trouble is that while many of the cityscapes are generic, many others are not: the representations of Venice (figure 9.10), Rome, Florence, Constantinople, and the major German cities, for example, are topographically recognizable; some even include architectural landmarks that are labeled. How did a reader who recognized Venice in this depiction of Venice decide that the

9.10 Nuremburg Chronicle, Venice.

9.11 Nuremburg Chronicle, Marseilles.

9.12 Nuremburg Chronicle, Athens.

representation of Marseilles in figure 9.11 was generic? It looks quite specific, including a domed building topped by a crescent moon – one would call it a mosque, except for the cross atop the apse – and a column bearing what appears to be the statue of a devil. Only when we find the same woodcut used for Trier, Padua, Metz and Nicaea do we become aware that the image is generic, not specific. The cityscapes, moreover, are not even limited to the depiction of cities; they do service for whole regions as well. The woodcut of Athens in figure 9.12, which also represents Pavia, Alexandria, and the capital of the kingdom of the Amazons, illustrates Austria, Prussia and the Roman province of Carinthia; that of Marseilles, Trier and so on, is also Lithuania; Damascus serves for Macedonia, Spain and the province of Hesse.

Readers were, in short, not being told "here you can read of a city," and the line between the particular and the general was much fuzzier than it is for us – the imagined generic looks very much like the particular. The modern focus on the topographical woodcuts, moreover, misrepresents the book: it is, as I have said, not primarily topographical, it is iconologic; that is, *everything* is illustrated, and arguments about specificity and generalization focus too narrowly on subject matter. The most obvious quality of the Chronicle is the overwhelming number and disposition of its illustrations; and perhaps this is the point: not to signal us that we are reading about cities, but a signal precisely that the book is overwhelmingly illustrated, that typography can produce books that are as lavishly illustrated as the most beautiful manuscripts – that, as with manuscripts, imagery is an essential component of the look of the page, whatever the subject matter. In fact, the integration of type and woodcuts is astonishing in this book – in figure 9.13, Strasbourg cathedral towers into the typography, and the townscape ignores the page margins. Such examples indicate not only how closely printing depended on the manuscript tradition at this period, but even more how insistent the early printers were to declare their control of the new technology, and especially their independence of its constraints. The fact that in this book everything is illustrated, that is, makes an assertion not about the look of everything, but about the art of the book.

Such an argument separates the book's technology from its subject matter, or even makes the book a "metabiblos," its own subject matter. The repetition of illustrations strikes us as inept, an index to the inadequacies of early printing, though in terms of design it might actually be considered a virtue. That it was at least considered an available visual convention is clear from one of the most extraordinary pieces of early English book illustration, John Heywood's *The Spider and the Flie*, 1556, with astonishing woodcuts by an unknown artist. These play on the idea of identity and repetition, with changes so slight that the work of reading is also a work of detailed visual analysis. The

13 Nuremburg Chronicle, the city of Argentina (i.e. Strasbourg).

three images in figure 9.14 are consecutive, though separated from each other by several pages; it requires a good deal of flipping back and forth to realize that they are not, in fact, identical. Numerous other images in the volume, on the other hand, are identical; the point is clearly to make the transformations look as much as possible like the repetitions.

But now consider a different kind of example. In 1517 the Roman printer Giacomo Mazzocchi published a volume of portraits of famous ancients derived from his own coin collection; the book is discussed in an essay by Sean Keilen, who called it to my attention.[2] Each woodcut is provided with a brief biography by the distinguished historian of Roman antiquities Andrea Fulvio. The book, entitled simply *Illustrium Imagines*, appeared under a draconian license from Pope Leo X threatening anyone anywhere in the world who published a competing volume "in the same or larger type" with excommunication – the relation between typography and heresy here is notable; so is the implication that the actionable element is the size of the type.

9.14 Three consecutive woodcuts in John Heywood's *The Spider and the Flie*, 1556.

The collection is systematic only in that it is roughly chronological and groups members of the same family together. All the figures are historical with the exception of Janus, who appropriately begins the book, and all are Roman with the exception of Alexander the Great and Cleopatra. Not all emperors are present, however, and there is no attempt to fill in the blanks, or to make the iconology comprehensive. The book gives the impression of a real coin collection, though only the obverses, showing the illustrious faces, are recorded, and, while the profiles are in fact quite accurate, the woodcuts nevertheless show what we might call a certain negotiation with verisimilitude. For example, the Alexander portrait in figure 9.15 is certainly based on a coin of Alexander, much elaborated, but on real Alexander coins his name is on the reverse, not the obverse, and of course in Greek. The armed head, moreover, is a portrait of Athena, not the emperor – though Mazzocchi would not have been aware of this: it was taken to be a portrait of Alexander until the eighteenth century. But the book contains three striking anomalies. Julius Caesar is grouped with various members of his family, including four wives: Cornelia, Pompeia (these two are shown in figure 9.16), Calpurnia and Cossutia. Now Cossutia was not in fact Caesar's wife. According to Suetonius, she was engaged to him, but the engagement was terminated in favor of a more politically advantageous marriage to Cinna's daughter Cornelia, who became Caesar's first wife: this is laconically explained in Cossutia's caption. Nevertheless, coins were issued by both Cossutia's family and Caesar's describing her anticipatorily as "Uxor Caesaris" – hence, no doubt, the confusion. But Cossutia's picture, in figure 9.17, is blank. What does it mean? Perhaps that Mazzocchi knows such coins exist, but his collection does not include one. But then why include her at all? The collection as a whole is, as I say, neither systematic nor complete – and if

9.15 Alexander the Great, from Andrea Fulvio, *Illustrium Imagines*, Rome, 1517.

9.16 Cornelia and Pompeia, Caesar's wives, from Andrea Fulvio, *Illustrium Imagines*, Rome, 1517.

one were going to omit a wifely coin, Cossutia's would surely be the obvious candidate: she was not Caesar's wife. An ideal of numismatic completeness, however, is apparently being implied here, and, as Keilen shrewdly remarks, the blank portrait serves as evidence of the authenticity of the entire enterprise – Cossutia has been neither omitted nor invented. She is the exception that proves the rule.

9.17 Cossutia, Caesar's fiancée, from Andrea Fulvio, *Illustrium Imagines*, Rome, 1517.

Two other lacunae show the same scholarly tactics in reverse. The heads of Antonia Augusta and Plaudilla Augusta, in figures 9.18 and 9.19, are depicted, but without captions. Now both these names are problematic. The honorific Augusta stamps them as the wives of emperors, but no such empresses exist. Plaudilla should in fact be Plautilla: she is Fulvia Plautilla, the wife of Caracalla, called Plautilla Augusta on her coins – was Mazzocchi's example worn or otherwise partly illegible, and was she therefore unidentifiable? Antonia Augusta, however, is altogether anomalous – she is apparently the elder daughter of Mark Antony and Octavia: they had two daughters, both named Antonia, Antonia Maior and Antonia Iunior, and Antonia Iunior appears a few pages later. Antonia Maior was not an empress, but perhaps

9.18 Plaudilla Augusta, from Andrea Fulvio, *Illustrium Imagines*, Rome, 1517.

9.19 Antonia Augusta, from Andrea Fulvio, *Illustrium Imagines*, Rome, 1517.

she was called Augusta as the niece of Augustus; however, I can find no record of any coins bearing her portrait. In any case, Andrea Fulvio certainly recognized both her name and Plaudilla's as anomalies. Once again, both coins could simply have been omitted, but the lacunae testify to the project's scholarly integrity.

What happens next? In 1524, François Juste, in Lyons, published a new edition of *Illustrium imagines* – as it happens, in smaller type, perhaps to be on the safe side of excommunication. It follows the format of Mazzocchi's volume quite precisely, with one significant exception: while Plaudilla and Antonia remain unidentified, the space for Cossutia's picture is no longer empty (figure 9.20). It has been filled with the portrait of the emperor Claudius who, unbearded and boyish, looks feminine enough. As the Alexander/Athena coin indicates, however, gender in such cases was less significant than attributes.

9.20 Cossutia and Claudius, from Andrea Fulvio, *Illustrium Imagines*, Lyons, 1524.

The substitution of Claudius for Cossutia would have been impossible with the 1517 woodcut, in which Claudius is crowned; whereas his 1524 laurel wreath is equally suitable to Cossutia. Only Claudius's name poses a problem. In both my own copy and those of the Harvard and Newberry libraries, and I assume therefore in all, it has been obliterated with printer's ink, apparently by hand, and in the printing house – the woodcut itself could not simply be altered, since it had to be used again for Claudius. *Illustrium Imagines* has here ceased to be a coin collection, a record of images drawn from the material remains of the past, and has become an iconology, fanciful when necessary; and, as in the Nuremberg Chronicle, everything, even the missing things, is illustrated.

And now the third step: starting in 1525 and extending into the 1550s the Strasbourg printer Johann Huttich issued a series of new editions of the book, initially under the title *Imperatorum Romanorum Libellus*. These follow Mazzocchi's original edition in leaving Cossutia's picture blank, though they also tidy things up by omitting the baffling Plaudilla and Antonia. But, for Huttich, Cossutia has in a sense become the norm: the Strasbourg collection

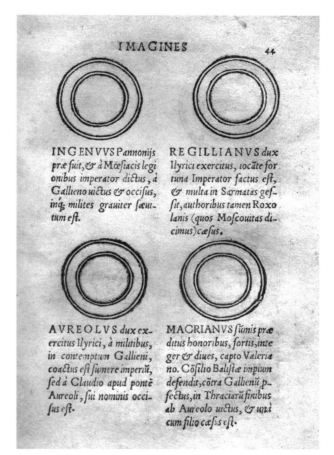

IMAGINES 44

INGENVVS *Pannonijs præ fuit,& à Mœsiacis legionibus imperator dictus, à Gallieno uictus & occisus, inq́, milites grauiter sæuitum est.*

REGILLIANVS *dux Ilyrici exercitus, iocăte fortuna Imperator factus est, & multa in Sarmatas gessit, authoribus tamen Roxolanis (quos Moscouitas dicimus) cæsus.*

AVREOLVS *dux exercitus Ilyrici, à militibus, in contemptum Gallieni, coactus est sumere imperiu, sed à Claudio apud ponte Aureoli, sui nominis occisus est.*

MACRIANVS *sūmis præ ditus honoribus, fortis, integer & diues, capto Valeriano. Côsilio Balistæ impium defendit, côtra Gallienu pfectus, in Thraciaru finibus ab Aureolo uictus, & uni cum filio cæsis est.*

9.21 Blank coins from Johann Huttich's *Imperatorum et Caesarum Vitae*, 1534.

is greatly expanded, largely by the addition of blank heads (figure 9.21). This effectively turns the book back into a coin collection, with the blanks to be filled by the individual collector; the book's greatest value is its record not of what is there, but of what is lacking: it is the reader's coin collection now. But it also transforms the nature of the book as a testimony to the historical reality of material objects. The evidence Huttich's missing heads provide is the evidence of things not seen, things to be sought.

These examples indicate the extent to which the Renaissance book was less a product than a process. Figure 9.22, from yet another archeological iconology, is an even clearer example. Guillaume du Choul's *Discours de la religion des anciens romains*, published at Lyons in 1556, is an exquisite piece of bookmaking, as expansive as Mazzocchi's volume is abbreviated. The care and planning that have gone into its production are evident on every page; the

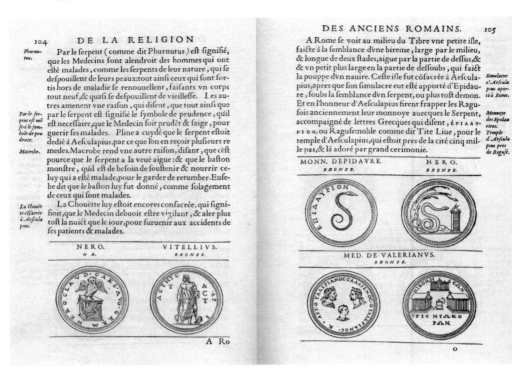

9.22 Guillaume du Choul, *Discours de la religion des anciens romains*, Lyons, 1556, pp. 104–5.

typography is varied and elegant, the illustrations finely balanced, often, as here, two against one; this is an entirely typical opening. A note at the end of the volume, however, reveals that page 105 is not as it should be: "Lecteur, la medaille qui se treuue auoir esté mise apres celle de Nero à la pag. 105. ou est insculpé le Serpent & vne are, est demeurée sans interpretation pour l'absence de l'Auteur, laquelle depuis il a faict mettre cy dessoubs en la maniere que s'ensuit" (Reader, the medal placed after that of Nero on page 105, depicting the serpent and an altar, lacks a commentary because of the absence of the author, which he has since provided as follows). The book, that is, continued without the author. Not until the second edition, in 1567, was the process finally complete.

I turn now to the illustration of classic narrative. When Caxton printed his second edition of *The Canterbury Tales* in 1484, he included 22 woodcuts illustrating the pilgrims. When Pynson issued his edition in 1492 he copied the blocks, and in 1526 had a set of new copies made. William Thynne's 1532 edition was based on Pynson's, and used the same blocks. In 1561 John Wight published a new edition of Chaucer, edited by John Stowe, the antiquary. This was issued in two versions, one with the illustrations from Pynson's edition, the other without illustrations. The illustrated version has generally been considered the first, though David Carlson reverses this scheme and argues plausibly that Wight reset the Prologue to include the illustrations when he belatedly obtained them.[3] The most recent discussion, by Seth Lerer and Joseph Dane, however, using some ingenious bibliographical detective work, suggests that the traditional order of the editions is the correct one.[4] What was it that made these very old woodcuts desirable, perhaps even desirable enough to warrant resetting the entire Prologue?

The illustrations are as generic as pictures can be without being identical. From Caxton's versions on, many of the male figures, with the obvious exception of the knight, could be substituted for each other, and as for the women, though from Caxton through Thynne the Wife of Bath is definitively worldly, with a fashionable traveling hat and an inviting smile (figure 9.23), in Stowe's edition the Prioress and the Wife are the same woodcut (figure 9.24), the feminine trumping the distinction between sacred and secular. In Thynne's edition of 1532 the woodcut in figure 9.25 does service for the Merchant, Summoner, Franklin and Manciple. The Clerk of Oxenford, however, is an anomaly: figure 9.26 shows him in Thynne – with his bow and arrows, and not a book in sight, he is clearly not an Oxford don. And when, thirty-two pages later, the Canon and his Yeoman join the pilgrims, we find the same woodcut used for the Canon's Yeoman. Now there is no more textual authority for the bow and quiver in this case than in the case of the Clerk, but the reason that Thynne's Clerk and Canon's Yeoman are identical has nothing to do with the text and everything to do with the history of the book. To begin with,

9.23 The Wife of Bath in Caxton's *Canterbury Tales*, 1482.

9.24 The Prioress and the Wife of Bath in John Stowe's edition of *The Canterbury Tales*, 1561.

9.25 The Merchant, Summoner, Franklin and Manciple from William Thynne's edition of *The Canterbury Tales*, 1532.

9.26 The Clerk of Oxenford in Thynne's Chaucer.

9.27 The Knight's Yeoman in Caxton's Chaucer, 1484.

9.28 Caxton's Clerk of Oxenford, 1484.

9.29 Caxton's Canon's Yeoman and Shipman, 1484.

9.30 Pynson's Knight's Yeoman, 1492.

9.31 Pynson's Clerk of Oxenford, 1492.

in Caxton's first illustrated edition of 1484, the representations of the Clerk and the Yeoman – not the Canon's Yeoman, but the one who accompanies the Knight, and is with the original party – are very similar (figures 9.27 and 9.28). Both carry bow and quiver, and the only attributes distinguishing them are the Yeoman's horn and sword. Either figure would make good textual sense for the Yeoman, since Chaucer specifically cites his bow and arrows in the Prologue: "His arwes drouped nought with fetheres lowe/ And in his hand he baar a mighty bowe" (ll. 107–8). Caxton, for whatever reason, had produced two versions of the Yeoman and used one for the Clerk. As for the Canon's Yeoman in Caxton, he is a different figure entirely (figure 9.29), characterized only by his sash of beads and his high-stepping horse; the same woodcut also serves for the Shipman.

Pynson, in 1492, adapting Caxton's woodcuts, gave the Yeoman his bow and arrows (figure 9.30), but also obviously saw the need to distinguish him from the similarly accoutred Clerk. The simplest way would have been to remove the Clerk's weapons and give him one of his beloved books; but that is not what Pynson's artist did. Instead he produced the image in figure 9.31: he retained the bow and arrow, but gave the pilgrim a banner with the motto "The Scients" – the term means "The Liberal Arts." This is the only figure with a label, and it is supplied for him out of a felt necessity: because the image is both specific and wrong. But since the pictures are being recut anyway, why did Pynson not correct the image by simply omitting the bow and arrow? Why provide the label that contradicts the attributes? Because Pynson is following a double and contradictory authority, Caxton and Chaucer.

Wynken de Worde in his 1498 Chaucer also saw the problem, and dealt with it by omission: only one of his pilgrims carries a bow and arrows. It is, however – perhaps predictably by this time – the wrong one: de Worde uses the woodcut in figure 9.32 for the Clerk, and, since he illustrates only the tales, not the Prologue, his edition does not illustrate the Yeoman at all, because he tells no tale. De Worde's Canon's Yeoman, who does tell a tale, is, reasonably enough, the beaded figure with the high-stepping horse (figure 9.33), Caxton's and Pynson's Canon's Yeoman/ Shipman. Thynne, in short, in 1532, simply picked the wrong Yeoman. He did, however, also use de Worde's Canon's Yeoman – but this time only for the Shipman. And for Stowe's Chaucer John Wight, in 1561, though he actually commissioned one new woodcut, for the Summoner, still adhered to the pictorial tradition of bow and arrows with lettered banner for the Clerk (figure 9.34) – the image is Pynson's woodcut of 1492.

All this suggests that Chaucerian illustration has less to do with Chaucer's text than with the look of the book and the history of its production. A page of the Wight/Stowe Chaucer is shown in figure 9.35. As a piece of printing, it looks to a modern eye crowded and ungracious, printed in double-columned heavy black-letter type with meager margins. If we like this we will call the typeface bold and the look of the page architectural, but such claims strike me as unconvincing: by 1561 English printing, though still doubtless somewhat crude by continental standards, was a good deal more elegant than this. So was illustration, as the *Cosmographical Glasse* title page of 1559 testifies (see figure 9.5). Both typography and illustration here are deliberately archaic, but the point is not simply to make Chaucer's works look like a very old book – this is not a sixteenth-century Kelmscott Chaucer. The woodcuts have more to do with the history of printing than with any sense of medieval style: they replicate Caxton and Pynson and Wynken de Worde, not Chaucer and the

9.32 Wynken de Worde's Clerk of Oxenford, 1498.

9.33 Wynken de Worde's Canon's Yeoman, 1498.

9.34 The Clerk of Oxenford from Stowe's Chaucer, 1561.

Bathes Prologue. Fol.xxxiij.

Men may deuine, and glofen vp and doun
But wel I wotte expreffe without lie
God badde vs for to wexe and multiplie
That gentil text can I well vnderftonde
Eke wel I wote (he faid) myn hufbonde
Should leaue father & mother, & take to me
But of numbre no mencion made he
Of bigamie or of octogamye
Why shoulde men speake of it villany?

Lo he the wife king Salamon
I trow had wiues mo than on
Is would god it lefull were to me
To be refreshed halfe fo oft as he
Whiche a gifte of god had he, for his wyuis
No ma hath fuch, that in this world a liue is
God wote this noble king, as to my witte
The firft night had many a mery fitte
With eche of hem, fo well was him aliue
Bleffed be god, I haue had fiue
Welcome the firte when euer he shall
Forfoth I woll not kepe me chafte in all
When myn hufbonde is fro the world ygon
Some chriften man fhal wedde me anon
For than the apoftel faith, that I am fre
To wedde a godeshalfe, where it liketh me
He faith, that to be wedded is no finne
Better is to be wedded than to brinne
What recketh me though folke fay villany
Of shrewde Lameth, and of his bigamy
I wote wel Abraham was an holy man
And Jacob eke, as fer as euer I here can
And eche of hem had wiues mo than two
And many another holy man also
Where can you fay in any maner age
That euer god defended mariage
By expreffe wordes? I praie you tell me
Or where commaunded he virginite?
I wote as well as ye, it is no drede
The Apoftel, when he fpake of maidenhede
He faid, therof precept had he none
Men may counfaile a woman to be one
But counfailing is no commaundement
He put it in our owne iudgement
For had god commaunded maidenhede
Then had he damphed wedding out of drede
And certes, if there were no fede fo we
Virginite than wherof should it growe?
Poule durft not commaund at the lefte
A thing, of whiche his mafter yafe none hefte
The darte is fet vp for virginite
Catche who fo may, who renneth beft let fe.
But this worde is not taken of euery wight
But there as god lift yeue it of his might
I wotte well that the apoftel was a mayde
But netheles, though that he wrote & faide

He would that euery wight were fuch as he
Al nis but counfaile to virginite
And for to ben a wife, he yaue me leue
Of indulgence, fo it be not to repreue
To wedde me, if that my make die
Without excepcion of bigamie
Al were it good no woman for to touche
He ment as in his bedde or in his couche
For peril is, both fire and towe to affemble
Ye know what this enfample may refemble
This is al and fome, he helde virginite
More parfite than wedding in freelte.
Freelte clepe I, but if that he and fhe
Would lede her life all in chaftite
I graunt it well, I haue none enuye
Though maidenhede preferre bigamye
It liketh hem to be clene in body and goffe
Of mine eftate I wol make no bofte
For well ye knowe, a lord in his houfholde
Hath nat euery veffell all of golde
Some ben of tre, and don her lorde feruice
God clepeth folke to him in fondry wife
And eueriche hath of god a proper gifte
Some this, fome that, as him liketh shifte
Virginite is great perfeccion
And continence eke with deuocion
But Chrifte, that of perfeccion is well
Badde not euery wight he should go fell
All that he had, and giue it to the poore
And in fuche wife folowe him and his lore
He fpake to hem, that would liue parfitly
And lordinges (by your leaue) that am nat I
I wol beftowe the floure of al myn age
In the actes and fruite of mariage
Tell me alfo, to what conclucion
Were membres made of generacion?
And of fo parfite wife a wight iwrought
Trufteth well, they were nat made for nouzt
Glofe who fo wol, and fape vp and doun
That they were made for purgacion
Of vrine, and other thinges fmale
And eke to knowe a female from a male
And for non other caufe, what fay ye no?
The experience wotte wel it is not fo
So that the clerkes be not with me wrothe
I fay that thei were maked for bothe
This is to fayn, for office, and for eafe
Of engendrure ther we not God difpleafe
Why should men els in her bokes fette
That man should yelde to his wife her dette
Now wherwith fhuld he pay his paiment?
If he ne vfed his fely inftrument
Than were they made vpon a creature
To purge vrine, and eke for engendrure
But I fay not that euery wight is holde

G.iii.   That

9.35 A page from Stowe's Chaucer, 1561.

Middle Ages. Whether David Carlson is right, and they were added to the book or, as Lerer and Dane contend, deleted from it, what they register is what we might call a sense of the material continuity of this English classic.

Similarly, Sebastian Brandt's magnificent woodcuts made for a Strasbourg Virgil in 1502 bring a sense of high chivalric style to the quitessential epic of love and war (figure 9.36). These images were still being found appropriate by mid-century continental printers. This is always explained as medievalizing Virgil, but maybe what it is really doing is preserving the conventions of a very famous book. In contrast, when Hugh Singleton needed suitably archaic illustrations for *The Shepherd's Calendar* in 1579 (the April woodcut appears in figure 9.37), he commissioned new ones that, for all their country simplicity, are devised in a style that accords with the book's elaborately modulated

9.36 Sebastian Brandt, woodcut illustrating *Aeneid* VI, Strasbourg, 1502.

9.37 Edmund Spenser, *The Shepherd's Calender*, 1579, illustration to April.

The Shipmans tale.   Fol. 64.

9.38 A page from Thomas Speght's Chaucer, 1602.

9.39 Speght's engraved portrait of Chaucer, 1602.

typography and testifies to the developing canons of Elizabethan taste – *The Shepherd's Calendar*, after all, is the vanguard of a poetic revolution. But why is *The Shepherd's Calendar* illustrated at all? Not because pastorals are illustrated – for the most part they aren't – but because calendars are; and the very fact of illustration thus connects the book both with the newest continental poetry and with the most traditional of native forms.

Chaucer continued to be archaic not through illustration but through typography: Thomas Speght's two editions of 1598 and 1602 are printed in a now quite anachronistic black letter (figure 9.38), which was still being used for Chaucer as late as 1687. Speght's editions are bigger and better in that they offer additional poetry and a glossary of archaic words, but the real innovation is a sense of the author: they include a biography, a coat of arms, a family tree and a portrait – in 1602, the portrait is engraved (figure 9.39). The author portrait and the move to engraving are the real breaks with tradition here. Textually, however, the 1598 edition is so close a reprint of 1561 that it even repeats errors in folio numbering. As for the illustrations, Speght retained only Pynson's woodcut of the knight.

These editions indicate that claims for the revolutionary aspects of printing really do not take enough into account: books like Stowe's and Speght's Chaucer are profoundly conservative. So are the Spenser folios of 1611 and 1617, which carefully preserve the printing history of the 1590 and 1596 quartos, not only providing a new title page for *The Second Part of the Faerie Queene* (figure

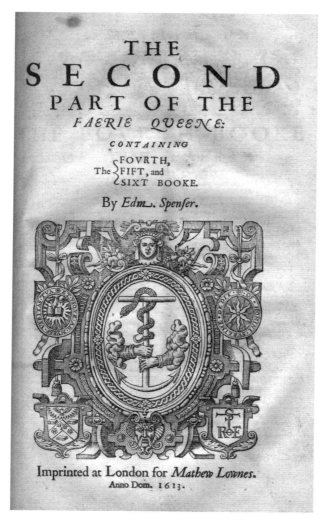

9.40 Edmund Spenser, *Workes*, 1611–13, title page to *The Faerie Queene*, Part 2.

9.40), quite pointless for a one-volume edition of the whole work, but even retaining both sets of final dedicatory poems from the two quartos – thereby repeating three of them. Equally conservative, in their way, are the Shakespeare folios: the 1632 second folio is a page for page reprint of the 1623 first, even preserving the mistakes, such as the placement of the prologue to *Troilus and Cressida* before the title of the play. This is, no doubt, not without its element of editorial ineptitude; but the point is the desire to replicate not simply the text but the physical book. Half a century later, in 1685, the fourth folio, with seven additional plays, still preserves the format of 1623.

Having begun with title pages, I really should conclude with colophons. These in a sense epitomize the sort of material I have been discussing. Colophons encode essential information about both the book's history and its construction – who printed it, when, what the order of the gatherings is to be – but they reveal nothing whatever about the book's subject matter; they are exclusively concerned with authority and technology. I turn instead, however, to a final example that may bring us back from typography to illustration, and indicate that these issues extend well beyond the Renaissance. One Jonson play, *The New Inn*, is omitted from the 1640 folio, doubtless because the 1631 octavo was still in print. The 1692 folio rectifies the omission, but does so by printing the play as an addendum, at the very end of the volume, after even *Timber, or Discoveries* and *The English Grammar*. This is done, clearly, to preserve the 1616/1640 format, but it also prevents *The New Inn* from taking its place among Jonson's plays, which he so pointedly and notoriously had placed first among his collected *Works*.

In 1716 Jacob Tonson published an elegant octavo Jonson in six volumes, on the model of Nicholas Rowe's Shakespeare of 1709. And like Rowe's Shakespeare, the plays are embellished with frontispiece engravings – figure 9.41 is the plate for *Volpone*. This is the first illustrated Jonson, as Rowe's is the first illustrated Shakespeare: illustrations complete the canonical text for the genteel taste of the eighteenth century, just as they did for Caxton's, Pynson's, de Worde's, Thynne's, Stowe's readers of Chaucer. But whereas all of Shakespeare's plays, even the spurious ones like *Locrine* and *The Yorkshire Tragedy*, are illustrated, Tonson illustrates only eleven Jonson plays; he excludes the later works, from *The Devil is an Ass* onward. The illustrations here seem to imply a value judgment – the unembellished plays were the ones that came to be referred to as Jonson's "dotages." The order of the works in 1716, however, adheres strictly to the order of the folios: textually, Tonson simply reprinted the 1692 folio – which means that the plays are not grouped together: the plays of the 1616 volume are followed by the poems and masques of 1616, and the plays of the 1640 volume follow these. And

9.41 Ben Jonson, *Works*, 1716, frontispiece to *Volpone*.

9.42 Ben Jonson, *Works*, 1716, frontispiece to *Cynthia's Revels*.

The New Inn keeps its place as an addendum, at the end of volume 6, after *Timber* and *The English Grammar*.

Clearly it is important for Tonson to retain the canonical order, however illogical this may be in a six-volume octavo edition – Rowe's Shakespeare similarly follows the order of the 1685 fourth folio. It is, however, not so much the placement of the plays as the illustrations that present Jonson to the eighteenth century and are the signifiers of his dramatic canon. The pictures are not only in the best modern style; they also represent the plays as if in performance, Jonson's drama as a living tradition. This was no doubt a potent selling point: Jonson was, throughout the Restoration, a more popular playwright than Shakespeare. Nevertheless, by 1716 a good deal of Jonson's theater was quite as obscure as *The New Inn* – of the eleven plays that Tonson's illustrations declared to be the major ones, *Cynthia's Revels* (figure 9.42), *The Poetaster* and *The Staple of News* had not been performed since the closing of the theaters, and *Every Man Out of his Humour, Sejanus* and *Catiline* had not been seen for half a century. For more than half the plays, that is, the stage history the illustrations record is entirely imaginary; they are realizations of printed texts – the same is true of about two-thirds of Rowe's Shakespeare canon. Tonson's engravings have more to do with the history of books than with Jonson's theater, and they derive their authority, their power to signify, from the history of printing, the construction of the previous century's folios.

Notes

1 A. Hyatt Mayor, *Prints and People* (New York, 1971), plate 44.
2 Sean Keilen, 'Exemplary Metals: Classical Numismatics and the Commerce of Humanism,' *Word and Image,* vol. 18 (2002): 282–94.
3 David Carlson, "Woodcut Illustrations of the *Canterbury Tales*", *The Library*, 6th Series, vol. 19, no. 1 (March 1974).
4 Joseph Dane and Seth Lerer, "Press Variants in John Stowe's Chaucer, 1561," *Transactions of the Cambridge Bibliographical Society*, vol. 11 (1999): 468–79.

10

Not his picture but his book

In 1574 Philip Sidney, then 19, was in Venice. His mentor and dear friend Hubert Languet, whom Sidney had recently left in Vienna, had wished for a portrait to ease the pain of their separation. Sidney made inquiries, and determined that Tintoretto and Veronese were the best local portraitists. Tintoretto was by far the more affordable of the two, even boasting that he could supply Veronese portraits for half the price. Sidney characteristically chose the more expensive option, and sat for Veronese. The sittings took only three or four days – all that was required for the preliminary sketches and a detailed drawing of the features. Five months later the portrait was delivered to Languet in Vienna by two of Sidney's friends, to whom it had been entrusted. Here is Languet's letter of thanks, as translated from the original Latin by Roger Kuin:

> Master Corbett unwrapped your portrait for me, and in order to feed my eyes I kept it by me for several hours; but looking at it has increased my longing for you, rather than diminished it. It seems to me rather to represent someone who looks like you than you yourself, and at first I thought it was your brother. Most of your features are quite beautifully rendered; but it is far more youthful than it should be. I think you must have been not unlike this when you were twelve or thirteen years old.[1]

A year later, however, Languet has changed his opinion of the painting. After he and Sidney finally parted in Frankfurt, upon Sidney's return to England, Languet writes that

> my longing for you made me ... set it up in a place where I could see it. Since that has been done, I find it so elegant, and such an excellent likeness of you, that already I have nothing among my possessions dearer to me ... .

There was now, however, a new complaint about the portrait:

> The painter has portrayed you slightly sad and thoughtful. I should have
> preferred to have had your face more composed to laughter … .

Languet contemplated his beloved friend's too youthful, too pensive portrait
for another seven years. He died in 1581, in the house of his onetime protégé
and close friend Philippe de Mornay, whose book on the truth of Protestantism
Sidney had been translating. The portrait then passed to Mornay, and was
recorded as hanging in his great gallery in 1619 – he too must have treasured
it, since he is also recorded as owning miniatures of Sidney and his sister the
Countess of Pembroke.

The portrait subsequently disappeared, though Roger Kuin, in a beautifully
methodical piece of forensic documentation, has persuasively traced it down
to 1697, in Normandy, where it was sold at auction. The lost Veronese
portrait of Sidney is a touchstone for the complex interrelation of art and
literature, a metonym for the absence of the author, that increasingly significant
lacuna, which frontispiece portraits throughout the seventeenth century were
insistently called upon to supply.

What do we want Sidney to look like? Ben Jonson's remark to Drummond
that "Sidney was no pleasant man in countenance, his face being spoiled
with pimples and of high blood"[2] has been taken to reflect more on Jonson's
meanspiritedness than on Sidney's appearance. Critics regularly observe that
Jonson is unlikely to have seen Sidney, but this is certainly not the case: Jonson,
as a boy at the Westminster School from 1579 to the mid-1580s, might have seen
Sidney on his way to and from Whitehall any number of times. The claim is
also said to be contradicted by the portraits, which show Sidney with a clear
and delicate countenance. But little can be argued from the portraits. To begin
with, all derive from only two, or possibly three, prototypes, and though the
claim is unquestionably true of the standard likeness, in figure 10.1, there is
no way of knowing how flattering this work was intended to be – portraits
are more likely to finesse blemishes than to reveal them. Roy Strong, who
has done the most recent comprehensive survey of the Sidney iconography,
has identified the original of this portrait as the version now at Longleat.[3]
This would have dated from 1577–78, when Sidney was about twenty-two,
painted either in the course of or just after his return from his second trip to
the continent, as ambassador to the Emperor Rudolph. Subsequent portraits,
however, show him as rather coarse-featured – figure 10.2 is the basic model,
now at Penshurst, ascribed to John de Critz. Sidney was only thirty-one when
he died, so the age difference between these two subjects cannot be more than

10.1 Anonymous. Sir Philip Sidney at the age of about twenty-two, 1577–78.

10.2 Attributed to John de Critz, Sidney at the age of around thirty, c. 1586.

10.3 The National Portrait Gallery painting (figure 10.1) before cleaning.

a few years. The lack of facial hair in the earlier one is significant. Katherine Duncan-Jones, author of the standard modern biography of Sidney, has observed to me how striking it is that Sidney at twenty-two, freshly returned from his embassy to the Emperor, is presented as clean-shaven, or even too young for a beard. She goes on to speculate that he, or his uncle the Earl of Leicester, may well have wanted to emphasize his youth, drawing attention to his precociousness, and thereby underlining the prodigiousness of heading so important a mission at such an early age. It is, therefore, also significant that an early copy of this portrait, formerly at Woburn, showed Sidney with a delicate moustache and beard (figure 10.3). The painting was subsequently acquired by the National Portrait Gallery, and the facial hair disappeared in cleaning (a tiny wisp of the moustache is still visible on the left); but when were they added, and why? Did they represent a back-formation from the mature portrait, or were they an attempt to make the picture more like the man – or more like the man the retoucher wished Sidney had been?

What do we want Sidney to look like – manly or boyish? The romantic youth, the precocious statesman, the marginalized courtier, the Protestant hero, the soldier cut off in his prime, or – least likely – the famous poet and novelist? For two centuries, starting with George Vertue in the 1720s, figure 10.4 was a portrait of Sidney at some country house (certainly not Wilton or Penshurst, the family properties), musing over the composition of *Arcadia* and *Astrophil and Stella*, an aristocratic aesthete. But the costume clearly dates the picture to the 1590s, a decade or more too late: thanks to the rise of costume history as a discipline, by the 1950s this contemplative figure could no longer be construed as Sidney. Nor was there, in the creation of Sidney's literary legacy, much interest in the features of the author: no English edition of Sidney's works included a portrait until 1655. The French translation of *Arcadia*, however, published in Paris in 1624, had as its frontispiece the elegantly classicized engraving in figure 10.5, by Crispin van de Passe, Sidney crowned with the poet's laurel. It is based on the rather less elegant engraving in figure 10.6, also by van de Passe, from Henry Holland's *Herologia* (1620), which, judging from the ruff and doublet, looks like a romanticized version of the de Critz painting. George Vertue early in the eighteenth century records

10.4 Isaac Oliver, Unknown young man, c. 1595.

10.5 Crispin van de Passe, frontispiece to *L'Arcadie de la Comtesse de Pembrok*, 1624.

10.6 Crispin van de Passe, Sir Philip Sidney, from Henry Holland, *Herologia*, 1620.

10.7 Frontispiece to *Arcadia*, 1655.

an annotation on a copy of the engraving indicating that it was indeed based on a drawing by John de Critz. De Critz was active as an artist by 1582, so the drawing could have been done from life – which means that triangulating the Longleat portrait with these two very different images might be the closest we can come to the real Sidney's features. In England, when the 1655 *Arcadia* finally included a portrait, it was the much more manly military image in figure 10.7, based on the least romantic of the prototypes. The iconographic tradition in England, even in providing a frontispiece for his imaginative writing, largely ignored the Sidney of poetry and romance.

Let us return now, very briefly, to the lost Veronese, the one that was too youthful and too pensive. Roger Kuin, in the article I mentioned earlier, points out that there is a surviving portrait of the right period and style that nicely fits Languet's description, the lovely work in figure 10.8, in the Boston Museum of Fine Arts. The trouble, Kuin observes, is that it is by Tintoretto, not Veronese.[4] Its authenticity has never been questioned, but its provenance is traceable only to the mid-nineteenth century, when it was acquired as a Tintoretto by a Scottish collector. I imagine that if it had been acquired as a Veronese, nobody would have objected: after all, Tintoretto boasted that he could paint Veronese portraits. If Kuin is correct that the Sidney portrait remained with de Mornay's effects until it was sold at auction in 1697, that would have been a logical time to attach an artist's name to it (in the family history, it would not have been a Veronese, but simply a portrait of Sidney) and Tintoretto would have been as reasonable an artist's name as Veronese – either would have done, but a name in the auction catalogue would have significantly increased its value. I am not, needless to say, insisting that this is what happened or when it happened; but only that if we really want the Veronese portrait of Sidney, Boston is a good place to look.

It is not, however, easy to look there. When I was first writing this essay, I sent two inquiries about the painting to the Boston Museum, which went unanswered. After a brief version of this argument was published in the *Times Literary Supplement*, I finally received a letter from a curator informing me that the painting was not even by the right Tintoretto, but by Jacopo's far less distinguished son Domenico. I returned my thanks, and asked whether

10.8 Attributed to Domenico Tintoretto, Portrait of a young man.

we might pursue the subject a little further: was the ascription to Domenico based solely on stylistic grounds, or was there some documentary evidence; and what was known about the painting's provenance? To this message I once again received no reply. So as far as I am concerned, the case necessarily remains open.

John Donne, who cared and knew a good deal about art, was eighteen, even younger than Sidney, when he first had himself painted, probably by Hilliard. That painting has disappeared, but a version of it is preserved in the frontispiece to the 1635 edition of his *Poems* (figure 10.9). The legend of his passionate youth seems embodied in an anonymous chiaroscuro portrait in his early 20s (figure 10.10), smoldering romantically beneath the shadow of his great hat – the sitter was identified as Donne only in 1959: it had previously been labeled a portrait of Duns Scotus, in a very unlikely outfit for a medieval philosopher. Donne kept a close watch over his image: there is a small group of portraits, precisely chronicling his changing fortunes and increasing seriousness – figure 10.11 shows him by Isaac Oliver in 1616, in his mid-40s. He maintained the same sort of authority over his poetry: except for three elegies, he published no verse during his lifetime, because, he said, if it were in print he would be unable to control who read it. Donne was a manuscript poet, who circulated his work to a well-defined group of friends, acquaintances and, perhaps most important, potential patrons in search of a witty, charming, well-educated secretary.

The posthumous quarto edition of his collected poems published in 1633, two years after his death, includes no portrait – indeed, it does not even include his name: the title page has only, discreetly, "Poems by J. D." By 1635 the success of the volume prompted a change to the more popular and portable octavo format, and the embellishment of the engraved frontispiece by William Marshall, after the miniature of Donne at 18, the presumed Hilliard portrait that has now disappeared. The same frontispiece continued to adorn editions of the poems until the 1650s, though the discreet initials remained (the author did not become John Donne until the edition of 1669, at which point the octavo format became larger and the engraved portrait disappeared). There were a number of other frontispiece options available for the *Poems*, portraits of the mature and serious churchman and intellectual, such as the classicized bust in figure 10.12, at the age of about forty, used as the frontispiece for an edition of his *Letters* in 1651, and subsequently in Walton's *Lives*, which derives from an anonymous oil portrait now in the Victoria and Albert Museum; or engravings deriving from the beautiful Oliver miniature, such as the portrait in the frontispiece for his *LXXX Sermons* (1640), in figure 10.13. Even the startling engraving in figure 10.14, of Donne in his shroud, the frontispiece to *Deaths Duell* (1632), would have been a possible choice – half the poems, after all, are religious; many are meditations on death.⁵ But what the publisher of the poems wanted was just what Sidney's editors did not want: the poet as a romantic youth, Donne the courtier-lover at the age of 18, wide-eyed, earringed, his fist clutching the hilt of his sword, which looks as if it is about to explode with excitement.

10.9 John Donne in 1591 at the age of eighteen, engraved by William Marshall after a lost Hilliard miniature. Frontispiece to *Poems By J. D.*, 1635.

10.10 Anonymous. John Donne in his early twenties.

10.11 Isaac Oliver, John Donne, 1616.

10.12 Peter Lombart, Donne aged about forty. Frontispiece to Donne's *Letters*, 1651.

10.13 Matthäus Merian after Isaac Oliver, frontispiece to *LXXX Sermons*, 1640.

10.14 Martin Droeshout, Donne in his shroud, frontispiece to *Deaths Duell*, 1632.

10.15 Abraham
Blyenberch, Ben Jonson
aged about fifty.

Sidney's and Donne's portraits, or at least the iconographic assumptions
embodied in them, are an essential part of their literary history. Ben Jonson
constitutes a significant counter-example. Donne and Jonson were close
friends, and moved in the same circle; Isaac Oliver was Jonson's neighbor
when both lived in Blackfriars. Oliver not only painted Donne, he painted at
least two ladies in the costumes they wore in Jonson's masques; and he and
Jonson must have known each other. But Jonson, Hilliard and Oliver seem
not to have inhabited the same cultural world. The only surviving portraits
of Jonson, whether painted or engraved, all apparently derive from a single
prototype, of which an early version, or possibly the original, is now in the
National Portrait Gallery (figure 10.15). It was for many years considered a
copy of an original ascribed to Gerard Honthorst, until the middle of the
twentieth century when someone noticed a painting of Jonson by Abraham
Blyenberch listed in a 1635 inventory of the Duke of Buckingham's pictures at
York House, upon which this, or perhaps a copy of it, became the Blyenberch

portrait instead: the identity of artists is no more stable than the identity of sitters; moreover, the conceptual distinction between an original and a copy was far less rigid than it is now. The proliferation of copies after lost originals surely implies that one of the functions of originals was precisely to serve as prototypes for copies; and there is, indeed, no reason to assume that the Duke of Buckingham's Blyenberch was the original.

Blyenberch is not recorded as working in England after 1622, and in any case the painting would have been done before Jonson's disabling stroke in 1628. His age, therefore, was around fifty. Visually, this is Jonson's immortality, but no allusion to Blyenberch (or Honthorst) or the portrait survives in Jonson's work – apparently it simply did not mean much to him. (If Buckingham's version was the original, I would think it was he, not Jonson, who commissioned it. Buckingham and Jonson became close in 1621, during the complex preparations for Jonson's masque *The Gipsies Metamorphosed*, commissioned by Buckingham and performed three times before the king at estates belonging to Buckingham and his family. This would have been a logical time for Buckingham to want a portrait of his poet – the Portrait Gallery assigns a date of 1617 to the painting, but this is very unlikely.) The only portraits memorialized in Jonson's poetry are two completely lost ones. Of the first, by his friend Sir William Borlase, Sheriff of Buckinghamshire and not otherwise known as a painter, Jonson says in a poem called "The Poet to the Painter", "You made it a brave piece, but not like me."[6] The other is the miniature described in the poem "On His Picture Left in Scotland" – left there by his beloved "Charis" – which was entirely too much like him, accurately depicting his "hundred of grey hairs" and "rocky face" at the age of forty-seven (as a miniature, it probably did not show what the poem also ruefully chronicles, his "mountain belly"). It is surely not irrelevant that in his prefatory poem to the Shakespeare folio – with its author's portrait, quite anomalously, displayed on the title page rather than facing it as a frontispiece – Jonson admonished the reader to "look/ Not on his picture, but his book." Jonson did not want his portrait in his books. The great folio of his *Workes*, clearly designed to Jonson's specifications, discussed in "Textual icons" on pp. 161–4 (see figure 9.3). The engraving shows not the author's face but his mind and the context he wanted for his art.

After Jonson's death in 1637, however, his image became essential to his works. The version of the Blyenberch portrait engraved by Robert Vaughan (figure 9.4), faced the title page of the second edition of his folio *Workes*, published in 1640. He is dressed more elegantly than Blyenberch's Jonson, and is now crowned with the poet's laurel. The motto on the cartouche declares him "the most learned of English poets." The engraving had been done many

10.16 William Hole, John Florio, from the second edition of his translation of Michel de Montaigne, *The Essayes*, 1613.

10.17 William Hole, George Chapman, frontispiece to *The Whole Works of Homer*, 1616.

10.18 William Hole, Michael Drayton, frontispiece to *Poems*, 1619.

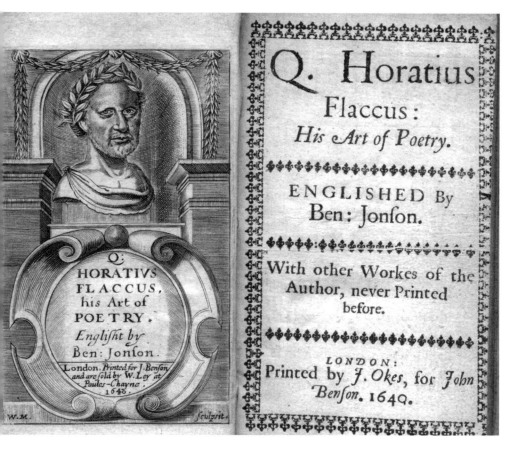

0.19 William Marshall, Ben Jonson, frontispiece to *Q. Horatius Flaccus: His Art of Poetry*, 1640.

years earlier – it was in existence by 1627 – and book collectors by the end of the century began regularly adding it to their copies of the 1616 folio, as if something were missing. In fact, Jonson's resistance to being identified with his picture, rather than his book, was, even during his lifetime, outmoded. The 1613 edition of John Florio's translation of Montaigne included the handsome bust of Florio in figure 10.16 (though not one of Montaigne); George Chapman's 1616 Homer showed the translator as semi-divine, with his head in the clouds and a hint of a halo (figure 10.17); and Michael Drayton's 1619 *Poems* had a grimly elegant frontispiece portrait (figure 10.18). In the light of such examples, Jonson's attitude must have seemed highminded but quixotic: quite simply, it was increasingly clear that author-portraits helped to sell books. The publishers, at least, believed so, and the appropriately classicized version of the

Jonson portrait in figure 10.19 duly adorned the elegant little duodecimo of his translation of Horace's *Art of Poetry* (1640), and a much grander revision of the portrait faces the title page of the massive 1692 folio.

Ironically, the Shakespeare and Jonson folios, despite Jonson's best efforts, made authors' portraits inescapable for large, expensive and, especially, posthumous dramatic collections. There were four such folios in the remainder of the century, devoted to the works of Beaumont and Fletcher (two volumes, published more than thirty years apart), Thomas Killigrew and Sir William Davenant. Killigrew, in figure 10.20, is shown with his favorite dog and a great many books – the named ones are his own plays – pensively reading under the cool gaze of his master the martyred king Charles. His taste and affluence are exemplified in the very style of the engraving, which has much more the look of a painting than of a frontispiece. Figure 10.21 is his chief theatrical rival Sir William Davenant, wearing the crown of his poet laureateship, and with his features perhaps somewhat extenuated: Aubrey says of Davenant, "He got a terrible clap of a black handsome wench,… which cost him his nose, with which unlucky mischance many wits were too cruelly bold".[7] The 1647 Beaumont and Fletcher folio, however, the grandest and most complex of such undertakings after the Shakespeare folio of 1623, posed a special problem. Both playwrights were long dead, and the publisher, Humphrey Moseley, was eager to commission a double portrait – he explains in a preface that he had initially considered collecting only Fletcher's plays, but "since [Beaumont and Fletcher were] never parted while they lived, I conceived it not equitable to separate their ashes." In fact, this overstates both the extent and intensity of their collaboration, which lasted at most a decade. Beaumont died in 1616, nine years before Fletcher; moreover, Fletcher worked throughout his career with several other playwrights, including Shakespeare and Massinger, as well as alone. But Beaumont served as a convenient synecdoche, summarizing (and eliding) the ambiguities and confusions of divided authorship, a common and unremarkable practice in the period; and he continues to do so.[8] For Moseley, Beaumont – or rather the concept of Beaumont – was indispensable to Fletcher, since there was no way of eliciting Fletcher alone from his collaborations, and the folio could obviously not be ascribed, however accurately, to *Fletcher and Others*. The two necessarily inseparable playwrights, therefore, are securely bracketed on the title page, a double author. The trouble was, however, that no portrait of Beaumont could be found, though Moseley says he "spared no enquiry in those noble families whence he was descended," and among Beaumont's former colleagues in the Inner Temple. So the frontispiece bust of Fletcher (figure 10.22) confronts the title in splendid solitude. As for the elusive Beaumont, Moseley takes refuge behind a thoroughly Jonsonian axiom: "the

0.20 William Faithorne after William Sheppard, Thomas Killigrew, frontispiece to *Comedies and Tragedies*, 1664.

0.21 William Faithorne after John Greenhill, Sir William Davenant, frontispiece to *Works*, 1673.

0.22 William Marshall, John Fletcher, frontispiece to Beaumont and Fletcher, *Comedies and Tragedies*, 1647, used again in the sequel *Fifty Comedies and Tragedies*, 1679.

best pictures and those most like him you'll find in this volume," in his works, not his image; and indeed, Moseley continues, almost undoing the work of the artist, even the portrait of Fletcher scarcely does him justice. "Reader, look/ Not on his picture but his book."

Notes

1 Roger Kuin, "New Light on the Veronese Portrait of Sir Philip Sidney," *Sidney Newsletter & Journal*, vol. 15, no. 1, p. 23.
2 Ben Jonson, *Conversations*, ll. 230–1.
3 Roy Strong, "Sidney's Appearance Reconsidered", in *The Tudor and Stuart Monarchy* (Woodbridge, 1995), vol. 2: 145–63.
4 Kuin says it is *signed* by Tintoretto. It does not, in fact, appear to be signed (Kuin tells me he is not sure whether it is signed, but only meant it was an authentic Tintoretto; requests to the Boston Museum for information have gone unanswered). The standard catalogue of Tintoretto portraits by Rodolfo Pallucchini, which reproduces the painting, says nothing about it being signed, and if it were, it would be quite anomalous: Tintoretto almost never signed his portraits. The very few exceptions are grand presentation pieces, not small commissions. If the painting were signed, that would be an argument against the assumption that it was Tintoretto who signed it.
5 *Devotions* (1634), has a full-length portrait of Donne in the shroud, but Donne was dead by that time. He was still alive when *Deaths Duell* was published.
6 Ben Jonson, *Underwood*, in *Poems*, ed. Ian Donaldson (London, 1975), 52.
7 John Aubrey, *Brief Lives*, ed. O. L. Dick (Ann Arbor, MI, 1957), p. 86.
8 The best overview of the subject is Jeffrey Masten's brilliant *Textual Intercourse: Collaboration, Authorship and Sexualities in Renaissance Drama* (Cambridge, 1997).

11

Plagiarism revisited

In 1975 I wrote an essay called "The Renaissance Artist as Plagiarist."[1] I was moved to write it by a puzzling crux in my work on Inigo Jones, an instance in which Jones's published statements about the genesis of a particular court masque seemed to contradict all the other evidence about the production. Two modern scholars of great learning and eminence had explained the contradiction by invoking the concept of plagiarism. This explanation, however, struck me as unconvincing on two counts: nobody could reasonably call what Jones had done in the masque plagiarism, and declaring it plagiarism didn't seem to me to explain anything. In the essay I came up with an alternative explanation, which didn't involve plagiarism and solved the puzzle to my own satisfaction; but the solution still left me wondering where the charge of plagiarism had come from, since it was, to my mind, so clearly irrelevant to the facts. I shall return to the specifics of this case, but I now summarize the rest of the essay, as the essential background of my remarks here. From the Jones masque I was moved to wonder what kinds of artistic imitation could reasonably have been called plagiarism in Jones's time, and what sorts of changes one could chart, historically, in the acceptable limits of artistic imitation. I have revised my thinking on the historical aspects of the matter a number of times, as I have been enlightened by classicists, medievalists and neo-Latinists; but I never felt moved to pursue the matter in print again, not least because it seemed to me that the essay had sunk without a trace. Nobody responded to it, I never saw it cited; so far as I was aware, no one took any notice of it at all.

Imagine my surprise, then, when twenty-four years later my old friend Christopher Ricks came to visit and announced that he was about to disagree with me publicly on the subject of plagiarism. And my even greater surprise at learning, when he sent me an offprint of his British Academy lecture "Plagiarism,"[2] that my essay was "influential." Really! It never seemed to me to have influenced anyone, except, of course, Ricks to object to it. I found, moreover, that when I read Ricks's essay I pretty much agreed with it – and certainly agreed that there were problems with my historical account, which I'd already revised for myself long before. So when I was subsequently asked whether I would agree to open a conference on plagiarism by participating in a debate with Ricks, I firmly declined. First of all, there seemed to me little to debate; second – and perhaps, to be honest, more compelling – Ricks and I have known each other for almost fifty years, and spent the first ten or so arguing, and I don't remember ever coming out ahead. I do, I suppose, come off fairly well in the present case: I am allowed to be, on the particular matter in question, muddle-headed and unpersuasive but basically well-intentioned, whereas most of the other people Ricks disagrees with are very bad news indeed – "weakly, wizenedly political," they "demean and … degrade moral thought." I'm extremely relieved not to be in this class. I can't, of course, match the intensity of Ricks's indignation – I never could – but I do certainly share his ethical principles.

My primary concern was with the historical and scholarly aspects of the subject, and I shall return to those; but since Ricks is chiefly concerned with the current practice of plagiarism and the decay of moral values in response to it, let me start with practical matters. I begin where most of us who teach begin, with how to deal with students who cheat. Ricks cites, as a kind of moral barometer of the modern condition, James Kincaid's story, in an article on plagiarism published in *The New Yorker*, of a student indignant over having ordered an original paper on the internet, and having been sold a plagiarized one.[3] "'Shit!' she said. 'I paid seventy-five dollars for that.'" Ricks's indignation is directed primarily at Kincaid's cool and cynical reaction, but what interests me is that he also swallows the story whole. The story is certainly outrageous; but it certainly is not original. The same story was making the rounds when I was a graduate student at Harvard in the 1950s, and when I was teaching at Berkeley in the 1960s – long before the internet there were outfits supplying papers on demand and students buying them (the *Encyclopedia Britannica*'s research service was an egregious supplier, widely used at Harvard), and this tale is a piece of American academic mythology, invented, I imagine, a few minutes after the first student bought the first paper. The only thing Kincaid's version adds to the story is the shit. I venture no opinion about whether or not such an incident actually happened to Kincaid, and/or to some Harvard or Berkeley colleague; I've recently heard a version of it at Stanford, where the price has dropped to $60: perhaps it happens all the time these days – imitation is the essence of life, as of art. How significant is the truth or falsehood of this story – why isn't originality an issue for Ricks here? Because everything depends on the genre: its primary function in this discourse is not factual, but as a classic exemplum, a rich subject for moralization, both Kincaid's and Ricks's.

My own plagiarism story is much less epigrammatic, though it is original. Nobody could have thought it up. Stanford operates on an honor system, which means that students formally subscribe to a code of ethics. I'm not allowed to proctor exams, and students who are aware of other students cheating are required to turn them in. I have never known this to happen, but I also don't put the system under much pressure – for the kinds of exams I give, it doesn't do you any good to look over somebody's shoulder, and my essay topics are usually too specific for anyone except a student in the class to write them. Still, there are opportunities – optional papers, which can be on anything; short papers for section meetings where the student picks the topic. The only culprits I can catch, of course, are the inept ones – students who copy the introduction to the text we're using, or crib from essays I've assigned so that I'm bound to recognize them. If the plagiarist takes a paper off the internet (or, in the old-fashioned low-tech way, out of the sorority files), I have no way of knowing it. I may decide the paper is too good for this particular student, or doesn't match the style of her other work, but the only way for me to be sure that she hasn't been suddenly transformed by my teaching into a first-class critic is to extract a confession.

In my twenty years at Stanford, I've had only one such case, in 1998. In contrast to the banal predictability of the *New Yorker* story, mine seemed to me positively surreal; but it is directly relevant to Ricks's insistence that we all know and have always known that the crucial element in plagiarism is the intention to deceive. One of my section leaders in a Renaissance survey course asked her students to write a page about any aspect of the Shakespeare sonnets, as a basis for class discussion. A student turned in a page copied verbatim from Hallett Smith's introduction to the sonnets in the Riverside Shakespeare. When confronted, the student freely admitted cribbing the material, but exculpated himself by explaining that his Oxford tutor had taught him to write papers that way. (Mentioning Oxford or Cambridge at Stanford is usually enough to silence any criticism.) The Oxford tutor was reported to have told her charges that one could never hope to write something original about great poetry, so one should find excellent critical work and copy that. But surely the tutor hadn't said one should copy it without acknowledgment! Yes, he insisted, she had. I declined his offer to put me in touch with the tutor, and the section leader and I contented ourselves with making sure he understood the local rules he had agreed to about the citation of sources, gave him a stern warning, elicited an apology, and considered the matter closed.

A month later the section leader presented me with a paper on *Paradise Lost* by the same student. It was cribbed verbatim from a book which happened to be by a former student of mine. The section leader, who had been suspicious of the prose, had found the original instantly because the paper had the same title as the book – this was not, you can see, a very sophisticated plagiarist. This time, however, the Oxford tutor was not invoked; the student flatly denied any knowledge of the original, though eventually, confronted with the absolute identity of the two texts in question, he agreed that he must have, sometime, looked at the book and forgotten about it. Here the exculpatory explanation was in his method of taking notes: he copies good things from critical works into the margin of his text; since these are simply reading notes he doesn't indicate their source, and doubtless he simply mistook these passages for ideas of his own. His copy of *Paradise Lost*, which he was asked to produce, did not, in fact, include such marginalia – he thought perhaps the text he had used was home in Maryland, or had even, unfortunately, been disposed of – but he did show me his copy of *The Tempest*, the margins of which were indeed full of good bits, copied directly from my own critical prose. I pointed out that this method of taking notes practically guaranteed that his papers would be plagiarized, but he replied coolly that the crucial element in plagiarism was intention, and he had no intention of deceiving anyone.

The whole matter meanwhile had been referred to the university's judicial board, which after an extended investigation and a very long hearing declared him guilty. It then went through several appeals, all of which he lost. Throughout the many months that all this took he maintained his innocence, and seemed baffled that nobody believed his explanations. He was especially aggrieved at me for refusing to pass him in the course – this was a real blow, since it meant he had to register for an extra term, which at Stanford is an expensive business. This was the only point at which he seemed to take the matter seriously, the point at which it turned out that it was going to cost him money. I never succeeded in getting him to admit that he had done anything unethical; he remained throughout courteous, patient, slightly pained but unflappable. His metaphor for what had happened was that, entirely unexpectedly, a brick wall had fallen on him. He had never, he assured me, been accused of lying in his life. You will perhaps not be surprised to learn that he intended to go to law school, though I am told that with an ethics violation on his undergraduate record he will have difficulty being accepted (I was surprised to learn this).

However inept this student was, he perfectly understood that intention here was everything, originality nothing. I turn now, for an oddly parallel case, to two of my most prized possessions, a pair of Dürer engravings. The first, the famous and mysterious *Melancholia I*, I bought in 1968 during a year when I was working at the Warburg Institute. It was in a box of Northern Renaissance prints at the late, lamented Craddock and Barnard on Museum

Street, and I was thrilled to find it. It is a beautiful, crisp impression, signed in the plate with the monogram AD and the date 1514; but even my minimal expertise was sufficient to tell me that there was something not right about it. The something was that it was priced at £12, and even in 1968 Craddock and Barnard didn't sell Dürers for £12. It is, in fact, not by Dürer, but by an expert copyist working in the latter half of the sixteenth century named Jan Wierix. With a magnifying glass and the original print, it is possible to see slight differences – in hatching and such – and there is one real giveaway, though it's difficult to spot unless you know what to look for; but the copy is a very expert one. My second Dürer, of the Holy Family, I found a couple of years later, also at Craddock and Barnard, and paid £8 for it. I was on to Wierix by this time, but this time also there was no question about it: Wierix had signed the print with his monogram and the date, IHW 1566 – though he had also included Dürer's original monogram. It is a very accurate copy, but it does declare itself a copy.

Wierix made his living, not to put too fine a point on it, both as a copyist and as a forger; and I take it that the first of my Dürers is a forgery, intended for sale as an authentic Dürer, the second a copy, intended for sale to those who wanted the Dürer print but couldn't afford it. (In fact, both pictures were produced in both signed and unsigned versions.) These two prints, then, inhabit quite different ethical worlds. Does this affect my feeling about them? Not at all: I am delighted with both. Would I have bought them if Dürer hadn't been an issue – if I knew nothing of Dürer but simply liked the pictures? I believe I would; I'm a sucker for nice Renaissance pictures, and usually buy them first and find out about them afterward. But then if I merely like the picture, would any copy do? What about a perfect digitalized reproduction, which would be an even closer approximation to the original than my Wierixes? Well, no, that wouldn't give me the same kind of pleasure. Part of what I like is the simple age of the objects, the fact that they're real survivals from the sixteenth century, but a significant part too is the genuine craftsmanship involved, the excellence not merely of the copy but of the copyist.

So the fact of the forgery doesn't bother me at all? No: the print was misrepresented by the artist, but not by the dealer, who wasn't selling it as a Dürer. *I* wasn't cheated; the fraud – and there certainly was one – was back in the sixteenth century; it's history. But what if I had been cheated, either by a dealer who hadn't done his homework on the *Melancholia I* or had lied about it? It's the same picture in either case; wouldn't I like it just as much? Well, perhaps not *just* as much: the fact of the fraud would matter. I'd be very angry, and not only because if it had been sold as an authentic Dürer I'd have paid a great deal more money for it. Ah, but what about the difference in cost? The extra money would then have been paid not for Dürer's inimitable expertise, since the engravings looked to me virtually identical, but merely for his name. Yes: it's the intangible that would matter here, and not even because it affects the resale value of the print: I'm not a dealer, and have never sold a print of mine; I buy them exclusively to look at. My outrage would be purely moral; there would be nothing at all practical about it. And I would grind my teeth and do my best to extract some satisfaction from the ignorant or fraudulent dealer; but I suspect that I'd keep the picture on the wall and continue to look at it with undiminished wonder.

These, however, are the simple cases. The most successful forgeries have been those with no original, those that do not copy the work of art but impersonate the artist, such as Van Meegeren's notorious Vermeers. Forgeries like these are especially subversive because they call into question the whole system of artistic value. This is not to say that questioning the system, or indeed subverting it, is necessarily a bad thing; and it may be that, given the way the art market works, such forgeries constitute the only way to question it. To observe that in this case, and any number of similar ones, the experts were mistaken, or deceived, or even defrauded, is also to concede that the usefulness of expertise in such cases is extremely limited. Picasso himself was constantly being asked by dealers to authenticate his own work, and was often found declaring the same picture to be both real and fake at different times. The later Picassos especially must be very easy to imitate; one even feels, in those thousands of quick sketches, Picasso imitating himself. In an art that depends on imitation in this way, what constitutes authenticity? It is not that there is no answer to this question, but that the basis of the answer, indeed the possibility of an answer, keeps changing. The most basic answer would certainly invoke the concept of misrepresentation – a commonsense answer – and there are clearly many such cases everyone could agree on. But even these bear so heavily on the question of what constitutes value that even the most obvious of them need a harder look: the problem is precisely the Picasso problem – that there is an unclear and uncertain relation between authenticity and authentication, and it is not always possible to know whether something is being misrepresented. An unknown painting by Vermeer is worth a great deal more than an unknown painting in the style of Vermeer, even when it is the same painting. This suggests that the issue is not the quality of the painting but the construction of the artist, what is taken to constitute an authentic painting by a particular painter. Rubens was quite open about this, selling paintings by his own hand and paintings from his workshop at very different prices. We might say that there is no problem as long as nothing is misrepresented; but there will inevitably come a point at which the documentation is lost and you can only tell by looking, and the question then will have to do not with the craft of painting or the ethics of the artist or the dealer, but with the art (and ethics) of attribution. In a recent sensational international art forgery case, the crucial forgeries were not the paintings, which were fakes, but the documentation – it was the paper trail that constituted authenticity.[4] Had the paintings been authentic, the dealer might have found it no less desirable to fake their provenance.

I return now to history – and to Christopher Ricks. I was wrong to suggest that plagiarism wasn't an issue before the late seventeenth century, but the issue was rather different from what came later. There is very little discussion of the subject in the Middle Ages, and what there is tends to be concerned with fears about the dissemination of corrupt texts rather than with authorial usurpation: Petrarch worries about plagiarism precisely because he assumes that the purloined and corrupted works will continue to be marketed as his – assumes, that is, that his authorship constitutes the crucial element in the text's value. Medieval poets employed a variety of methods of asserting and maintaining their authority over their writing. Dante not only made himself the hero of the *Commedia*, he numbered the lines of the poem and alludes to the numbering within the text to preclude revisions and interpolations. Chaucer didn't merely compose his tales, he represented himself as narrating them. There are even cases of poets embedding their names in their poems, so that the author would remain an integral element of the work – these are rare, but the fact of their existence at all is to the point. I doubt that any of these can be seen primarily, or even significantly, as strategies designed to prevent plagiarism, but they all involve notions of intellectual property and authorial control, and these in themselves imply a concept of plagiarism.

The Renaissance revival of the classics, however, was also a revival of the classical sense of plagiarism, which was clear and explicit; and the smoking gun in Ricks's account, the proof that, far from being a post-Renaissance phenomenon, plagiarism has been a serious moral crime since ancient times, is Martial. Here the account, I think, needs some fine tuning. Ricks points out that it is to Martial that we owe the application of the term *plagiarius*, the abductor of somebody else's slave, to literary theft, and he cites epigram i.66. Here it is in a 1695 translation by Henry Killigrew:

> Thou sordid felon of my verse and fame,
> So cheap dost hope to get a poet's name,
> As by the purchase barely of my book
> For ten vile pence eternal glory rook?
> Find out some virgin poem ne'er saw day,

> Which wary writers in their desks do lay
> Lock'd up, and known unto themselves alone;
> Not one with using torn, and sordid grown.
> A publish'd work can ne'er the author change,
> Like one ne'er pass'd the press, that ne'er did range
> The world trimly bound up: and such I'll sell,
> Give me my price, nor will the secret tell.
> He that another's wit and fame will own,
> Must silence buy, and not a book that's known.[5]

This certainly condemns plagiarism, at least in the opening lines; but is it about plagiarism in general or in particular – is it, that is, really about a case of somebody stealing Martial's poems and taking credit for them? If so, why isn't the culprit named, and what poems did he steal? What's the point of attacking someone who is appropriating your work if you don't reveal his identity and say which purloined poems are yours? And if it is an actual case of plagiarism, how outraged really is Martial about it? He certainly starts out sounding indignant – the plagiarist is "fur avare," a greedy thief of Martial's work. But by the end of the poem Martial is actually offering himself as a ghost writer: the passage literally says, "a book already known (i.e., one that has been published) cannot change its author; but find an unpublished one and buy that – I have some, and no one will know: anybody who wants to become famous by reciting somebody else's poems must buy not a book but the author's silence." Martial ends by declaring himself quite willing to participate in the deception as long as he is paid; it's not the deception that bothers him, but the fact that he's been left out of it. This is nicely ironic, but it's also quite cynical, and doesn't look like a smoking gun to me. It should be added that all of it depends on a totally constructed persona: Martial, as a gentleman poet, does not in fact write for money – he doesn't even sell his books, he gives them away.

In i.72, Martial does name names, attacking a plagiarist named Fidentinus. Once again, the crime seems more generic than particular: it appears that this is not the name of someone real, but a symbolic name – according to Peter Howell's commentary on Martial, it is "intended to hint at the bearer's shamelessness."[6] *Fidens* means audacious or fearless, and *fidentinus* is a diminutive of it – something like calling him Rambino instead of Rambo. The *–tinus* ending, moreover, was a frequent marker of the names of ex-slaves; so the name also implies that the *plagiarius*, the slave-stealer, is a former slave himself. Here is the poem, again in Henry Killigrew's translation:

> For verses, Fidentine, thou stealst from me,
> A poet fain thou wouldst reputed be;
> Old Aegle so, well-tooth'd would yet be thought,
> When she a set of ivory teeth hath bought;
> Painted Lycoris to her self seems fair,
> Who only with a gypsie can compare,
> On like account, a poet thou art nam'd,
> And may'st, tho' bald, for youthful locks be fam'd.[7]

How bad, in this poem, is the false poet's theft? As bad, says Martial, as old women wearing dentures, or unattractive women wearing makeup, or bald men wearing wigs.

As bad as that! Not, at least to a modern eye, in the same league with kidnapping, or even with theft. Both these poems certainly address a danger faced by anyone pursuing a poetic career, but the danger is represented as being built into the system, and Martial sees himself in every sense as part of the system – just as this most social of poets remains part of the society in which women use cosmetics and want nice-looking teeth, men wear wigs, and rich phonies pay ghost writers. (There is actually no word for theft in the epigram; the opening lines say literally "Do you believe you'll be thought a poet with my verses?" – Martial has a lighter touch than Killigrew.) There are several other Martial epigrams on the subject, all of which strike me more as ironic and cynical than as ethically fervid; the indignation is there, but it turns immediately to wit. It should be noted that the word *plagiarius*, from which all future uses of the term applying to literary appropriation derive, appears in only one of them, i.52, where the purloined poems are conceived as Martial's slaves, whom he has freed by publishing them, and whom the plagiarist is attempting to re-enslave. This is where the metaphor comes from, and it is represented as something being done to the poems, not to Martial.

The plagiarism in all this strikes me as curiously disembodied – curiously, when I consider how outraged I feel when a student does it, to say nothing of when it's done to my own work (as it once was, in a conference paper, to my face – I emphatically did not feel like writing an amusing epigram). Consider this even more disembodied example in an epigram by Sir Thomas More entitled *Ad Gallum Sublegentem Veterum Carmina*, "To a Frenchman Stealing the Poetry of the Ancients" – the word used for the plagiarism here, *sublego*, is a straight theft word, meaning carry off secretly, so there's no question about whether what More is objecting to constitutes criminal behavior. Here is the poem:

Frenchman, surely you in our time have the same wit and inspiration
that the ancient poets had, for you write the same poems, and frequently
word for word.[8]

This is quite witty: is it really an attack on some anonymous Frenchman? Is the
saintly More really contenting himself here with condemning the fault and not
the actor of it? Or is this epigram perhaps a way of distinguishing himself as
a poet from all the poetasters who shall remain nameless – perhaps even from
that whole nation of poetasters across the Channel – the defining feature of
poetasters being precisely that they have no wit of their own? The trouble is,
however, that the defining feature of humanist poetry is precisely how closely
and accurately it replicates the ancients. Maybe this is not really a francophobic
barb but a sly joke about humanism itself, the thieving Frenchman as the
reductio ad absurdum of the humanist ideal. Many of More's own epigrams
are direct translations from the *Greek Anthology*; sometimes this is made clear,
but sometimes it is not. More surely would say that any properly educated
humanist would recognize the poems as homage, not theft – but so, doubtless,
would the Frenchman. Whatever plagiarism is here, it is not a danger – nobody
is stealing from More, and the condemnation, despite the charge of theft,
produces irony and wit, but not outrage.

None of this, I think, gets us anywhere near accounting for Sir Thomas
Browne's extraordinary effusion on plagiarism, which I cited in the influential
essay but didn't spend much time over, and which has continued to fascinate
me. Something did change in the seventeenth century. In Chapter 6 of
the *Pseudodoxia Epidemica* Browne deplores "a peremptory adhesion unto
Authority, and more especially the establishing of our belief upon the dictates
of Antiquity," which he calls "the mortallest enemy unto knowledge, and that
which hath done the greatest execution upon truth." What is pernicious about
this is not simply that it impedes the possibility of any skeptical empiricism
of our own, but even more that there is nothing about classical writers
that *entitles* them to be considered authoritative: their "volumes are meer
collections, drawn from the mouthes or leaves of other Authors," and here we
come to the real point:

Not a few transcriptively; subscribing their names unto other mens
endeavours, and meerly transcribing almost all they have written. The
Latines transcribing the Greeks, the Greeks and Latines each other.[9]

He then gives a compendious list of classical offenders, including many of the
monuments of ancient literature, history and science: Aristotle, Pliny, Lucian,

Apuleius, Aelian, Athenaeus, "and many more," he says. And then, hitting his stride,

> the wittiest piece of Ovid [the *Metamorphoses*] is beholding unto Parthenius Chius; even the magnified Virgil hath borrowed almost all his works: his Eclogues from Theocritus, his Georgicks from Hesiod and Aratus, his Aeneads from Homer; the second Book whereof containing the exploit of Sinon and the Trojan horse (as Macrobius observeth) he hath *verbatim* [note that *verbatim*] derived from Pisander. (p. 125)

Browne then moves on to the classics of his own profession, with ancient medical writers cribbing from Galen and from each other. Here is the moralization he draws from this catalogue of thievery:

> Thus may we perceive the Ancients were but men, even like ourselves. The practice of transcription in our daies was no monster in theirs: Plagiarie had not its nativity with printing ...

And lest we say that none of this is *really* plagiarism, since none of it involves the crucial intention to deceive, Browne blocks that exit too:

> Nor did they only make large use of other Authors, but often without mention of their names. *Aristotle*, who seems to have borrowed many things from *Hippocrates*, in the most favourable construction, makes mention but once of him, and that by the by, and without reference unto his present Doctrine. *Virgil*, so much beholding unto *Homer*, hath not his name in all his Works; and *Plinie*, who seems to borrow many Authors out of *Dioscorides*, hath taken no notice of him. I wish men were not still content to plume themselves with others feathers.

Browne does not even allow the distinction between plagiarism and allusion, or acknowledged borrowing, to be a real one:

> Fear of discovery, not single ingenuity [simple honesty] affords Quotations rather than Transcriptions ... . (p. 126)

The only reason people put things in quotes is not that they're honest but that they're afraid of being found out. "The ancients were but men, even like ourselves": everybody is guilty here – and one of Browne's modern editors remarks tartly, predictably, about this passage, "his comments were not very original."[10] Plagiarism is the original sin, the sin we are all guilty of. The only reason Homer is not indicted is that Browne does not know whom he copied from. What Browne says is that the price of literature, the price of a written tradition, is plagiarism; without plagiarism there is no Homer, no Aristotle, no Virgil, no Ovid ... . This is not, obviously, being offered as an argument in favor of plagiarism, but it also is not a claim, as it well might be, that plagiarism is a necessary evil, that the sin that makes us mortal also makes us human. Plagiarism is the symptom, not the disease: the attack on plagiarism becomes almost at once an attack on Virgil, Ovid, Aristotle. That is the disease: literature, culture, the classics, are precisely the problem. They are the stronghold of the pernicious adherence to authority, the enemy of experience and empirical science. Virgil imitated Homer because Homer was a classic, the poetry he cared most about, the center of the canon; and that is what has to go – the canon, the tradition, the desire to preserve and renew the greatness of the past. I really don't think Christopher Ricks wants Sir Thomas Browne as an ally.

What I find fascinating here are the totalizing aspects of this passage, especially coming from someone as genuinely literary as Browne, whose writing is so deeply and obviously imbued with a rich and detailed sense of – love of – the literary tradition, and is the product of great learning, and long and wide reading. The argument is undeniably perverse, and is not without its nonsensical side (how can Virgil's Latin be cribbed *verbatim* from Pisander's Greek?); but I find it nevertheless curiously compelling and moving. It indicates how much strain the scientific revolution – or, more precisely, construing Baconian science as a revolution – put on the whole concept of culture. There is no way of arguing that Browne doesn't really mean what he says, but his convictions run counter to his deepest beliefs, what he cares most about. The implied dialectic between science and culture is a striking expression of a particular moment of intellectual history, comparable to Milton's dialectic between his praise of, indeed identification with, Galileo, "the Tuscan artist"[11] (this is the only use of the word artist in Milton's poetry) and Raphael's rebuke to Adam for asking questions about astronomy.

I return now to Inigo Jones. Here is the story, summarized from my 1975 article. In 1638 Jones and Sir William Davenant produced two masques for the court. The first, *Britannia Triumphans*, danced by the king in January, celebrated the imminent success of the royal scheme of Ship Money. In 1629, outraged by what he took to be continual inroads on the crown's authority, frustrated by inadequate revenues and the failure of numerous proposals for new taxes, the king had dissolved parliament and determined to rule without it. His Attorney General William Noy scoured the statute books for sources of money. One such source was the revival of an Elizabethan tax on coastal towns for the support of the navy – such towns were targets of pirates and Spanish marauders, and were, in effect, paying for protection. In 1633 the tax was extended to the rest of the country, and met with considerable resistance, the opponents arguing that the imposition of ship money constituted taxation by royal fiat. The test case, *Rex versus Hampden*, was argued in 1637. In January 1638 the famous trial was about to reach its conclusion in the Star Chamber, with a narrow victory for the crown; this is what *Britannia Triumphans* proleptically celebrated. Three weeks later, at Shrovetide, the queen danced in *Luminalia*, Jones's most elaborate scenic spectacle up to that time. The complexity of the engineering was all the more impressive, Jones tells us in the published text of the masque, because it had to be devised very quickly:

> The King's majesty's masque being performed, the Queen commanded Inigo Jones ... to make a new subject of a masque for herself, that with high and hearty invention might give occasion for variety of scenes, strange apparitions, songs, music, and dancing ... . This being suddenly done and showed her majesty, and she approving it, the work was set in hand, and in all celerity performed in shorter time than anything here hath been done in this kind.

Modern scholarly opinion has been very hard on *Luminalia*, and Enid Welsford, the first British historian of the court masque, believed she had found the source of its poetic and dramatic deficiencies: "in no other masque," she writes, "is the plagiarism so blatant and so extensive. *Luminalia* is in fact nothing else but a clumsy adaptation of Francesco Cini's *Notte d'Amore*" (this being a Florentine production of 1608).[12]

Leaving aside the question of whether an adaptation from a foreign language, much less a clumsy one, can be considered an example of blatant plagiarism, clumsiness is not the only problem faced by the critic of *Luminalia*, because Jones's account of its sudden inception and hasty preparation, if it means what it seems to mean, cannot be true. Court correspondence in November and December of 1637 reported that the queen was preparing a Shrovetide masque, so the project had been under way for many months. Gerald E. Bentley believed that this contradiction, like the production's structural flaws, could also be explained by invoking the concept of plagiarism:

> No doubt Jones was in a great fret, first getting his masquing hall finished, then cleaning it all away before he could set his men to work on the elaborate constructions for *Luminalia*, but he did not need to wait

all this time to begin on the designs ... . Perhaps his uneasiness about
the plagiarism led him to magnify and advertise the pressure of time.[13]

Bentley's explanation for the apparent conflict between Jones's account and the
other evidence seems to run this way: Jones was sufficiently uncomfortable
about the plagiarism to want to cover himself by pleading extenuating
circumstances; and he did so by producing a lie which everybody who had
been at court since November would have known to be a lie.

This strikes me as very implausible. We have no way of determining
what really happened, but with the same information I can devise a more
credible hypothesis. All that the court correspondence tells us is that, in the
autumn, the queen was planning a Shrovetide masque. It says nothing about
what the subject was to be, how elaborate the spectacle was, how complex
the engineering. But we know that the king's masque in January, *Britannia
Triumphans*, was an exceedingly elaborate one, with multiple scene changes
and lots of machinery; it included visions of hell, the Palace of Fame, a
sea-triumph of Galatea, the fleet in full sail. And Jones tells us that after the
queen saw this masque, she commanded him "to make a new subject of a
masque for herself, that with high and hearty invention might give occasion
for variety of scenes, strange apparitions," and so forth. This account suggests
to me that the queen wanted just what Jones says she wanted: "a new subject
of a masque" – not the masque they had been planning, but a new and much
more elaborate one that would compete in splendor with the masque Jones
had devised for the king.

In this hypothesis, it will be seen that the question of plagiarism has become
a red herring. In fact, I was and continue to be puzzled about where it came
from, because what Welsford discovered behind *Luminalia* was not a smoking
gun, it was simply a source. There are few Stuart masques, and indeed few
Stuart plays, that are not similarly based on earlier examples of the genre. If
Luminalia constitutes plagiarism, so does Shakespeare's use of old plays like
Hamlet, old romances like *Romeus and Juliet*, old novels like *Rosalynde*. There
is nothing in Welsford or Bentley attacking Shakespeare on such grounds, and
I speculated that the charge of plagiarism was here doing service for something
else – for all those other qualities of Inigo Jones's that displease the modern
critic but somehow don't seem sufficiently actionable: preferring spectacle to
poetry, disliking Ben Jonson enough to get him fired. (Bentley actually doesn't
like Jonson's interest in the masque much either, and finds the form on the
whole trivial and immoral. Declaring a masque plagiarized is a good way of
removing it from serious consideration.)

Ricks didn't contest my analysis of this material, and I imagine he doesn't disagree with it. My interests in the subject, however, are really the opposite of his. Ricks finds a general tendency nowadays to excuse or overlook or argue away plagiarism; I am concerned with a general tendency in modern scholarship to invoke it as a universal explanation. Here are a couple of other examples, which are also cited in my original article. Don Cameron Allen discovered a particularly flagrant example of plagiarism in that indispensable classic of Elizabethan literary criticism, Francis Meres's *Palladis Tamia*. Allen demonstrated that the book was a pure pastiche, and that its material derived, moreover, not even from classic or obscure sources, but from absolutely standard Renaissance compilations of the sort that were used as school texts. This established, for Allen, the meretricious worthlessness of the book, and became the basis of an attack not only on the ignorance of modern critics, who take Meres seriously, but on the whole Renaissance educational system which, grounded as it was exclusively in the practice of imitation, fitted a student like Meres (and, it presumably follows, like Jonson and Shakespeare) precisely for nothing better than plagiarism.

Here, the facts seemed to me incontrovertible, but the conclusions did not follow. What did the Renaissance reader see in this blatant rehash? If Meres's material was cribbed from standard schoolbooks, weren't contemporary readers aware that they'd heard it all before? Why was the book popular? It went through three editions, the last as late as 1636, and it was only one of a great many such compilations in the period. Were Renaissance readers simply being deceived? Or did they find in the book precisely the force of the *commonplace*, a term that suggests to us a thing not worth saying, but implied to the Renaissance a universal truth? The volume's full title is *Palladis Tamia, or Wit's Treasury*. Did anyone buying a book called *Wit's Treasury* think he was paying for originality?

The commonplace book, indeed, was a commonplace undertaking in Renaissance culture, and everyone understood its conventions. Ben Jonson's *Timber, or Discoveries* was his commonplace book, duly published in the second volume of the 1640 folio among his works. There are original thoughts in this miscellaneous compilation, but Jonson mingles his own ideas with a good deal of continental wisdom, to which his only contribution is a translation into English. There is rarely any indication of the source of the quotations, and therefore no way of knowing, without a good deal of detective work, what is original with Jonson and what comes from the great *copia* outside his head. I doubt that the question of deception is relevant here, any more than it is with Meres: it is clear that this is a commonplace book. What is striking and significant for us is surely that Jonson apparently did not want, or require, a record of where his wisdom came from.

I observed in the essay that modern critics are usually willing to allow Renaissance authors their sources provided they are sufficiently classical. If *Luminalia* had been based on Ovid, rather than on Francesco Cini, Welsford and Bentley probably wouldn't have felt they had a case. Even with classical sources, however, the idea of intermediate texts disturbs us. Allen has it in for *Palladis Tamia* not because it's a pastiche of classical passages, but because Meres didn't go to original texts.[14] He used contemporary handbooks and anthologies, and Allen therefore believed that his intention was to deceive the reader into thinking he was a scholar. Ernest W. Talbert used the same line of argument to level a charge of plagiarism against Ben Jonson.[15] Talbert discovered that Jonson's learned citations are often copied from Renaissance dictionaries and encyclopedias; Jonson's learning, Talbert felt, was thereby impugned. On this basis he accused the poet of lying when he claims, in the dedicatory epistle to *The Masque of Queens*, that he wrote the work "out of the fullness and memory of my former readings." But (I am quoting myself; the point still seems to me valid) every age has its reference books, and a more scrupulous generation than ours may criticize us for failing to acknowledge our use of bibliographies and periodical indexes – to say nothing of the internet – as if we were thereby pretending to carry all the relevant scholarship in our heads.

I find these examples more offensive than amusing, and what offends me in them is the way invoking plagiarism enables these scholars to condescend to their material – indeed, D. C. Allen's characteristic attitude toward much of the work he spent his life editing and elucidating was one of amused condescension. Talbert's charges seem to me particularly offensive, impugning not only Jonson's ethics but his learning. Literally hundreds of volumes of the classics survive from Jonson's library, many with copious marginalia in his hand. It is simply preposterous to claim that Jonson wasn't familiar with the texts he cites because he sometimes cites them from secondary sources. As a poet who habitually lived beyond his income, he was always selling off books and buying new ones as he could afford them, and he used whatever texts were conveniently available. The fact that Talbert was eventually forced by Percy Simpson to back down seems to me only to reveal how clear the case is. Invoking plagiarism was the first, automatic response, the one that came without thinking.

Talbert's charge against Jonson was in fact, as I pointed out, anticipated 250 years earlier by Aphra Behn. For Behn, it formed part of an invidious comparison between Jonson and Shakespeare, the invidious point being that since the uneducated Shakespeare wrote better plays than the learned Jonson, and since the only intellectual advantage men have over women derives from their education, there was no reason why women should not be as good playwrights as Shakespeare, and better than Jonson. But, for Behn, the trouble with Jonson goes deeper than his erudition: she goes on to argue – a little self-contradictorily – that Jonson wasn't even all that learned,

> for I am informed his learning was but grammar high (sufficient indeed to rob poor Sallust of his best orations) ... .

Jonson clearly has to be disposed of, not simply demoted; but as a way of disposing of him, this is a very odd example. The Sallust quotations are used by Jonson in his tragedy *Catiline*. They are Catiline's speeches, and Jonson includes them because, according to Sallust, they are what Catiline actually said. To accuse Jonson of plagiarizing from Sallust makes about as much sense as accusing Sallust of plagiarizing from Catiline.

Idiotic as Aphra Behn's plagiarism claim certainly is, it isn't merely idiotic: there is an agenda behind it. The agenda is largely self-serving, concerned with establishing her own credentials, and thereby those of any woman, as a playwright, but Behn is completely open about that; moreover, she is clearly having a good time. There is also an agenda behind Welsford, Bentley, Allen and Talbert, but it is unacknowledged. It has to do with the kind of control modern scholarship has wanted to exercise, the kind of moral superiority we have wanted to assert, over the material we work on; with our general attitude toward the past; and ultimately with the kind of attitude toward literature and culture that we have wanted to inculcate in our students. It treats the past as a childish or recalcitrant or incomplete version of ourselves; it fails to acknowledge the ways in which early modern societies were genuinely different from ours and their terms significantly untranslatable – requiring us, that is, not to "modernize," but to learn their language. In this agenda, charges of lying and bad faith become simply a routine way of disposing of whatever we do not like or understand. Most of all, it ignores or suppresses any cultural differences that might call our own standards into question, and resists any contemplation of the standards and assumptions from which we regard the past. It is an agenda that seems to me admirably characterized by Ricks's phrase "weakly, wizenedly political." As to whether current academic moral standards really represent a decline from this ethical eminence I hesitate to say. But certainly if the history of our response to plagiarism constitutes an ethical barometer, it is several centuries since we had anything to be proud of.

Notes

1 Stephen Orgel, "The Renaissance Artist as Plagiarist." *ELH*, vol. 48, no. 4: 476–95. The essay is reprinted in my collection *The Authentic Shakespeare, and Other Problems of the Early Modern Stage* (New York, 2002).

2 Christopher Ricks, "Plagiarism," *Proceedings of the British Academy, no. 97*: 149–68.

3 "Purloined Letters: Are We Too Quick to Condemn *Plagiarism*?" *The New Yorker*, vol. 72, no. 43 (January 20, 1997), pp. 93–7.

4 See Peter Landesman, "A 20th-Century Master Scam," *New York Times Magazine* (July 18, 1999): 30ff.

5 [Henry Killigrew,] *Epigrams of Martial Englished* (London, 1695), numbered 67.

6 Peter Howell, *A Commentary on Book One of the Epigrams of Martial* (London, 1980), p. 168.

7 Killigrew, *Martial*, numbered 73.

8 Thomas More, *The Latin Epigrams*, ed. Leicester Bradner and Charles Arthur Lynch (Chicago, 1953), no. 220.

9 *The Prose of Sir Thomas Browne*, ed. Norman Endicott (Garden City, NY, 1967), p. 124.

10 Ibid., p. 558

11 *Paradise Lost*, I.288.

12 Enid Welsford, *The Court Masque* (Cambridge, 1927), p. 236.

13 G. E. Bentley, *The Jacobean and Caroline Stage* (Oxford, 1956), vol. 3, p. 209.

14 See the Introduction to D. C. Allen, *Francis Meres's Treatise "Poetrie"* (Urbana, IL, 1933).

15 E. W. Talbert, "Current Scholarly Works and the 'Erudition' of Jonson's *Masque of Augurs*," *Studies in Philology*, vol. 44 (1947), pp. 605–24; see also the earlier article "New Light on Ben Jonson's Workmanship," *Studies in Philology*, vol. 40 (1943), pp. 154–85. The argument was called to account by Percy Simpson in *Ben Jonson* (Oxford, 1950), vol. X, p. 640. Talbert implicitly recants in D. T. Starnes and E. W. Talbert, *Classical Myth and Legend in Renaissance Dictionaries* (Chapel Hill, NC, 1955), p. 212, but not without some amusingly self-defensive scholarly gobbledygook in n. 69, p. 432.

Part IV

The visual arts

12

Devils incarnate

My title refers to Roger Ascham's famous aphorism, that Italians are wicked, but the Italianate Englishman is the devil incarnate; and I begin with two obviously Italianate Englismen, Inigo Jones and Ben Jonson. In 1613 and 1614 Jones accompanied the Earl and Countess of Arundel on a trip to Italy, serving as their cultural guide and interpreter – his qualifications were primarily in his aesthetic expertise, though he also knew the country, having spent some time in Italy a decade earlier. His sketch book from the Arundel trip survives, a fascinating record of an English artist teaching himself to be Italianate. To compare the Jones of the first decade of the seventeenth century, for example a nymph for an unidentified entertainment of about 1605 (figure 12.1), with a page of the sketch book (figure 12.2), shows him learning not only a style but how to make a sketch book that looks Italian (so it includes a couple of examples of older men leering at attractive youths, an exemplary case for the English of the Italian devil incarnate). Jonson, at his most acerbic in the quarrel with Jones, calls him *Iniquo*. The pun is particularly insulting precisely because it is Italian.

On a practical level, what did it mean for Jones to be Italianate? His architectural practice is generally described as classicizing, but the classical in Queen's House, Greenwich, or in the Banqueting House (figure 12.3), is obviously learned less from the classical Vitruvius than from the contemporary Alberti, Serlio and Michelangelo, and in any case, certainly not from any Roman remains. Jones's Italian classicism also included a great deal of hybridization, the Italian grafted onto the English, sometimes perforce, as in the new west façade he erected on old St Paul's cathedral (figure 12.4); but sometimes by design, as in the setting for Oberon's palace in Jonson's masque *Oberon*, performed in 1611 (figure 12.5). Whether one considers the Italian elements here a refinement or a corruption will depend not only on one's taste, but on which side one took in the current debate over British history – whether Britain was authentically Roman because it was founded by the legendary

12.1 Inigo Jones, winged masquer, design for an unknown entertainment, c. 1605.

12.2 *(opposite)* A page from Inigo Jones's Roman sketchbook, 1613–14.

Brutus, grandson of Aeneas; or whether the Romans were, on the contrary, not ancestors to be revered but aliens and invaders, oppressors rather than civilizers. Jones's treatise on Stonehenge declares Jones's position quite clearly: the ancient British monument (figure 12.6) is a Roman temple dedicated to Coelus, and preserves the most basic of the classical architectural orders, the Tuscan – the ancient Italian style is, for Jones, more quintessentially classical than the standard Greek orders of architectural classicism, Doric, Ionic and Corinthian. By his return from the Arundel trip, his stage designs have taken the Serlian models completely to heart. The quick sketch of "a street in fair

12.3 The Whitehall Banqueting House, from Thomas H. Shepherd, *London and its Environs in the Nineteenth Century*, 1831.

12.4 Wenceslaus Hollar, Inigo Jones's west portico of old St Paul's, from William Dugdale, *The History of St Paul's Cathedral in London*, 1658.

12.5 Inigo Jones, Oberon's palace from Ben Jonson's masque *Oberon*, 1611.

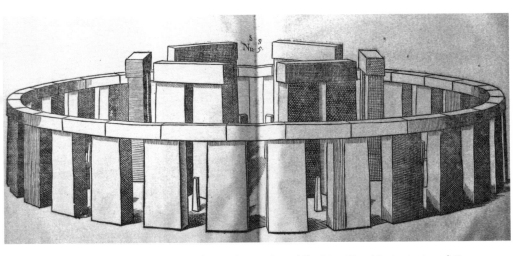

12.6 After Inigo Jones, reconstruction of Stonehenge, from *The Most Notable Antiquity of Great Britain, vulgarly called Stone-Heng*, 1655.

12.7 Inigo Jones, "A street in perspective of fair building," stage design for Ben Jonson's masque *The Vision of Delight*, 1617.

12.8 Inigo Jones, stage design for the Sieur de Racan's *Artenice*, 1626.

perspective" for Jonson's *Vision of Delight*, 1617 (figure 12.7), is purely Italian, and the elegant setting for the court pastoral *Artenice*, 1626 (figure 12.8), combines the elements of the Serlian tragic, comic and pastoral scenes into a beautifully realized synthesis. This is a style that Jones has clearly made his own.

The Italianate Jonson is, obviously, more directly classical – Jonson's Italy is the Italy of Martial, Horace, Terence, not least, of course, because he had never been there – but his masques show a clear awareness of recent Florentine models, possibly derived from the returning traveler Inigo Jones. The visual arts, however, provide Jonson with a touchstone for the taste that he craves as much as the diabolical Iniquo. "The pen," Jonson wrote in his commonplace book *Timber, or Discoveries*, "is more noble than the pencil; for that can speak to the understanding, the other, but to the sense" (1528–30). The invidious comparison here is between the written word and pictorial art; but the synecdoche itself shades the two into each other: Inigo Jones did his drawings in pen and ink, while the books that survive from Jonson's library include many with marginalia in pencil – the instrument of Jones's invention was the pen, that of Jonson's understanding the pencil. In fact, the passage, *Poesis et pictura*, goes on to praise picture more highly than poetry. It is "the invention of heaven: the most ancient, and most akin to nature." The two arts, moreover, are indissolubly linked, just as sense and understanding are; and "whosoever loves not picture is injurious to truth, and all the wisdom of poetry" (1536–38).

But what pictures does Jonson have in mind? Many of them are certainly, if not fictitious, at least exclusively textual, such as those lost masterpieces of Apelles and Zeuxis described by Pliny, or Philostratus's gallery of *Icones*. Jonson's sense of modern masterworks similarly derives from descriptions and catalogues – it is unlikely that he read Vasari, though he certainly knew people who did; but his account of ancient and modern painting comes quite directly from Antonio Possevino's *Bibliotheca Selecta*, published in 1593, a guide to the history of the arts and sciences. *Timber* is, after all, a collection of authoritative opinions; but the authority behind them is rarely Jonson's. In this sense, his praise of picture is a praise of ekphrasis, and the pen and the pencil are one.

In a peculiarly indicative passage Jonson cites a list of the best artists of his own time, "six famous painters who were excellent, and emulous of the Ancients." The six are in fact seven: Raphael, Michelangelo, Titian, Correggio, Sebastiano del Piombo, Giulio Romano and Andrea del Sarto. The list – including the erroneous number – is copied from Possevino, who in turn is copying G. B. Armenini's *De' Veri Precetti della Pittura* (Ravenna, 1586), and the slip in the numbering suggests that Possevino's sense of painting is no less textual than Jonson's: Armenini in fact names eight excellent artists, and implies that there are many more; his list starts with Leonardo, who is his benchmark, includes the seven cited by Jonson, and concludes with "molti altri." Possevino, however, translating the passage into Latin, streamlines Titian's name as it appears in Armenini, "Titian da Cadoro" (i.e., from his birthplace, Cadore) to simply "Titiano," and omits the comma between him and "Antonio Corrigiensi," making Titian and Correggio appear to be a single artist, Titiano Antonio Corrigiensi – though they would appear so, obviously, only to someone who had never heard of Correggio and knew too little about Titian to know his full name. This, therefore, must be the case with Possevino, unlikely as it would seem in a late sixteenth-century Italian Jesuit writing a handbook of the arts. Jonson, on the other hand, clearly knows that Titian is not Correggio, because he re-inserts the comma; but he still follows Possevino in numbering the seven great painters six. Authority is not to be lightly rejected.

What visual experience is there behind this textual praise of painting? What pictures would Jonson have seen? Not, certainly, many originals by the artists on his list – though also not necessarily none. The collecting instinct was starting to burgeon in England. Leicester was said to have owned some Venetian paintings, though there is no record of what they were, and Sidney knew enough to sit for Veronese when he was in Venice, though the portrait's recipient, his friend Hubert Languet, was not happy with the result, and the picture has since disappeared. Robert Cecil, Earl of Salisbury, Jonson's patron on more than one occasion, was a notable connoisseur (he was furnishing Hatfield House), and owned works by both Italian and Netherlandish artists, as did two other patrons of Jonson's, the Earl of Somerset and the Duke of Buckingham. Prince Henry, under Salisbury's guidance, became a passionate collector of paintings and bronzes. The Earl and Countess of Arundel formed the greatest art collection in Jacobean England, and acquired works by Leonardo, Michelangelo, Raphael, Giulio Romano and Annibale Carracci to display beside their inherited Holbeins.

There was, in fact, a good deal of information circulating in Jonson's England about who were the right artists to admire and invest in – Possevino would have been, for Jonson, at most a convenience. Richard Haydocke, translator of Paolo Lomazzo's *Trattato dell'Arte della Pittura*, published in English in 1598 as *A Tracte conteining the Artes of Curious Painting*, noted "many noblemen then furnishing their houses with the excellent monuments of sundry famous and ancient masters, both Italian and German" – it is perhaps indicative of how essentially literary Jonson's sense of the artistic canon is that it includes only Italian names. But Jonson's best source of information, along with whatever entree he may have had to the works themselves, would certainly have been Inigo Jones, at least as long as they remained on friendly terms. Jones was by 1615 a genuine expert. Even before the Italian trip with the Arundels he was advising the Prince of Wales and the Earl of Rutland on artistic matters, and after his return his major clients, in addition to the Arundels, were Prince Charles and the Duke of Buckingham.

Still, whatever pictures Jonson saw, he mentions painters but no paintings. The only actual works he refers to by any of the artists he singles out for praise are Giulio Romano's notorious set of sexual positions, *I Modi*, which circulated as prints, accompanied by the salacious sonnets of Pietro Aretino. Lady Politic Would-Be uses them in *Volpone* to show off her familiarity with Italian culture:

> But for a desperate wit, there's Aretine
> Only his pictures are a little obscene. (III.4.96–70)

If Jonson had left it there, this would be simply a joke at the expense of the expatriate nouveau-riche Englishwoman. But three scenes later the uxorious Corvino, who certainly knows his Italian pornographers, worries about "some young Frenchman, or hot Tuscan blood,/ That had read Aretine, conned all his prints" (III.7.59–60). And five years later, in *The Alchemist*, the world's expert on pornographic painting Sir Epicure Mammon imagines his "oval room/ Filled with such pictures as Tiberius took/ From Elephantis, and dull Aretine/ But coldly imitated" (II.2.43–4). Jonson, in short, seems to be under the impression that the pictures are by Aretino. Possibly Jonson had read the sonnets, which were easily available, but had not seen the prints, which were suppressed; nevertheless, turning Aretino into a visual artist and eliding Giulio Romano is surely the most complete triumph of ekphrasis the Renaissance offers.

Ignorance is, of course, no impediment to the deployment of artistic allusion. Giulio Romano is, notoriously, the only modern artist named by Shakespeare, who knew so little about him that he made him a sculptor, the creator of Hermione's lifelike statue in *The Winter's Tale*. Giulio did no sculptures; but the name of the great artist alone is sufficient to establish Paulina's (or Shakespeare's) credentials as a connoisseur. Jonson's list of names from Possevino would doubtless have been similarly sufficient to certify Jonson's expertise – even, perhaps (since *Timber* is his own commonplace book), to certify it to himself.

I pause over this only because Jonson's praise of "picture" is so genuinely magnanimous, but at the same time so relentlessly unspecific. For comparison, Donne, in "The Storm," reveals an equally unspecific but nevertheless much more direct knowledge of contemporary painting:

> ... a hand or eye
> By Hilliard drawn, is worth an history
> By a worse painter made ... . (ll. 3–5)

The engraved frontispiece portrait of Donne in the 1635 *Poems* is apparently based on a lost Hilliard miniature, and a superb Isaac Oliver portrait of Donne survives; I have discussed the iconography of the Donne portraits in the essay "Not His Picture But His Book," in this volume. Donne and Jonson were close friends, and Oliver was Jonson's neighbor when both lived in Blackfriars. The three must have known each other. But, as I observe in the essay on frontispiece portraits, they seem not to have inhabited the same cultural world. Jonson had no interest in investing his immortality in the visual arts, and admonished the reader of Shakespeare's works to "look/ Not on his picture, but his book" (ll. 9–10).

Let us return now to the invocation of Giulio Romano in *The Winter's Tale* to create the surpassingly lifelike statue of the late queen Hermione, commissioned by the noble Paulina, connoisseur and architect of the play's reconciliations. In the final scene, the statue is revealed, and brought to life. The invocation of Giulio Romano is striking for a number of reasons: this is the only allusion in Shakespeare to a modern artist and, indeed, one of the earliest references to Giulio in England – Shakespeare here, as nowhere else, appears to be in touch with the avant-garde of the visual arts. But Giulio was not a sculptor, and in fact the name is all the play gives us – as it turns out, there is no statue; the figure Paulina unveils is the living queen.

The relation between art and life is particularly direct here, and the ability of the great artist to restore the losses of the past and reconcile the present to them is represented as axiomatic. But the name of the artist is essential, the name of an artist renowned for his skill at producing the illusion of life; and a modern artist, moreover, not a historical figure like Phidias or Zeuxis, who might be expected to be supplying art treasures in ancient Sicily, where *The Winter's Tale* is set. The formidable model for Paulina is surely the Countess of Arundel, depicted in figure 12.9 by David Mytens before her gallery. She and the Earl formed the greatest collection of art works in Jacobean England. They owned, indeed, a number of Giulio's drawings, including preparatory sketches for the luxuriantly lifelike frescos at the Palazzo Tè, though these had not been acquired by 1610.

12.9 Daniel Mytens,
Alathea Talbot Howard,
Countess of Arundel,
c. 1618.

English collectors in the first decade of the seventeenth century began for
the first time to be serious connoisseurs, dispatching experts to the continent
to buy for them, and concerned with acquiring expertise of their own. On
the continent conspicuous collections of great art had for more than a century
been an attribute of princely magnificence, and Henry VIII had to some extent
undertaken to emulate his contemporaries Francis I and Charles V in this
respect: there were no Titians in the Tudor royal gallery, but the Holbeins and
Torrigianos suggest a very high standard of artistic taste. The taste, however,
was obviously not genetic: Queen Mary's court painter was Antonio Mor,
not a bad choice, but hardly in the league of Holbein; and neither Elizabeth
nor James had much interest in the arts as such, nor had they any interest

whatever in increasing the royal collection. James's son Henry, Prince of Wales, promised to change all that.

Prince Henry seems to have been introduced to connoisseurship around 1610, when he was sixteen, by Robert Cecil, Earl of Salisbury, and Arundel. Cecil already had a notable collection, and at Henry's request he sent a group of paintings for the prince's attention; it went without saying that one of them would remain with the prince as a gift to form the nucleus of a royal collection

12.10 Palma Giovane, *Prometheus (or Tityus) Chained to the Rock.*

that would stamp this prince as a true Renaissance monarch. Cecil was to accompany the pictures and expound their merits (and presumably ensure that Henry chose the right one to keep with the Earl's compliments). The painting Cecil gave the prince was Palma Giovane's *Prometheus Chained to the Rock* (figure 12.10).[1] It had been acquired for him in 1608 by Sir Henry Wotton, the English ambassador in Venice. This is a painting that is not much regarded now, and it *is* rather grim. Nevertheless, it really can be considered one of the foundational works of English artistic taste, a touchstone that almost by itself established the market for Venetian painting in England. Wotton, indeed, had sent it to Cecil in the first place in order to establish his own credentials as an artistic agent and broker. Palma's *Prometheus* was the work that made everyone want big dramatic Venetian paintings, not just Palmas, but the bigger (and more expensive) names: Titians, Veroneses, Tintorettos. Thereafter it was made clear that gentlemen desiring Prince Henry's favor could do no better than give him paintings.

The prince's own taste, insofar as one can judge it, was eclectic, voracious, and, it has to be admitted, relatively uninformed. The largest purchases were Dutch and Flemish, but that was only because the market was closer and the agents more familiar: he was in fact the first large purchaser of Venetian paintings in England. When he asks for gifts from continental princes eager to curry favor with the next king of England, the requests are little short of megalomaniac: not merely miniature bronzes by Giambologna – in response he received a number of miniature *copies* of Giambologna statues – but even the *Rape of the Sabines* in the Piazza Signoria in Florence, and a Michelangelo ceiling from the Palazzo Medici in Siena. (There is neither a Michelangelo ceiling nor a Palazzo Medici in Siena, so in this case a refusal was easy.) He also asked for and was sent portraits of illustrious men, such as had graced the royal gallery of Cosimo de' Medici (being a Renaissance prince meant imitating the lifestyles of the rich and famous); scenes of famous battles both on land and sea, night pieces, exercises in perspective and *trompe l'oeil* combining art with the new science of optics; even scientific instruments themselves were included, for example a model of a perpetual motion machine constructed by the Prince's resident magus Cornelius Drebbel (it worked by changes in barometric pressure, and was somehow supposed to demonstrate the validity of the Ptolemaic system against the claims of Copernicus and Galileo). Indeed, the request for the miniatures and the Michelangelo ceiling was accompanied by further requests for a new type of magnet and the latest book by Galileo (was the prince unpersuaded by Drebbel's machine?), as well as for the plans of Michelangelo's staircase in the Laurentian library, and the formula for a new cement capable of sealing pipes so that they could carry water uphill without leaking. The art gallery was also to be a historical and scientific museum, a cabinet of wonders, perhaps most of all an architectural masterpiece including elaborate fountains and waterworks.

Figure 12.11 is the companion piece to Mytens's portrait of the Countess of Arundel. The Earl's own collection was less eclectic than Prince Henry's, but here again it was not simply a reflection of the new connoisseurship, and, despite the obvious pride expressed by the two portraits of the Earl and Countess posing before their treasures, it was really not what we would call an art gallery. The Arundel Marbles seem to us the forerunners of the Elgin Marbles; but they looked quite different to contemporary observers. Arundel's protégé Henry Peacham, the author of *The Compleat Gentleman*, praises the statues in terms that are indicative: there is nothing about ideal Greek bodies or perfect proportion or *contrapposto*; they bring the past to life – what they give the observer, he says, is "the pleasure of seeing and conversing with these old heroes ... ." As for Arundel House, Peacham calls it "the chief English scene of ancient inscriptions ... ."[2] It is rather startling to us to take up John Selden's book entitled *Marmora Arundelliana* and to find in it not depictions of the sculptures but pages like that reproduced in figure 12.12. Peacham continues, "You shall find all the walls of the house inlaid with them and speaking Greek and Latin to you. The garden especially will afford you the pleasure of a world of learned lectures in this kind".[3] A world of learned lectures: the collecting passion was not simply aesthetic; it also involved a profound interest in recovering and preserving the past, an education in history; and, significantly, connoisseurship has become the essential mark of a gentleman, marked as much by his taste as by his lineage.

Such a claim involves quite a new notion of both gentleman and artist. In 1628, the year in which Selden published the *Marmora Arundelliana*, Rubens wrote from London to a friend in Paris of "the incredible quantity of excellent pictures, statues, and ancient inscriptions which are to be found in this Court" – notice how the inscriptions are mentioned in the same breath as the works of art. His highest praise was reserved for one of Arundel's sculptures: "I confess that I have never seen anything in the world more rare, from the point of view of antiquity."[4] As the last bit suggests, to collectors like Arundel and artists like Rubens a primary value of the visual and plastic arts was their memorializing quality, their link to the past and the vision of permanence they implied. This is why Peacham emphasizes the importance and rarity not only of the statues but of the inscriptions: they were an essential element of the artistic power of the past. The word established the significance, the authority, of classical imagery, and modern masterpieces – the work of Giambologna, Michelangelo, Rubens – existed in a direct continuum with the arts of Greece and Rome.

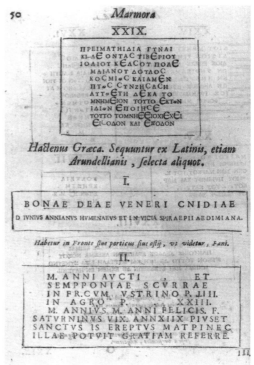

12.11 Daniel Mytens, Thomas Howard, 2nd Earl of Arundel, c. 1618.

12.12 John Selden, a page of inscriptions from *Marmora Arundelliana*, 1628.

Here is a very clear example of the relation of the verbal and visual arts in the period. Arundel conceived his collection not simply as a private matter, treasures for his personal enjoyment, but as an education in taste for the nation – as such, it would also serve, of course, as a monument to his own taste and magnificence. To this end he commissioned Wenceslaus Hollar to produce etchings of the principal masterpieces, with a view to publishing a volume of them. One of the first that Hollar completed was a rather grisly scene from ancient history, *King Seleucis Ordering his Son's Eye to Be Put Out*, after a sketch by Giulio Romano for a fresco in the Palazzo Tè (figure 12.13). The subject was a moral story about the perquisites and obligations of power – the son had committed adultery, the stipulated punishment for which was that the perpetrator's eyes were to be put out. The father, as king, could have repealed the sentence, but instead he chose merely to mitigate it by ordering that only one of his son's eyes be blinded. The etching could

12.13 Wenceslaus Hollar, etching after Giulio Romano, *King Seleucis Ordering his Son's Eye to Be Put Out.*

certainly have stood on its own, a record of an exemplary work by one of the greatest Renaissance history painters, but it comes accompanied with a set of inscriptions. First Henry Peacham moralizes the scene in a Latin epigram which effectively suppresses the fact that the story is as much an instance of judicial nepotism as of justice tempered with mercy: one always had to be told how to take historical examples, which have an uncomfortable tendency to imply the wrong morals along with the right ones. Below this Hollar places a dedication to Arundel establishing all his credentials: his hereditary titles, his position as Earl Marshall, his Garter knighthood, the fact that he is the greatest amateur, collector and promoter of the visual arts in the world; and then establishing his own claims to artistic eminence: "This picture, first drawn by Giulio Romano" – notice how long it takes to get to the artist – "now preserved in Arundel House, and here engraved after the original, Wenceslaus Hollar humbly dedicates and consecrates...", and so on. The drawing comes accompanied with both a pedigree and an ethical commentary, a "learned lecture"; these are both essential to the picture.

Arundel's pictures served him as a species of validation, establishing not only his taste but his authority within his own history as well. Early in his career he began collecting Holbein portraits, of which a number had come to him by inheritance. Holbeins were very expensive in England at this time, as much for nationalistic reasons, the artist's record of Henry VIII and his court, as for his artistic excellence. But he had a particular connection with the Arundels, having painted many of the Earl's ancestors, including the unfortunate Henry Howard, Earl of Surrey, who had been executed for treason; so the expense was also undertaken to assemble a visible family history. It undeniably helped to establish the Earl's fame as a connoisseur – Arundel House contained over thirty Holbein oil portraits – but here, again, the history was as important as the aesthetics, as the following story shows. In 1620 Cosimo de' Medici II, the Duke of Florence, wrote requesting one of the Earl's Holbeins as a gift. He offered to send any of his own paintings in exchange. He was, he wrote, "passionately set upon having a work by this artist." Arundel dispatched a splendid portrait of Sir Richard Southwell (figure 12.14), duly furnished

12.14 Hans Holbein the younger, Portrait of Sir Richard Southwell.

with appropriate inscriptions praising the artist, memorializing the sitter, and identifying the donor and recipient connoisseurs by their coats of arms – once again, the inscriptions are essential.

Now, for Arundel, the Southwell portrait was a piece of family history in the worst way: Southwell had been instrumental in the arrest and execution of the Earl of Surrey. If the decision to purge the art collection of an old enemy seems logical, however, this in fact was not Arundel's motive. He at once commissioned a copy of the painting, and it continued to hang among the ancestors Southwell had betrayed. However demonic the sitter, whatever else the painting was, it was history. For Cosimo, on the other hand, it was both art and an index to his own power as a collector, and he hung it among the greatest treasures of the Uffizi, where it still resides.

After Prince Henry's death in 1612, Prince Charles inherited most of his brother's treasures, and, with the advice and encouragement of two of his father's favorites, Somerset and Buckingham (Charles and Arundel were on the whole not on good terms), added constantly to them, both by purchasing other collections and by commissioning paintings from the major artists of the day, most significantly Rubens and van Dyck. Figure 12.15 shows van Dyck's triple portrait of him, prepared for Bernini: of course Charles wanted the greatest Italian sculptor to immortalize his head. The ironies are obvious; and the bust, destroyed in a fire at Whitehall in 1698, was no more immortal than its original. By the mid-1630s the Caroline royal pictures constituted one of the greatest art collections in the world. There was more in this acquisitive passion than aesthetics and conspicuous consumption. Just as, in the sixteenth century, artists came increasingly to be considered not mere craftsmen but philosophers and sages (thus the greatest artist of the age is referred to, in the account of his funeral, as "the divine Michelangelo"), so increasingly in the period great art was felt, in a way that was at once pragmatic and quasi-mystical, to be a manifestation of the power and authority of its possessor. Great artists became essential to the developing concept of monarchy and to the idealization of the increasingly watered-down aristocracy, to realize and deploy the imagery of legitimacy and greatness.

The extent to which the power of art became a practical reality in England at this time may be gauged by a brief comparison of two large royal expenditures. In 1627, in the midst of the long and disastrous war England waged with Spain and subsequently with France, the Duke of Buckingham led an expedition to relieve a trapped Huguenot garrison at La Rochelle. But his troops proved insufficient, and, in urgent need of reinforcements and pay for the soldiers, he appealed to the king. Charles believed wholeheartedly in the cause, but money was difficult to find; after three weeks, £14,000 and 2,000

12.15 Sir Anthony van Dyck, Triple Portrait of Charles I.

additional troops were committed to the enterprise. These proved utterly inadequate, and Buckingham was forced to retreat ignominiously. Throughout this period, however, Charles was eagerly negotiating for the magnificent art collection of the Gonzaga Dukes of Mantua, which had recently come on the market, including Mantegna's vast *Triumph of Caesar*, one of Charles's most important artistic purchases, still in the royal collection. For this he paid, in 1627 and 1628, a total of £25,500. To this monarch, a royal gallery full of Italian masterpieces was worth far more than a successful army.

But, to a generation of Britons, Charles himself was the devil incarnate – Milton compared him with the diabolical Richard III, and Milton's Satan, with his ardent patronage of Mammon, shared Charles's aesthetic tastes. One of Cromwell's first acts upon declaring himself Lord Protector was to sell off the the Titians, the most famous and valuable paintings in the royal collection, and thus purge the realm of this most visible evidence of Italian culture.

Notes

1 The painting was also referred to as *Tityus*, and may be found catalogued under either title.
2 Henry Peacham, *The Compleat Gentleman*, 2nd edition (1634), pp. 110, 112.
3 Ibid., p. 112.
4 *Letters of Peter Paul Rubens*, ed. R. S. Magurn (Cambridge, MA, 1955), pp. 320–1.

13

Ganymede Agonistes

Ganymede figures in one of a large number of contingent narratives about love and lust interpolated by Ovid into the story of Orpheus in Books 10 and 11 of the *Metamorphoses*. They include some of the best-known Ovidian myths: Pygmalion and the statue, Venus and Adonis, Atalanta and Hippomenes, Apollo and Hyacinthus. The narratives are contingent in the sense that they are interrelated, and for the most part interdependent, often family histories, and they explain how love, such as that of Venus and Adonis, came to be normatively, if not inevitably, tragic. But the stories are not presented simply as histories. They are also the archetypes of poetry, the songs the archpoet sings; they constitute the eloquence that so ravishes the animals and woods and stones that they stop their own lives to listen to him. They do this because these stories of cosmic lust speak directly to the passions of the world of nature: these are the songs that tell us – all of us, people, animals, trees, rocks – what we are; and they say that our essence is desire, we are our lust.

For the Renaissance, the stories in this group most often depicted by artists are those of Orpheus himself (particularly the journey to hell, Orpheus singing to the animals, and his death), the love of Venus and Adonis, and the story of Ganymede – surprisingly, not the story of Pygmalion, though that would seem a natural subject for artists. I am framing my discussion with an especially interesting and not very well known Ovidian iconology engraved by Johann Wilhelm Baur, published between 1639 and 1641, and then copied and adapted many times throughout the seventeenth century – considering its great popularity, it has received surprisingly little attention.

Figure 13.1 is Baur's version of Orpheus in Hades. The Orpheus story starts where love stories usually end, with a marriage. Orpheus summons the wedding god Hymen at the opening of Book 10 to celebrate his union with Eurydice, but the ceremony is ill-omened and the bride is dead scarcely ten lines into the book. Orpheus's story is about the power of love, but not in the usual sense: love here sends the bereft poet to hell, both literally and

13.1 Johann Wilhelm Baur, Orpheus pursues Eurydice to the Underworld, from *Ovidii Metamorphosis* 1639–41.

13.2 Eurydice disappearing among the shades, detail of figure 13.1.

figuratively, in a vain attempt to reclaim his bride. His song of grief and longing moves the infernal powers to tears, but his own impatience, all too human, defeats him. He has been given an impossible stipulation, not to look back at the wife he loved and lost – impossible because it is inhuman, and Orpheus's passion is the condition of humanity. Baur's Orpheus story begins in Hades, and focuses on Orpheus at the moment of Eurydice's disappearance back among the shades, or devils as they appear to be here (figure 13.2): she is, appropriately, as Baur imagines the scene, almost indiscernable.

So he grieves, forgoing the love of other women because his Eurydice is irreplaceable, and seeking instead the love of young men – he was, Ovid says, for the people of Thrace, the *auctor*, both founder and poet, of the love of men for tender youths. Very few iconologies acknowledge this part of the story, though it is of the essence. Figure 13.3 is an early example that does acknowledge it, from the fifteenth-century French Ovid *La bible des poètes*, re-used in the next century to illustrate the Orpheus story in Boccaccio's *Genealogiae*, with the poet's death accounted for by the male love scene in the

13.3 Woodcut illustrating the Orpheus story, from *Boccace de la genealogie des dieux*, 1531.

13.4 Albrecht Dürer, The death of Orpheus, 1494. Pen and brown ink.

13.5 "Orfius der Erst puseran" ("Orpheus the first bugger"), detail of figure 13.4.

foreground. Dürer's version, in figure 13.4, omits the love scene but similarly justifies the murder with an inflammatory motto on the ribbon above (figure 13.5), where the archpoet is succinctly identified as "Orfiuss der Erst puseran" – the first bugger. I myself identified the Giulio Romano drawing in figure 13.6, always called Apollo and Cyparissus or Hyacynthus, as Orpheus and a youth menaced by a maenad – the woman's gesture, biting her finger, is glossed by the symbologist Pierio Valeriano as the gesture of revenge, and Giulio used it at least twice more in the same way.[1]

I want to pause over Dürer for a moment, since his version of Orpheus's death is particularly and uncompromisingly moralistic – in modern terms, blatantly homophobic. Consider another Dürer image, apparently quite unrelated. Figure 13.7 is a silverpoint portrait of Dürer's closest friend Willibald Pirckheimer, done around 1503. Pirckheimer was a major humanist scholar, one of a group of Nuremberg humanists with whom Dürer was intimate. He was a great intellectual resource for the artist, supplying him with imagery drawn from his study of ancient symbolism, and advising him on its interpretation. This is one of several portraits Dürer did of his friend. The special thing about this one is that it includes a faint Greek inscription across the top, legible to the naked eye, but not in a photograph. I have superimposed the inscription on my reproduction of the drawing. It reads, "arsenos te psolé es ton prokton," which means, as literally as possible, "with a man's prick up your anus." I shall parse this, to make it clear that I am not sensationalizing this bit of humanist Greek. "Arsenos" is a man; the "prick" word is "psolé", and I have translated it prick rather than penis because it is the closest thing Greek has to a dirty word for the penis. The usual word is phallos. Psolos means an erect penis, more specifically one with the foreskin retracted, so that the glans is visible – this was considered especially obscene, involving seeing the penis in action. (The word was also used for a circumcised penis, which the Greeks considered similarly obscene.) And "te psolé es ton prokton" means not just in your anus, but going into it, being shoved into it – es is the word for "in" used with verbs of action, "into." So this is not simply an inscription like "fuck you," or "up yours"; it is quite specific about the sodomitical act being invoked.

Needless to say, over the centuries art historians haven't wanted to deal with this curious aspect of the drawing, and have either ignored it or treated it as a bit of later vandalism. But a group of technologically sophisticated researchers at the Louvre, trained as both physicists and art historians, who have developed a way of identifying pigments, inks, and the like, recently decided to examine the drawing with their analytic instruments.[2] What they found is that the inscription was written with the same silverpoint pencil that made the drawing. My informant in all this, the physicist Guillaume Dupuis,

13.6 Giulio Romano, Orpheus and a youth menaced by a maenad (catalogued as Apollo and a youth).

who worked on the project, had initially assumed that the inscription was by Dürer, and that, at the very least, some sexual connection with Pirckheimer was implied.

But the inscription cannot be by Dürer, who knew no Greek. It must, however, be strictly contemporaneous with the drawing, made by someone

Αρσενος τη ψωλη ες τον πρωκτον

13.7 Albrecht Dürer, Portrait of Willibald Pirckheimer. Silverpoint drawing.

with access to Dürer's studio, and to his drawing materials – one of the humanist circle with whom Dürer and Pirckheimer were intimate; or even, as several recent art historians not panicked by the idea that Renaissance humanists talked dirty have suggested, by Pirckheimer himself. And what then does it mean? Is it a bit of straight locker-room humor? Is it implying

13.8 Albrecht Dürer, Self-portrait naked.

something about Pirckheimer's – or Dürer's – sexual tastes? If Pirckheimer is the scribe, does it express what he wants from his best friend, or what he wants to do to him; or is it a negative comment on the drawing itself – I look as if I've got a prick up my ass? At the very least, it implies a degree of specificity about homosexual practice in Dürer's circle that we ought to keep in mind when we look, for example, at the teasing sexuality of Dürer's very naked self-portraits, such as that in figure 13.8 – the eyes here are clearly the mirror to the cock. How much projection, then, does that motto on the Orpheus engraving, "der Erst puseran," the first bugger, imply?

I return now to the first bugger. Despite his own distinctive sexual tastes after the death of Eurydice, Orpheus's grief, expressed through his songs, encompasses all of human eroticism, whether chaste, promiscuous, polymorphous, heterosexual, homosexual, bestial, incestuous, gentle, or savage. The stories he recounts are offered by Ovid on the whole without moralizing. Tragic endings in these tales are often accidental, and, if the gods are offended by the behavior of mortals, the fault has generally been either inadvertent or compelled – as Venus deliberately inspires lust in Atalanta and Hippomenes, and then punishes them for succumbing to it. Orpheus's own death, at the hands of the women whom he has rejected, is in context less a moral about the unnaturalness of homosexuality than a warning about the dangers of unsatisfied women. And, more than a moral, it serves, as the whole book does, to explain how things got to be as they are, how so simple an emotion as love came to be so fraught, conflicted, frustrating and destructive.

If the meaning of Orpheus's life lies in the death of Eurydice, his own death gives the story as a whole its meaning, with the severed head that goes on singing figuring the poetry that survives the grave. Orpheus dies at the hands of women because of his surpassing love for one particular woman, because of his presumptuousness in believing the woman he loved was unique, and therefore irreplaceable. The young men to whom he turns for love are not replacements for Eurydice; the point is that Eurydice is irreplaceable. That is what enrages the women: not his interest in youths, but his indifference to *them*, his refusal to accept a substitute or alternative woman, to equate other women with his woman.

The implied corollary, however, is the dangerous part: Orpheus's choice reveals that men require love, but they do not necessarily require women. The Ganymede story is thus directly predicated on the death of Eurydice, and it says something about mankind in general, not about Orpheus alone. "The king of gods," Ovid says, "once burned with love for Phrygian Ganymede," and this utterly transformed Jove: all at once there was something – the Latin says "*inventum est aliquid*," "something was discovered" – "that Jove would rather be than what he was."[3] For once it is not the object of love that is transformed, but the god himself, metamorphosed by lust into an eagle to ravish his prey, but also, for the first time in history (and, Foucault to the contrary notwithstanding, not at all anachronistically), metamorphosed from straight to gay: something was discovered, something that Jove would rather be than what he was. The boy is both what he wants and what he wants to be; and, as the passive voice implies, the discovery is made not by Jove alone, but by the world at large: something was discovered. The model for Orpheus's homoeroticism is Jove himself. "He cleft the air with his lying wings and carried off the Trojan boy, and even now, against the will of Juno, he mixes the nectar and tends to the cups of Jove."[4] The love that Orpheus taught the Greeks transforms even the king of gods. It also remains a perpetual affront to women and to marriage, even the marriage of the queen of heaven.

IN DEO LAETANDVM

Aspice ut egregium puerum Iouis alite pictor
Fecerit Iliacum summa per astra uehi.

13.9 Ganymede,
from Andrea Alciato,
Emblemata, Augsburg,
1531.

13.10 Ganymede, from
Emblemes d'Alciat,
Lyon, 1549.

13.11 Ganymede,
from Achille Bocchi,
Symbolicarum
Quaestionum, 1555,
emblem 78.

DIEV, OV RELIGION.
En Dieu se fault esiouyr.
EVIDENCE.

ΓΑΝΝΥΣΘΑΙΜΗΔΕΣΙ,

GANYMEDES.

Voyez comment l'Aigle porte à grand ioye
Dessus les cieulx, le bel enfant de Troie?
Qui ne croiroit Iupiter estre attainct
D'amour d'enfant? D'ond l'ha Homere sainct?
Qui au conseil de Dieu est esiouy
Au souuerain Iupiter est rauy.
　Rauissement d'esprit à Dieu, sans separation de corps,
est côtentemét de l'ordônance de Dieu en toutes choses.

CLXVI　　　LIB. III.

VERA IN COGNITIONE DEI,
CVLTVQ. VOLVPTAS.

Symb. LXXVIII.

CLXVIII **LIB. III.**

SCVLPTORIS IAM NVNC GANYMEDEM CERNE
LEOCRÆ
PACATI EMBLEMA HOC CORPORIS, ATQ.
ANIMI EST.

Symb. LXXIX.

13.12 Ganymede, from
Achille Bocchi, *Symbolicarum
Quaestionum*, 1555, emblem 79.

Perhaps the oddest things about this story, given its immense and complicated critical history, are its brevity and its uncompromisingly happy ending. It occupies far less space in Ovid's narrative than the two other homoerotic exempla described by Orpheus in the same passage, the love of Apollo for Cyparissus and for Hyacinthus – Ganymede's story is a brief paragraph, a mere seven lines, separating the extended, circumstantial and very romantic accounts of these two tragic love affairs, in which the god of poetry is accidentally responsible for the deaths of his two young lovers. For moralists preaching the destructiveness of homoeroticism, either of these would seem a preferable, or at least a more natural, subject.

But from the beginning Ganymede has been the really fearful example, providing a name, and an ideal, for every teenage hustler across two millennia – fearful, surely, precisely because of the spectacular success of the homoerotic escapade, because this boy is not raped and discarded, or immolated, or translated into a beast like Jove's women, or turned into an ominous natural monument to Apollo's lust, like the hyacinth or cypress or laurel, but ravished clear out of nature to the skies, there to serve as a perpetual pleasure to Jove, and an eternal outrage to Juno, and decent folk, and the sanctity of marriage.

The ambivalent iconography of this myth for the Renaissance has been admirably and courageously, if cautiously, discussed by James Saslow in a genuinely pioneering book, *Ganymede in the Renaissance* – the courage and the caution are amply accounted for by the reticence and outright suppression accorded the subject in traditional art history.[5] Leonard Barkan, in an eloquent, original and seriously underappreciated book, *Transuming Passion*, places the subject in a broader humanistic context.[6] If I pursue the

13.13 Nicholas Beatrizet, engraving after Michelangelo, *The Rape of Ganymede*, c. 1530.

GANIMEDIS·IVVENIS·TROIANVS·RAPTVS·A·IOVE

matter a little further here, and a little less cautiously, it is because Saslow
and Barkan have enabled me to do so. In fact, the sexuality that is avoided in
depictions of the death of Orpheus is often quite explicit in versions of the
Ganymede story, despite its usual moralization as an allegory of the mind
ascending to heaven through divine love. This is generally described as a
neoplatonic reading, but the neoplatonic allegory moves from the sensual and
physical to the intellectual and spiritual, and it only makes sense if you really
do start with the sensual and physical. That is precisely where Andrea Alciato
starts (figure 13.9). The earliest version of the Ganymede emblem, in the first
edition of the *Emblemata*, 1531, shows the youth as a putto riding on an eagle
(the illustrations were provided by the book's German publisher – Alciato did
not intend it to include pictures, and was not consulted about the iconography).
There is nothing remotely sexual about the image; the verse, however, at once
acknowledges the unthinkable:

> See how the excellent painter has shown the Trojan boy Ganymede
> borne through the highest stars on Jupiter's wings. Who would believe
> that Jupiter was touched by the love of boys? Say, from what source did
> old Homer create this? He whose joy is in the mind and judgment of
> God is conceived to have been carried up to Jove.

By the 1549 French edition, in figure 13.10, the boy is older, and though
undraped so that he is sexually exposed, he seems now to be resisting the
eagle's abduction. Achille Bocchi's *Symbolicarum Quaestionum*, published
in 1555, gives two versions of the scene (figures 13.11 and 13.12), seemingly to
exemplify the divided life of the myth. In the first, the boy is again naked and
exposed, but entirely passive; in the second he is not merely draped, but fully
clothed (the garment even has sleeves).

This group of images is based on a well-known Michelangelo composition
that does not survive. Figure 13.13 is Nicholas Beatrizet's engraving of the
whole work. What survives is two versions of Michelangelo's famous drawing
of around 1530; figure 13.14 shows the version now in the Fogg Art Museum
at Harvard. Erwin Panofsky's influential account of the drawing is relentlessly
evasive. Though his larger argument acknowledges both the physical component
of the iconology and its explicit use in reference to homosexuality, the drawing
itself in Panofsky's description is resolutely sanitized:

> It shows Ganymede in a state of trance without a will or a thought of
> his own, reduced to passive immobility by the iron grip of the gigantic
> eagle, the posture of his arms suggesting the attitude of an unconscious

13.14 Michelangelo, Ganymede (detail). Drawing. Black chalk on off-white antique laid paper.

person or a corpse, and his soul really *rimossa dal corpo* ... . Thus it cannot be questioned that this drawing symbolizes the *furor divinus* ... .[7]

Well, yes, it can be questioned. Barkan minces no words, observing that "this serenity of Michelangelo's Ganymede is also sexual passivity, so traditionally definitive of the role of the catamite (an alternative form of the name Ganymede)."[8] Saslow's description of the image is even more explicit about its obvious sexual content:

The Ganymede drawing reveals Michelangelo's sexual reading of the myth by depicting the boy as if the eagle were physically penetrating him. In contrast to earlier, less erotic visualizations of Ganymede's abduction, Michelangelo introduces a front-to-back positioning of the boy and eagle and greatly increases the proximity, overlapping, and

13.15 Ganymede, hellenistic marble sculpture. Museo Archeologico, Venice.

intertwining of their bodies. In addition, he shows the youth entirely nude, in a full frontal pose that for the first time exposes Ganymede's genitals.[9]

Well ... not really for the first time. I found the Hellenistic marble in figure 13.15 hanging above a doorway in the archeological museum next to the Sansovino library in Venice, one of those wonderful galleries that used to let you take photographs. The ancient tradition was not at all squeamish about the boy's genitals.

Nor were Renaissance artists squeamish about eroticizing the rest of the youth's anatomy. Figure 13.16 is a ceiling painting by Lelio Orsi, done between 1546 and 1557. The fainting youth's legs are spread and raised to expose both his genitals and buttocks. In Damiano Mazza's painting of c. 1570–90 (figure 13.17), it is clear that the viewer's interest in the subject is not in platonic

13.16 Lelio Orsi, *The Rape of Ganymede*, c. 1546–57.

philosophy. Figure 13.18 is perhaps the most overtly sexual of the variations on the Michelangelo image, a mid-sixteenth-century example which adds three other naked young men to the original composition. This is signed with the initials I. B. and a dove, and is attributed to a shadowy figure called Giovanni Battista Palumba, otherwise known to art history, wonderfully, as The Master I. B. With the Bird. In the airborne love scene, the youth has been flipped on his back, and the Jovian eagle is mounting him between his raised legs – if this image is about platonic philosophy, it is also quite explicit about sex.

13.17 Damiano Mazza, *The Rape of Ganymede*, c. 1570–90. Oil on canvas.

13.18 Giovanni Battista Palumba, *The Rape of Ganymede*, c. 1505–15. Engraving.

For Henry Peacham, in 1612, platonic philosophy was entirely beside the point. His Ganymede emblem in *Minerva Britanna* (figure 13.19) is headed *Crimina Gravissima*, the worst of vices, and the youth is now in thrall to a less exalted but far more demanding bird:

> Upon a cock here Ganymede doth sit,
> Who erst rode mounted on Jove's eagle's back;
> One hand holds Circe's wand, and joined with it
> A cup top-filled with poison, deadly black;
> The other medals of base metals wrought,
> With sundry moneys counterfeit and nought.

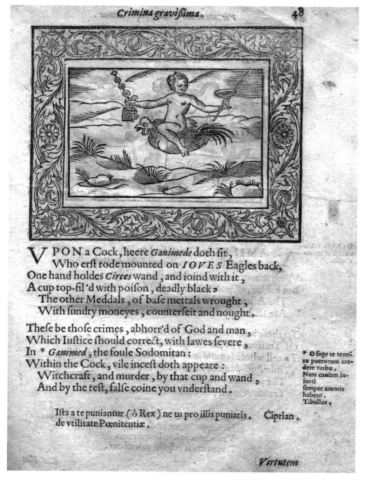

13.19 Henry Peacham, "Crimina Gravissima," from *Minerva Britanna*, 1612.

13.20 Johann Wilhelm Baur, *Ovidii Metamorphosis* 1639–41, Ganymede triumphant (detail).

These be those crimes abhorred of God and man
Which justice should correct with laws severe:
In Ganymede the foul sodomitan,
Within the cock vile incest doth appear,
Witchcraft and murder by that cup and wand,
And by the rest, false coin you understand. (p. 48)

No platonic ascent here; the youth's crimes move from buggery through incest, witchcraft, murder, and finally to counterfeiting. If the ending is, for modern sensibilities, rather a letdown, it at least testifies to the extraordinary breadth of the Ganymede story's applicability – divine love makes anything possible.

I return at last to Johann Wilhelm Baur. No iconographic version better expresses the unequivocal success of the story's outcome, whether for good

13.21 Johann Wilhelm Baur, *Ovidii Metamorphosis* 1639–41, the death of Orpheus.

13.22 Johann Wilhelm Baur, a maenad at the death of Orpheus (detail of figure 13.21).

or ill. In figure 13.20 Ganymede, naked and triumphant, rides the eagle, now fully in control – this Jove has been captured and tamed by the powerful and glamorous youth. In contrast, figure 13.21 is Baur's version of the murder of Orpheus. The deadly threat represented by women is explicitly, even blatantly, sexual, as the exposed, decidedly unclassical figure of the maenad in figure 13.22 reveals.

Notes

1 See my essay "Gendering the Crown", in my collection *The Authentic Shakespeare* (New York, 2002), pp. 112–17.

2 The analysis, by Ina Reiche et al., "Spatially resolved Synchroton-induced X-ray fluorescence analyses of metal point drawings and their mysterious inscriptions," is in the autumn, 2004, issue of *Spectrochimica Acta B* vol. 59: 1657–62.

3 Ovid, *Metamorphoses* 10: 155–61.

4 Ibid.

5 James Saslow, *Ganymede in the Renaissance* (New Haven, CT, 1986).

6 Leonard Barkan, *Transuming Passion* (Stanford, CA, 1991).

7 Erwin Panofsky, *Studies in Iconology* (New York, 1962), p. 216.

8 Barkan, *Transuming Passion*, p. 84.

9 Saslow, *Ganymede in the Renaissance*, p. 39.

Index

(Note: works are indexed under the author's name. British peers are indexed under their titles, not their family names, e.g. Robert Cecil, Earl of Salisbury, under Salisbury, not Cecil.)